DANTE'S *PARADISO* AND THE LIMITATIONS OF MODERN CRITICISM

DANTE'S *PARADISO* AND THE LIMITATIONS OF MODERN CRITICISM

A STUDY OF STYLE AND POETIC THEORY

ROBIN KIRKPATRICK

COLLEGE LECTURER IN ITALIAN AT UNIVERSITY COLLEGE DUBLIN

CAMBRIDGE UNIVERSITY PRESS

CAMBRIDGE

LONDON · NEW YORK · MELBOURNE

Published by the Syndics of the Cambridge University Press
The Pitt Building, Trumpington Street, Cambridge CB2 1RP
Bentley House, 200 Euston Road, London NW1 2DB
32 East 57th Street, New York, NY 10022, USA
296 Beaconsfield Parade, Middle Park, Melbourne 3206, Australia

First published 1978

Printed in Great Britain by
Western Printing Services Ltd, Bristol

Library of Congress Cataloguing in Publication Data

Kirkpatrick, Robin, 1943–

Dante's Paradiso and the limitations of modern criticism.

Bibliography: p.

Includes index.

1. Dante Alighieri. Divina commedia. Paradiso.

2. Paradise in literature. I. Title.

PQ4451.K5 851'.1 77–80839

ISBN 0 521 21785 7

CONTENTS

PREFACE

An earlier version of this book was presented in 1975 as a doctoral dissertation to the University of Cambridge, where I was fortunate enough to have as my supervisor Father Kenelm Foster. I am deeply indebted to Father Foster for the encouragement he has given me throughout, and know only too well how far short of his example my own work falls. I should also like to thank William Righter for the interest he has always shown in the progress of the book, Robert Lord for twice reading drafts of it at crucial moments, Patrick Boyde for an early conversation which now he probably will not remember, and Antonino Marrale for his comments upon the final draft. Reserving for my wife, Wai Heung, a better book than this, I should still wish to thank her for her patience and for her help in preparing the typescript. It is, I realise now, no mere formality to add that the opinions and faults to be found here are entirely my own.

The authorities of Hong Kong University gave me some assistance in the initial stages of preparation by way of study leave. However, my greatest debt is to the undergraduates with whom I first studied Dante's *Commedia*. This book is dedicated to them with gratitude and affection, to Au-Yeung Kwan, Tisa Ho, Sakina Hoosanally, Lorraine Law, Shelley Lee, Jennifer Mak, Poon Kok Fai, Tang Fook Ki, Tao Pei Lin and Yuen Tak Chuen.

R. K.

ACKNOWLEDGEMENTS

I should like to acknowledge the kind permission of Arnoldo Mondadori Editore to quote from the text of the *Commedia* edited by G. Petrocchi, and of the Studio Bibliografico Antenore to quote from the text of *De Vulgari Eloquentia* edited by P. V. Mengaldo. I would also like to express my thanks to Casa Editrice Professor Riccardo Pàtron (Bologna) for the use of *Il Convivio*, edizione critica a cura di Maria Simonelli.

ABBREVIATIONS

The following abbreviations are employed:

DANTE'S WORKS

Con.	*Convivio*
D.V.E.	*De Vulgari Eloquentia*
Inf.	*Inferno*
Par.	*Paradiso*
Purg.	*Purgatorio*

For the text of Dante's works, I have used the following: *Il Convivio*, ed. M. Simonelli (Bologna, 1966); *De Vulgari Eloquentia*, ed. P. V. Mengaldo (Padua, 1968); *La Commedia*, ed. G. Petrocchi (4 vols., Milan, 1966–7).

PERIODICALS etc.

(The full title of each reference is given in the bibliography)

AB	*Art Bulletin*
ACISD	*Atti del Congresso Internazionale di Studi Danteschi* (1965)
ACNSD	*Atti del Congresso Nazionale di Studi Danteschi* (1962)
ACNSR	*Atti del Congresso Nazionale di Studi Romanzi* (1960)
AISD	*Annali dell' Istituto di Studi Danteschi*
ALCGG	*Annali del Liceo Classico 'G. Garibaldi' di Palermo*
AMAT	*Atti e Memorie dell' Accademia Toscana di scienze e lettere, 'La Colombaria'*
BARLL	*Bulletin de l'Académie Royale de Langue et Littérature Francaises*
CL	*Comparative Literature*
CNL	*Cultura neolatina*
CS	*Cultura e Scuola*

CSD	*Cultura e Scuola*, IV (1965), Dante issue
CV	*Convivium*
DB	*Dante e Bologna nei tempi di Dante*
DCV	*Dante e la cultura veneta*
DDJ	*Deutsches Dante Jahrbuch*
DH	*De Homine*
DMC	*Atti del Convegno di Studi su Dante e la Magna Curia*
DV	*Divinitas*
ED	*Enciclopedia Dantesca*
FMLS	*Forum for Modern Language Studies*
FR	*Filologia romanza*
GCI	*Il giornale della cultura italiana*
GD	*Giornale dantesco*
GSLI	*Giornale storico della letteratura italiana*
HMN	*Humanitas*
HR	*Hudson Review*
IT	*Italica*
IS	*Italian Studies*
IV	*Il Veltro*
JAAC	*Journal of Aesthetics and Art Criticism*
JP	*Journal of Philosophy*
KR	*Kenyon Review*
LA	*L'Alighieri*
LC	*Letture classensi*
LD	*Letture dantesche*
LDS	*Lectura Dantis Scaligera* (1967–8)
LTI	*Lettere italiane*
MD	*Miscellanea dantesca* (Utrecht–Antwerp, 1965)
MLN	*Modern Language Notes*
MLR	*Modern Language Review*
MPSE	*Momenti e problemi di storia dell'estetica* (Milan, 1949)
MSD	*Miscellanea di Studi Danteschi* (Genoa, 1966)
NA	*Nuova Antologia*
NLD	*Nuove Letture Dantesche* (vols. V and VI, 1972–3)
PG	*Paragone*
PQ	*Philological Quarterly*
RI	*Rivista d'Italia*
RLI	*La Rassegna della letteratura italiana*
RP	*Romance Philology*
RR	*Romanic Review*
SC	*Società*
SD	*Studi danteschi*

SP	*Symposium*
SPHLS	*Studia Philologica et Litteraria in honorem L. Spitzer*
TP	*Terzo Programma*

A NOTE ON THE TRANSLATIONS

The translations both of Dante's prose works and of the *Commedia* that appear in this book are my own. They make no claim to elegance or artistic adequacy. But since I am concerned throughout with the close analysis of Dante's text, I have attempted to provide a translation which is not only literal but also preserves, wherever clarity permits, the word-order and lineation of the original. This, I hope, will assist those readers who have some acquaintance with Italian to recognise, when they return to Dante's text, the emphasis and articulation of his phrases. For a more fluent version of the *Commedia* the reader will naturally turn to J. D. Sinclair's excellent work.

INTRODUCTION

The subject of this essay is the poetry of Dante's *Paradiso*. And if the form of it now were the form I first intended it to have, I should be wholly occupied with the style of the canticle. Like many another reader, I had been impressed on turning from the final pages of the *Purgatorio* to the first of the *Paradiso* by an alteration in the character of the *Commedia*. There were, as I recognised, a variety of reasons why the concluding section should affect one differently from the first two. Yet it seemed to me that, as Dante addressed himself to his 'ultimo lavoro', a change occurred in the very fabric of his poetic utterance. It was this development that I set myself to delineate, assuming initially that I should be able to do so in the normal way, by the analysis of detail and of instances.

I soon realised, however, that analysis alone would not answer to the case. For the features which, in my view, were most essential in the style of the *Paradiso* proved, on examination, so thoroughly unusual that simply to describe them, in the terms at least of any current theory of poetry, would have tended surreptitiously to obscure their proper value and distort their force. There had arisen no such difficulty in the analysis of *Inferno* or *Purgatorio*. And that it should have arisen in regard, even, to a work as uncommon as the *Paradiso* may appear not a little surprising.

For what had attracted me in the canticle, broadly speaking, was the way in which the art of the poet had there been reconciled to the statement of an intellectual interest. And in respect of its intellectuality the *Paradiso* is by no means the problematical work that once it was supposed to be. Nonetheless, I was unable to discover in any recent discussion of the text a scheme which might elucidate the extreme originality of the poet's undertaking. My conclusion was that for an accurate description of the canticle it would be necessary not only to examine the qualities of its style, but to devise also a vocabulary appropriate to the work, and no less, to justify and define this vocabulary by a general consideration of poetic theory. Looking further still, I came to realise that Dante in his theoretical writings had himself partially suggested an explanation of his procedure in the *Paradiso*. These suggestions proved in their own way so stimulating and so surprising that at last I decided to give as much attention to them as to the detailed examination of the poet's style.

In its present state, then, this essay is concerned as much with questions of theory as with a reading of the text itself. And these theoretical considerations will present themselves in a twofold aspect.

In the first place, the purpose of the discussion will be to resuscitate certain features of Dante's own theoretical position. For as I shall argue the distinctive qualities of his style in the *Paradiso* are in no way accidental but derive rather from a deliberate decision, to pursue in the canticle a peculiar, even unexampled, principle of composition. Certainly, at the opening of Cantos One and Two the poet himself protests the unique gravity of his final enterprise. And precisely in point of such gravity, I think, the principle which guided Dante in the *Paradiso* is to be distinguished from that which he followed in *Inferno* and *Purgatorio*.

This principle, however, which in its theoretic aspect will allow to the poet a serious and effectual voice in matters of the intellect, is to be distinguished as well from any to which modern theoreticians have introduced us. Yet if one appreciates it fully, in its purposes and consequences, one will, I believe, be able not only to describe the *Paradiso* with a greater exactitude, but also to recognise in the art of poetry itself certain hitherto unheeded possibilities. The reader of this essay will be asked, therefore, to tolerate a tone of argument which is in some degree polemical. For I am convinced that the *Paradiso*, as the exemplar of a principle, has much of value to teach us in the present literary epoch.

What, then, is the principle that Dante follows in writing the *Paradiso*? I cannot, of course, offer a complete answer here. But I may at least indicate the outline of one by an analogy. For roughly Dante's procedure in the *Paradiso* will prove to be comparable, I suggest, to a procedure that occasionally one adopts in defining for oneself the crucial point of some philosophy. Attempting to grasp the force of a philosophical position – especially perhaps if one senses its bearing upon one's own train of thought – one will seek to devise a formula or a paraphrase by which in one's own way one can comprehend the argument and, so to say, appropriate its substance. Such a procedure could not strictly be called a logical one. Yet its success will depend upon one's being peculiarly careful in the construction of the interpretative phrase. And to that extent one's thinking will undoubtedly display a certain discipline. After all, the purpose of the paraphrase must be to define the point as truthfully and accurately as possible. Nor will one be satisfied unless the formula one does arrive at is, in some measure, authoritative. For as one continues, it is upon this formula that one will rely for clarity of thought. And one may also use it in communicating to others the special importance of one's understanding.

Now, in subsequent chapters, I shall argue that Dante, though not submitting to a process of logic in his verse, nonetheless does display a certain discipline – of the kind my analogy suggests – in the handling of words. In a particular sense, this discipline is such as to ensure the truthfulness and the intellectual authority of the poet's utterances. Even so, it is consistent, I shall maintain, with disciplines that are specific to the art of poetry. And here it may at once be apparent why an investigation of theory should be so necessary. For to speak at all of truthfulness, and of the relation between poetic utterance and the truth, is to raise directly questions of a philosophical character. It would not, I think, be impossible to translate the loose terms that I shall be using here into more exactly philosophical ones. However, the issues are of a kind that concern literature quite as much as they concern philosophy. And seeking only to demonstrate how Dante's own determination to be truthful affected his style in the *Paradiso*, I shall not attempt to pursue the matter beyond those regions where the literary theorist has already set foot.

Thus, for the present I may best advance my argument by suggesting briefly how the intellectual qualities of the *Paradiso* as I would represent them differ from the qualities which other critics have recently attributed to the work. After all, the general question is one which might appear long since to have arrived at a peaceable conclusion.[1] Thus A. Buck, reviewing the situation in 1965 can confidently assert that no one will understand either Dante himself or his poetry if he supposes, following De Sanctis, that there exists a conflict in Dante between the poet and the thinker. For 'Dante is a poet, and at the same time strives to be a philosopher' ('Gli studi sulla poetica e sulla retorica di Dante', *ACISD*, vol. 1, p. 264).

Now it is undoubtedly true that one's taste and tolerance for poetry of an intellectual cast has lately been enlarged by the stylistic studies, above all, of Giovanni Getto, and of others too, for example, Anna Chiavacci-Leonardi and, in one magisterial essay, Mario Fubini.[2] Yet in every such case, I think, the purpose of the critic has been to establish only that if, in Buck's phrase, a poet does 'strive to be a philosopher', the virtue of his poetry need not on that account be diminished. Poetry, they maintain, is entirely compatible with the exposition of doctrine and may co-operate fully with the movement of intelligence. Which is both true and undoubtedly important. Yet to argue thus is by no means to show that in the questions that it raises the *Paradiso* carries any intellectual weight or authority. The excitement of exposition is one thing, the responsibilities of affirmation quite another. And if one's concern is with the latter, it will be insufficient merely to indicate that there exists no antagonism between a poetic purpose and a theme or preoccupation of doctrinal bearing. One must decide rather whether a poet may ever claim for himself in the use he makes of his art an authority at all comparable to that of which the philosopher is possessed by the strictness of his method.[3]

My contention is that in the *Paradiso* an authority of this sort does indeed appertain to the poet. Yet one would not complain if the failure of the critics I have mentioned were a failure only to recognise this. There is, however, a more acute occasion for discomfort. For it happens that in recent work upon the *Paradiso*, the general question of what poetry is has rarely, if at all, been raised. Nonetheless assumptions as to the nature of poetry continue, of course, to reveal themselves. And these assumptions have, in the main, been of a kind actively to preclude so thorough an identification of poetic and intellectual procedure as the *Paradiso* requires.[4]

For instance, there survives a widespread agreement that the aesthetic power of the mind, in poetic creation, is constitutively separate from the intellectual power. Which is strange indeed. For among twentieth-century theoreticians the classic, though not unique, expression of this principle is to be found in Benedetto Croce's philosophy. And there are few critics or aestheticians who would not now declare a dissatisfaction with the Crocean etiquette. The fact remains that while many of Croce's particular judgements upon the *Commedia* have by now been discredited, his disaffected inheritors, when confronted with his aesthetic theory itself, – or theories which resemble it – seem concerned rather to mitigate and expand its more restrictive criteria, answering Croce with Croce, than to countenance any thorough reappraisal.[5]

To consider for the moment only the most important case, one finds that Getto repeatedly avails himself, while proposing modifications, of Croce's argument in 'La gioia dell'insegnare e dell' apprendere' (*Critica*, XXXIX (1941), 137–41) and in parts of *La*

Poesia di Dante. And when, in an influential passage, he describes the *Paradiso* as 'the epic of the inner life . . . the drama of the life of grace . . . the poetry of mystic experience' (*Aspetti della poesia di Dante*, p. 196), he echoes, with intent perhaps to challenge, the phrasing of the Heidelberg address, where Croce speaks of poetry as being characteristically 'epic and lyric at the same time – or, if one prefers, dramatic' ('L'intuizione pura e il carattere lirico dell'arte' in *Problemi di estetica* (Bari, 1910), p. 20). Getto's use of Croce is admirable, insofar as it shows how Croce's system does not disallow to poetry the choice of an intellectual or doctrinal subject – provided always that its form remains aesthetic and imaginative.[6] But, as will be seen, Getto himself, in regard to principle, advances scarcely any further. For him, as for Croce, the form of an intellectual poem will still be an expressive form, where imagination devises, for intellectual material, its own peculiar embodiment.

In the *Paradiso*, however, – though not, I think, in *Inferno* or *Purgatorio* – an intellectual subject is presented in a strictly intellectual form. And this, in fine, would be incomprehensible, if one supposed contentedly that poetry must always possess, in the Crocean sense, an expressive character. The damage of this supposition to one's reading of the *Paradiso* is bound to be considerable. But even apart from that, to persist in it is to settle for a concept of the relation between poetic and intellectual activity – and a concept indeed of poetry itself – which was commonplace even before the *Paradiso* returned to the canon of literary *exempla*.

So far I have spoken only of writers whose criticism is mainly stylistic in character. But these are by no means the only or even the most influential critics who have concerned themselves with the *Paradiso*. For since Croce, one of the most notable developments in the study of Dante's work has been the emergence of a new historical criticism, the especial characteristic of which is sympathy for the cultural circumstances in which the poet wrote, and for his own poetic theories.[7] By now, it may be thought, these would have enabled one to elude the preconceptions of modern aesthetic theory.

Yet even here there is a disappointment. To be sure, the questions which the *Paradiso* stimulates have been tackled with great vigour, notably in the discussion of 'Dante as prophet' and 'Dante as scribe of God'.[8] Yet precisely because the modern historian has been so concerned to justify the poetry of the *Paradiso*, his inclination has been to reconcile an historic view with the prevailing understanding of what poetry is. Time and again he emphasises the dramatic qualities of the work, or asks that we discover in it the peculiarly concrete embodiment of an intellectual position. Joseph Mazzeo, for instance, to whom I shall return, seems happy to confound the notions of inspired truth and imaginative truth (*Structure and Thought in the Paradiso* (Ithaca, N.Y., 1958) pp. 129–30). And in general even the best philologists such as Auerbach and Singleton are prone to something of the sort. Thus Auerbach, in his conception of 'figura', is sustained as much by a commitment – of considerable profundity – to the value of the dramatic as by any purely historical intent.[9] Likewise C. S. Singleton, in common with many who take as their theme the allegory of theologians, encourages not only an historic view of the *Commedia*, but also an appreciation of its concreteness and narrative force.[10]

Earlier I suggested that the terminology which critics of the *Paradiso* have employed has itself prevented a full appreciation of the canticle. By now it will be apparent that I had in mind especially the terms 'expressive' (in some such particular sense as Croce gives it), 'concrete', 'dramatic', and the like.[11] To these I would add 'organic', 'tension' and, in the end, even 'imaginative'. But it profits little to quarrel with the terms themselves. Undoubtedly they do have their value. And one's principal objection is that they perpetuate beyond its usefulness the theory that first gave rise to them. If, then, one is to propose any alternative, one must examine, as recent critics of the *Commedia* have not, the theoretical ground of our existing scheme,[12] seeking to identify its characteristic purposes and limitations.[13]

This I shall attempt to do in the following section. Then in Chapter One, turning to the *Paradiso* itself, I shall begin to consider the remedy which Dante's own procedure there has suggested. In Chapters Two and Three I shall consider certain aspects of Dante's own theory in the *Convivio* and *De Vulgari Eloquentia* to see what there is still to be learnt from these both about the *Paradiso* and generally about the writing of poetry. In Chapter Four I shall examine as a counterpart to the discussion of Chapter One how Dante expected his reader to respond to the *Paradiso*. Then in the last two chapters I shall apply the principles I have developed in the preceding chapters to the analysis of representative passages.

If, however, one is first to examine the origins of contemporary terms, where, one must ask, are these origins to be found? The inquiry may be conducted under three heads as, firstly, a question of artistic psychology, secondly of poetic form, and thirdly, of artistic truthfulness. And in Croce one will find, of course, the persistent notion that in the economy of the mind, poetry is a distinct and autonomous activity. It is not, however, with Croce's *La Poesia di Dante* that I shall be concerned but with his aesthetic philosophy. On the matter of form, I shall turn to the writings of T. S. Eliot, and on the question of imaginative truth, to those of Benevenuto Terracini, whom I include as one of several Italians who have learnt much from Ernst Cassirer.[14]

Save for the interest which all of these writers have in Dante, it may not immediately be apparent what they have in common. Indeed Eliot and Croce are not infrequently brought into opposition by students of the *Commedia*.[15] Yet in spite of certain undoubted differences, they all three in their own manner represent a phase of the theory of imagination,[16] whereby poetry is represented solely as an imaginative form, or, as a follower of Croce, Luigi Russo, has said, 'as a symbol wholly of itself . . . as a spiritual act that resolves the entire world in itself' (*La critica letteraria contemporanea* (Bari, 1946–7), vol. II, p. 200). And this, at root, is the notion I am concerned to question.

It will be obvious, of course, that the concept of imaginative symbolism has in recent years by no means gone unchallenged. Nor are the theoreticians I mention the most modern defenders of it.[17] Thus in what follows I shall have occasion to refer in particular to two Italians, Galvano della Volpe and Guida Calogero, who have in part anticipated my own objections.[18] Yet neither in their works nor elsewhere does one find, I think, a satisfactory alternative to the principles they are attacking. And my own argument will only be successful if it does suggest, in the end, where an alternative is to be found.

The first question, then, that I have to consider is whether poetry need be regarded always as the product of a self-sufficing activity or unique moment of the mind. This is not, of course, to ask whether poetry, considered purely *as* a product of the mind must itself be distinctive. For evidently it is, and, in some way, one expects it to be. Yet granted that we do associate with poetry certain distinctive qualities, one has still to inquire how these are brought about. For our judgement of any particular poem, as readers, will be influenced to some degree by the conception we hold of how a poet ought to conduct himself. And if, to take an extreme example, a poet were himself persuaded that the merit of his work arose, distinctively, from the *furor poeticus*, he would undoubtedly improve or cancel his composition in a different way from the poet whose inclination was to taste and measure.

Consider, then, how Croce understands the psychology of the poet. The principles of his position are, I think, sufficiently familiar for me to be brief.[19]

To Croce the poetic act and the aesthetic moment of intellection are identical,[20] and the distinctiveness of poetic creation arises precisely from this. For the aesthetic moment is a particular form of knowledge. As a form of knowledge, it must in the first place be distinguished from all the activities of the will, since in these we seek not to know the world as it is, but to alter it in some practical way.[21] Equally, however, aesthetic knowledge is to be distinguished from every other form of knowledge. This particular moment, lying in the scale of cognition below the conceptual and above perception and impression,[22] is, characteristically, 'il sogno della vita conoscitiva' (*the dream-phase of the cognitive life*) ('L'intuizione pura', p. 29).

From this, and especially from the 'sogno' metaphor, one may see at once the integral freedom which Croce attributes to the poetic act. At the same time, if the distinctiveness of poetry is to be explained thus, only as a reflection or function of aesthetic independence, the reader, particularly of a poem like the *Commedia*, can hardly fail to protest. For it would not seem possible in defining what is unique and constitutive to the *Commedia* to ignore the qualities of its author's conceptual design – as seen, for instance, in Dante's allegory – or to disregard the influence which a plainly practical interest in devotion or instruction may have exerted upon its formation. Obvious, however, as this objection may be, it is very easy in pursuing it to allow to Croce's contention less resilience and indeed less value than it actually possesses.

Thus from the first it is important to bear in mind that Croce, although concerned for the independence of poetry, in no way condones unruliness or irresponsibility. The 'sogno' of which he speaks is such as will submit to and evince its own intrinsic character and law. Specifically, it is a particular and individual image which claims for itself neither reality nor unreality (*Estetica come scienza dell' espressione e linguistica generale*, terza edizione riveduta (Bari, 1908) p. 6).[23] For in the aesthetic moment the mind may indeed apprehend a reality or a possible reality (*Estetica*, p. 6), but will seek to retain this only as an image, undisturbed by 'le nette distinzioni e i fermi contorni' (*the sharp distinctions and firm contours*) of a final judgement ('L'intuizione pura', p. 29). Nor, of course, is such an image to be comprehended in mere passivity, as an impression or a sensation might be. For the act of the pure intuition, which for Croce is the substance of art, is always simultaneously an expressive act (*Estetica*, pp. 8–12), so that in the forming of an image, one will intuit an individual state of things, and, at the same time, come to realise one's own individual standing in respect of this situation. Thus he writes that 'l'arte rifà idealmente ed esprime la mia istantanea situazione' (*art recreates in an ideal way and expresses my immediate situation*) ('L'intuizione pura', p. 27).

Poetry, then, if truly to be such, must depend upon an intensely active and intensely individual exercise in cognition. But here there arises – most acutely for the student of the *Commedia* – a dilemma. For Croce's conception of poetry has two consequences. The first is that he should discriminate in any work between what is and what is not poetry. Thus since, for Croce, the particularity of poetic apprehension will be seriously impaired by any dependence upon general concept or the received ideas of doctrine, it is natural, in discussing the *Commedia*, that he should propose a radical division of the structural and poetic elements. Yet from the self-same principle, Croce develops a most compelling account of poetic unity. Thus

> Ogni espressione è un'unica espressione. L'attività è fusione delle impressioni in un tutto organico. Ed è quel si è voluto sempre notare quando si è detto che l'opera d'arte deve avere unità.
>
> (Every expression is a unique expression. The activity is the fusion of impressions in an organic whole. And it is this that we mean to draw attention to when we say that a work of art must have unity.)
>
> (*Estetica*, p. 23)

Unity, it is important to note, is represented here not simply as the product but even as the spiritual condition of the aesthetic act. The wholeness and liberating activity of this moment is itself what we value in a work of art.[24] Indeed, for Croce to speak of the expressive intuition or of the 'sogno' is to speak precisely of aesthetic unity.

The difficulty is, however, that if one accepts in anything like a Crocean sense that unity is a distinctive quality of poetic production, one cannot without risk of contradiction maintain that a practical interest should contribute to its distinctiveness.[25] Thus when V. Cian,[26] reviewing *La poesia di Dante*, argues bluntly, against any objection to the practical manifestation of the poet's spirit, that the *Commedia* is above all a 'great spiritual organism and *therefore* a great poetic organism' (*GSLI*, LXXIX (1922), 64), he opens himself at once to attack from the school of Croce, as represented in Salvatore Breglia,[27] who, showing incidentally how in Croce's scheme the mere material of a poem may well be of a practical or intellectual nature, argues that an organic structure could not be created by any 'spirit', however rich and talented it might be, unless the energies of spirit were to converge and focus upon a single vision, 'unless among the multitude of its spiritual forces . . . there arose an idea and dominant sentiment that yoked these forces together and directed them to a single end' (*Poesia e struttura nella Divina Commedia* (Genoa, 1934), pp. 22–3). In a work of art, then, one looks, according to Breglia, for something other than that general coherence of thought and personality that satisfied Cian, concentrating rather upon the particular form into which the experiences and impulses of the poet have been drawn. That form itself will be the vital centre of artistic unity.

While this is not the place to revive the structure–poetry debate,[28] Breglia's observations in point of principle seem hard to fault. Certainly in reading a text, as will be seen from later chapters, an emphasis upon the unity of a work does appear inevitably to direct our attention away from any encounter with the author's individual intent towards the contemplation, precisely, of its informing idea. And to that extent it is indeed self-defeating to speak at once of unity in a work and the force of its author's practical presence.[29]

If, then, one is to give weight to the practical interests of a poet, it is important to ask whether unity itself is necessarily a feature of poetic creation. This question in one aspect concerns the matter of technical form, which I shall consider in the next section. But for Croce, as one has seen, it is a question above all of psychology. And what does concern me here is to ask whether, supposing that unity were a characteristic of aesthetic experience, one had even then explained what is distinctive in such experience. It is at this point that Calogero's aesthetic is of the greatest assistance.

For Calogero, arguing against Croce's central principle, maintains firstly that there is in fact nothing unusual about the unity of expression and intuition. Every intuition, he protests, is expressive, and every expressive intuition will have as its centre an image (*Estetica, semantica, istorica*, pp. 5–13). No such imaginative unity, therefore, will account for the sense that aesthetic experience is somehow exceptional and out of the ordinary. Indeed, in itself, any image that an artist offers could easily be approached in a spirit which obscured its peculiar status, as, for example, when a spectator's appreciation of a statue is be-clouded by directly erotic reactions (*ibid.* pp. 20–1), or (to invent an instance of closer relevance) when one entertains a fiction too intimately in the manner of a Madame Bovary or a Francesca reading her Galeotto.

How, then, *is* one to account for the quality of artistic experience, and above all for the detachment of mind which characteristically attends the conceiving and enjoyment of it? Should we not admit, asks Calogero, that to secure a disinterested view of the material before us, we are required to exert a definite act of the will?

Questa esperienza estetica fondamentale... non si risolve, allora, in un soggettivo atto di rinuncia, di voluta sospensione dell' urgenza di una certa imagine del desiderio? In un atto, cioè, che perciò non solo non si oggettiva e concreta in nulla di stabilmente valido, ma addirittura conserva un' essenziale indipendenza e arbitrarietà nei riguardi di quell'immagine passionale...

(Does not the fundamental aesthetic experience resolve itself, then, into a subjective act of renunciation, into the willing interruption of the urgent pressure that accompanies the mental image of desire. In an act, that is, which not only does *not* objectify itself or become concrete in some steady and valid form, but in fact preserves an essential independence and freedom of decision towards that 'felt' image.)

(*Estetica, semantica*, p. 20)

The suggestion is, then, that the peculiar disinterestedness of artistic experience, whether in creating art or appreciating it, will arise not in any simple moment of intellection, but as the consequence of a deliberate and decisive 'act of renunciation'.

But with this, one arrives at an answer to the initial question, and need no longer suppose that the experience of art will necessarily be associated with an autonomous function or particular faculty of the mind. For the renunciation of which Calogero speaks is evidently an act of choice and decision. To be sure, the decision itself is one which demands a certain suppression of our ordinary desires and responses. And, similarly, one will continue to regard aesthetic experience as distinctive by virtue of a certain disinterestedness. Nonetheless, the activity will be one which involves the self-possessed intelligence of the whole personality, as it turns deliberately away from the attractions of the 'passionate'. For both the artist and his audience must, if each is to appreciate the peculiar quality of the image or artistic object, choose to attend to it. And this conclusion one may readily support from experience. For plainly in the reading and still more in the writing of a poem one *is* more deliberately attentive than in the everyday reading or composition of a prose-work. And surely one does, in the former activities, tend to 'renounce' an interest save in what might prove exceptional.

As to the understanding of the *Commedia* itself, one may easily avoid in adopting Calogero's position the difficulties which Croce's system aroused – though Calogero himself does not extend his argument so far. For where Croce would ask whether a poet has sustained throughout his work a particular mode of apprehension, Calogero suggests rather that we decide whether in all parts of his composition, he has persisted in his own initial 'atto di rinuncia'. Indeed there is, as will be seen, a sense in which this very persistence may be a criterion in the appraisal of an author's accomplishment. Since, however, the act of renunciation is itself an act of moral and intellectual choice, there seems no reason why, in writing of doctrine or general concepts, the author, being directed by such an act, should not at once preserve the psychological character of his subject, and display as well a peculiarly disinterested, not to say philosophical, satisfaction in it. Of this I shall have more to say when I turn to the *Paradiso*.

Here, however, one may pause to consider the depth of the disagreement between Croce and Calogero, and the alternatives which their work makes available.

Most obviously of all, in Calogero's conception of it, art is an uncompromisingly sophisticated activity. For in consciously pursuing the exceptional the artist and his audience will need to exercise a most acute awareness both of the resources and possibilities of an art, and, no less, of themselves, as they maintain towards the image the purity of their concentration. And nowhere is this sense of sophistication more keenly apparent than in Calogero's objections to the 'panaestheticism' of Croce. Thus Calogero, extending his criticism of the expressive intuition, argues that Croce, seeing art only as the function of an innate and essential 'moment', might lead us to suppose that every moment of life were, potentially, a moment of art, and art itself an inevitable feature of existence (*Estetica, semantica*, p. 10). But against such confusion Calogero exclaims:

non c'è speranza che intenda poesia, chi crede che la poesia sia presente in ogni istante della giornata umana.

(there is no hope of anyone's understanding poetry if he believes that poetry is present at every moment in the human day.)

(*ibid.* p. 11)

Let it be said, however, that Calogero is attacking not a weakness but a strength in Croce's system. For Croce himself would undoubtedly have answered to the title of 'panaesthetist'.[30] Thus, in an important passage of *Estetica* (p. 18), where he pointedly reformulates the aristocratic conception *poeta nascitur*, he declares that there is nothing but a quantitative difference between the artistic genius and the common man. We do in fact believe, he insists, that great artists 'reveal us to ourselves'. And this revelation would be impossible were there not an identity between the artistic imagination and our own. Indeed, rather than saying *poeta nascitur*, it would be better, urges Croce, to say *homo nascitur poeta*, and to admit that while some men may be great poets, the ordinary man, in a small way, is himself a poet.

Poetry, then, being for Croce, the specific creation of a common power of imagination is to be regarded as a natural even necessary aspect of our primitive constitution. And one cannot deny the significance of this. For where a poet does commit himself to the power of the imagination, the strength of his writing will lie precisely in the stimulus it gives to a constitutive sympathy in the reader. Thus Dante himself, in the *Inferno* and *Purgatorio*, informs the very extremities of his cultural inheritance with a rhythm that evokes in the reader an awareness of the earth and air, and change and immobility.

Even so, among the qualities one recognises in art, one must certainly number those which, so far from possessing any necessary appeal, are rather to be called gratuitous and arbitrary. In one aspect, art is a game and a holiday. Indeed on occasion, the value of a work may derive precisely from one's knowing that the author was not obliged to give it the form he did – nor, for that matter to create the work at all – and, conversely, from the realisation that, deeply as one may appreciate the work, it exerts no claim which we could not, if we should so decide, gainsay.

It is this – which concerns me very nearly in the discussion of the *Paradiso* – that Calogero allows one to acknowledge without discomfort. For in conjunction with his argument that art demands of one an 'act of renunciation', there is, in his writing, an insistence upon the 'divina saltuarietà ed eccezionalità dell' esperienza estetica' (*divine discontinuity and unusualness of aesthetic experience*) (*Estetica, semantica*, p. 10). Art, in the fullest sense, is out of the ordinary and occasional. Yet precisely for that reason it will require no automatic or everyday response but rather an act of deliberate dedication. Art is 'domenica nella settimana della vita' (*Sunday in the week of life*) (*ibid.* p. 12). And if finally one compares this phrase with Croce's description of art as 'the dream-phase of the cognitive life', giving emphasis to the terms of each analogy, one may appreciate how thorough Calogero's reassessment of the question is.

For where in Croce's metaphor, art appears as an ineluctable revelation, Calogero indicates, with no diminution of gravity, the gratuitousness of art – insofar as 'Sunday', too, is a solemn exception to the pattern of the work-a-day week, and, to the religious eye, a pure concession. Likewise, where Croce would endow us with, so to say, a natural capacity for the exceptional, Calogero requires an act of willing and judicious admiration. For as Sunday imposes upon the faithful an attention to its ordained meaning, so art is 'doverosa' (*obligatory*) in demanding of us the act of renunciation.[31]

One has yet to see, of course, what the consequences might be in respect of formal properties if one did regard poetry thus as a form of playfulness and its creation as directed by the 'atto di rinuncia'. Nor, on this matter, is Calogero himself especially enlightening.[32] Yet if I have dwelt upon his argument, the reason, as will be seen in Chapters Two and Four, is that his account of artistic psychology is remarkably consistent, in certain important respects, with Dante's own. And unfamiliar as Calogero's argument now appears, it is by no means without a precedent.[33] For many a poet has, on his own account, been supported in his work not merely by his 'sogno' or his imaginative energy, but equally by a single-minded intention towards the wonderful and exceptional. Thus Milton, determining to write 'things unattempted yet in prose or rime', constructed a list of ninety nine subjects to which he might apply himself without disgrace. And Dante anticipates him in this, resolving with less circumspection to write of Beatrice:

quello che mai fue detto d'alcuna.

(That which was never said of any woman.)

(*Vita Nuova*, XLII)

Nor can there be any doubt that when, in the *Paradiso*, he declares:

Que' gloriosi che passaro al Colco
non s'ammiraron come voi farete,
quando Iasón vider fatto bifolco.

(Those glorious adventurers who made their way to Colchis/ did not marvel as you will do/ when they saw Jason made a ploughman.)

(*Par.* II, 16–18)

he is demanding of his reader a reverence, and an entirely willing attention to the worth of his achievement. Moreover if any part of Dante's writing is to be called sophisticated in its self-possession and emboldened self-awareness it is surely the *Paradiso*. Calogero indeed suggests this when with evident justice he speaks of Dante's 'gioire della verità' in the canticle as 'Apollonian' (*Estetica, semantica*, p. 117).

The second question concerns the formal properties of poetry. Are we, that is to say, justified in expecting, whatever the subject of a poem may be, that its form will in some sense be concrete, or that one may appropriately ascribe to it a quality of unity or imaginative coherence? Croce clearly would have it that we are. But if Croce's view were the only one, it would, of course, be needless to prolong the discussion. For the unity of which he speaks is a spiritual unity, and the aesthetic image in which the experiences of the poet are compounded is a spiritual image. Hence, to allow into composition, as Calogero does, an act of decision is to destroy at once the peculiar integrity that Croce wishes to attribute to it.

But need one after all be so exercised about poetic psychology? Might one not, in fact, leave aside the question as to whether the spirit was operating in the aesthetic phase, and ask only, on the evidence of the work itself, whether its detail and components are fully consistent with, so to say, the imaginative logic of the whole?[34] To this Croce might well have replied that one may, as long as one accepts the draining from poetry of the human presence.[35] And in spite of every other difference my own inclination on this matter would be to agree with him. Nonetheless, Croce is notoriously unsympathetic to questions which touch upon the technical or material form of the arts. And this, in the case of poetry, is to be seen in his positive antagonism towards the analysis of linguistic style.[36] As a corrective then to Croce one may turn at this point to T. S. Eliot, who of course deserves attention not only for his work on the *Commedia*, but also for the sake of his own 'intolerable wrestle/ With words and meanings'.[37]

The two principles of Eliot's critical thinking which especially concern me are, firstly, his representation of the poetic act as the creation of an 'objective correlative', and, secondly, his emphasis upon the value in poetry of the visual or broadly sensuous image. The two notions are, of course, related. For precisely in his descriptive vocabulary, or in the impressions which are organised in his words, the poet will establish an orderly correlative to his state of mind. The complexity of thought, emotion and impressions will be reflected exactly in the complexity of the artistic object.[38] However, since the act of writing is itself an act of rigorous and inward discipline, the spiritual complexity of the poet will emerge, in any satisfactory and successful poem, not as an 'undisciplined squad of emotion', but as a balanced and final entity. Thus in the *Four Quartets*, where Eliot discusses the purposes of poetry quite as thoroughly as in his regular criticism, he writes feelingly of the 'imprecision' which the poet must remedy, and declares:

> Only by the form, the pattern,
> Can words or music reach
> The stillness, as a Chinese jar still
> Moves perpetually in its stillness.
> (*Burnt Norton*, 140–3)

The poet then will seek to create in words an image, a finished and consummate form, in contemplating which the reader may attain to a disinterestedness and pure composure of experience. And this image is at once a mode of unity and of experiental precision.

In his emphasis, especially, upon the ultimate 'stillness' which attends the experience of art, it will be seen that Eliot is by no means out of sympathy with Croce in his emphasis upon its imaginative disinterestedness. At the same time, Eliot's position appears at first to be challenged less by the *Commedia* than Croce's is. For the *Commedia* indisputably is visual in many of its effects. And, certainly, for much of the poem what is thought and what is seen are profoundly inextricable. Furthermore, one need only consider the use that Eliot himself appears to have made of the *Commedia* – and above all of the *Paradiso* – in the *Four Quartets*, to see how he might have found there the pattern and precision of an objective correlative. For as Guidubaldi suggests the canticle must have seemed to him a 'true symphony', where no motif was separable from the whole, but all were unfurled in answer to a scheme of echoes and reciprocation ('T. S. Eliot e B. Croce: Due opposti attegiamenti critici di fronte a Dante', *Ævum*, XXXI (1957), 162). And undoubtedly, turning from the *Quartets* to the *Paradiso*, one would be alert to a certain 'musicality', in which word and phrase and theme circle continually before one, arousing, as they do in the *Quartets*, new impressions, and promoting their own resolution until the still point is reached, and the mind brought back to a healthy and original unity. The *Paradiso* has often been described as a 'symphony' of music and light. Does not Eliot's conception of form only refresh and deepen this venerable apprehension?

It may indeed. Yet when Helen Gardner, noting the formal perfection of the *Quartets*, observes that we are left at the end not with the thought of: 'the transitory Being who beheld this vision, nor with the thought of the vision itself, but with the poem, beautiful, satisfying, self-contained, self-organised, complete', and affirms that Eliot's paragon in all this was Dante (*The Art of T. S. Eliot* (London.

1949), p. 185), one must surely demur. Indeed, Croce might well have warned one against this very conclusion. For right as Gardner may be about Eliot, and harmonious as the structure of the *Commedia* undoubtedly is, one cannot imagine that the poet who wrote 'Se mai continga . . .' would have permitted his 'transitory Being' to be obscured by such a harmony. Still less would he have wished the 'thought of the vision itself', its content and significance, to be, even in the interests of a formal perfection, obliterated.

Similar objections arise if, following Eliot, one places too great an emphasis upon the visual components of the poem. To do so must perforce encourage a slackness of intellectual concentration, and Eliot himself has been censured for this. Thus, Mario Praz, noting that the design of *Ash-Wednesday* was probably suggested by Dante's writing, observes that Eliot would seem to have read Dante without paying any great attention to the sense, but rather abandoning himself to the impressions he received from a few, clear visual images ('T. S. Eliot e Dante', in *Machiavelli in Inghilterra*, 2nd edn, Rome, 1943, p. 263). This is to undervalue perhaps the rigour which Eliot himself would require of a poem, in the fitting of part to part and image to image.[39] However, it is unlikely that Dante's writing would admit of any precision which did not arise from a due 'attention to the sense', at least on the author's part.[40] And one may add that, while Dante's imagination no doubt is predominantly a visual one, it would even so be an error to suppose that the visual qualities of a work need always be imaginative in mode. Thus, in the *Paradiso*, I shall argue, one may in fact approach the intellectual presence of the author more closely and appreciate more fully the precision with which he pursues his own meaning, if one allows the visual features of the work to be, not in a strict sense imaginatively organised, but simply descriptive or decorative in quality.

Be that as it may, I would insist that Eliot's poetic theory, in the two aspects I have so far mentioned, severely limits the scope and function of the art. Thus following Eliot, one's inclination will be to value rather the aesthetic form of a work (or at best the aesthetic persona which it reveals) than the actual thought or deliberate affirmation of the author. And this could scarcely be otherwise. For the language of which an imaginative unity may be forged is a language at odds with the language of responsible statement.[41] And the besetting limitation in Eliot's notion of form – a limitation to which Croce and Terracini are equally subject – is that he will admit as proper to poetry only those functions of language which may broadly be called synthetic.[42] One may briefly note the consequences of this in Eliot's attitude, firstly, to rhythm, then to the poetic word itself, and, finally, to terminology.

Speaking, then, of the auditory imagination, Eliot emphasises how rhythm may penetrate:

far below the conscious levels of thought and feeling, invigorating every word; sinking to the most primitive and forgotten, returning to the origin and bringing something back, seeking the beginning and the end.
('Matthew Arnold', *The Use of Poetry and the Use of Criticism* (London, 1964), 2nd edn, pp. 118–19.)

There could be no clearer statement of the synthetic power of rhythm.[43] The rhythm of the poet's utterance, as the reader receives it, will stimulate in him a profound sense of primitive unity, releasing in every word and phrase a vigour which relates to the 'beginning and the end'. And there is no denying that the position is persuasive and, for many poems, accurate. Nonetheless, it is important to ask whether rhythm may perform only this function. For it is rhythm, if nothing else, that will distinguish poetry from other forms of discourse. And one's understanding of what poetry is will in large part depend upon one's understanding of the potentialities of rhythm. An alternative, however, to Eliot's view will only appear when one turns to Dante's work.[44]

That Eliot's view of the poetic word is consistent with his understanding of rhythm may best be seen in the *Four Quartets*, where 'every word' is 'at home', and where 'every phrase and every sentence is an end and a beginning':

The complete consort dancing together
(*Little Gidding*, 216–25)

By its participation in the pattern 'the word's life is preserved almost miraculously by art, in a kind of true life beyond its life in speech' (Gardner, *The Art of T. S. Eliot*, p. 7). Because of this, however, the value of the word will not reside in its carrying any simple significance. Its function will be to perform not referentially but dramatically, or as a chord, so to say, in the global activity of the synthesis.[45] Thus when Eliot writes:

Time present and time past
Are both perhaps present in time future . . .
(*Burnt Norton*, 1–2)

we are confronted with a phrase whose structure, depending upon an intrinsic paradox and the force of 'perhaps', is tentative and contingent, a phrase which relates to a synthesis of emotion, in

Eliot's personal diffidence, and to a larger pattern, in which its suggestions may finally be organised. That there are sentences of this type in Dante's writing, even in the *Paradiso*, I do not deny. All I need emphasise here is how remote such a sentence must remain from direct affirmation.

With the question, finally, of terminology, one approaches the centre of the argument I am pursuing. For by terminology I mean those words which carry the burden of a poet's philosophy and system of thought. And it is in his treatment of these that a poet is most likely to reveal his conception of the truth to which he believes a poet may attain. To this matter I shall return in the following section. What may be said, however, is that Eliot, although for most of his career a Christian, is even so unwilling to make any direct use of Christian terminology, preferring generally to devise for the word which his faith required an expressive equivalent. This is to say, precisely, that his Christianity is 'embodied' in an imaginative form. And there are good reasons, historical and cultural, why this should be thought a proper and a satisfactory procedure.[46] Nonetheless it is theory and not history which leads Eliot to assert that Dante, as a poet, 'never does any real thinking' ('Shakespeare and the Stoicism of Seneca', *Selected Essays* (London, 1951), 3rd edn, p. 136). This is a strangely brutal statement.[47] Yet Eliot's whole conception of poetic form could have led to no other conclusion.

By now it will be apparent that, to find an alternative to Eliot's position, one must prepare to abandon the notion that poetic language is necessarily synthetic. And if one's concern were with Eliot alone, one could turn at once for support in this venture to the writings of Yvor Winters.[48] However, in Italy a programme similar to Winters', though superior in force and implication, has been presented by Galvano della Volpe.

From my present point of view, the most important feature of della Volpe's argument – and the centre of his own polemic – is his attack upon the error of which not only Kant and Romantic theorists are guilty but also 'all their successors' (among whom one must clearly include Croce and Cassirer, and, however remotely, Eliot himself). This error, in della Volpe's opinion, consists of having exchanged

la *immediatezza semantica* della parola poetica . . . per e con un'*immediatezza sinonima di intuizione* o *immagine pura*.

(the semantic immediacy of the poetic word . . . with and for an immediacy that is identical to intuition or the pure imagination.)

(*Critica del gusto*, p. 164)

Thus, arguing that there is 'in a rigorously literal sense' such a thing as poetic discourse just as there is historical or scientific discourse (*ibid.* p. 20), della Volpe asserts that when we frame our experiences in a linguistic form, it is impossible that we should ever entertain an image without simultaneously organising our impressions in a rational and conceptual manner:

non può avere alcun senso ... il parlare ancora ... di una conoscenza artistica per 'immagini' o 'intuizioni' soltanto e non insieme organicamente per concetti.

(it is senseless to go on speaking of an artistic knowledge (*that arises*) only through 'images' or 'intuitions', and not, equally, in an organised manner through concepts.)

(*ibid.* p. 17)

Every word will naturally carry with it a 'concetto esplicativo' (*an explanatory concept*) (*ibid.* p. 14), which is sustained by the scheme of lexical and grammatical features (*ibid.* p. 17). And the cognitive value, even indeed the visual clarity of an image, will depend not upon the activity of the imagination, but upon the attention of the poet both to the syntactical structure of his utterances and to the lexical and semantic aspects of the words he employs (*ibid.* pp. 71 and 15–16). Thus he concludes that

il poeta per essere poeta, e cioè per dar forma alle sue immagini ... deve pensare e ragionare, nel senso letterale dei termini...

(the poet, if he is to be a poet – that is, to give form to his images – has to think and reason in the literal sense of these words.)

(*ibid.* p. 20)

Now della Volpe's emphasis upon the importance in poetry of lexical factors and even more of syntax is, I believe, indispensable if one is to appreciate the 'philosophical' potentiality of poetry. And from a study of Dante's own theory and the text of the *Paradiso*, it will appear that della Volpe's work, in the aspects I have mentioned, is sympathetic to Dante's own.[49] Indeed, the illustrations which della Volpe offers in the pages I quote, come mainly from Dante's 'petrose'[50] – which is remarkable, for of all Dante's writings, these are the works which would seem to respond most satisfactorily to the 'expressivist' poetic.[51]

As to the question of rhythm, too, della Volpe is illuminating. For against the age-old inclination to make of poetic rhythm a form of music, he objects:

essendo la poesia un fatto essenzialmente verbale, linguistico, il cosidetto ritmo in essa non può non essere in quanto elemento fonico che una sorta di *significante* ausilario; per cui il ritmo poetico è indistinguibile dal significato che esso serve.

(since poetry is essentially a verbal, a linguistic fact, the so-called rhythm of poetry, insofar as it is a phonic element, cannot be other than a kind of auxiliary significant. Poetic rhythm, then, is indistinguishable from the significate that it serves.)

(*ibid.* p. 140)

To this I would certainly agree. For, as will be seen, rhythm is an important element in the kind of analysis which a poet is especially capable of offering. Indeed a principal feature of my argument will be that a poet, through the emphasis of his rhythm, may articulate and stabilise his meaning even more thoroughly perhaps than the writer of prose. Yet on this point, finally, I should mention a disagreement between my own position and della Volpe's.

For della Volpe, in emphasising throughout the conceptual 'significato', is concerned to demonstrate the possibility of there being a sociological or materialistic basis for poetic values (*ibid.* p. 21). In fact, if della Volpe is known at all outside of Italy, it is probably as a Marxist critic.[52] Thus, he argues, in attending to the semantic logic of the poet's words, one will in fact engage oneself to the specific vocabulary of concepts which characterise the poet's cultural epoch, and enter thus into the 'pathos' of his historical situation.[53] And certainly it is important to consider how the concepts which a poet employs are given weight and definition. Yet, against della Volpe, I suggest that by his rhythm a poet may demonstrate, as a more significant feature than any sociological determinant, his own deliberate attention to the terms he uses, and his commitment to their force. So far from discovering here the instance of a sociological pressure, one may rather discern the affirmation of individual choice and judgement.

One evident danger in this position, as in della Volpe's, is, of course, that one should obscure the distinction between poetry and prose. Though I shall have no opportunity to consider this question at length, the danger is not, I think, a very real one. And one may note in conclusion that Dante's own poetic achievement would seem to have depended, in some measure, upon his introduction into poetry of the lessons he had learned in writing prose.[54] Aldo Vallone, indeed, has suggested that, even after the *Convivio*, it remained for Dante to acquire in his poetry:

un linguaggio apofantico, che solo un alto della *discretio* può dare. (a statement-making language, such as only a profound sense of 'discretion' can give.)

(*La prosa del 'Convivio'* (Florence, 1967), p. 83)

The final question and probably the most important to my argument is an ancient one, concerning the relation between poetic utterance and the utterance of a truth. The question is as complicated as any could be, involving among other things the whole problem of the nature and use of language. Yet one cannot avoid it if one is to do justice to the *Paradiso*. And in point of literary theory, the issue stands at the centre of the present debate. For implicit in the notions of poetic psychology and of poetic form which hitherto I have associated with Eliot and Croce, there lies a particular understanding of the truth to which a poet may attain. To illustrate this connection, I shall turn shortly to the writings of Benvenuto Terracini. Firstly, however, one may consider, in outline, the position of Terracini's mentor, Ernst Cassirer, in whom of late the philosophy of the creative imagination has found a most magnanimous champion.

For Cassirer, art is 'one of the ways leading to an objective view of things and human life' (*An Essay on Man* (New Haven, 1944), p. 13). It is a process 'by which we ascertain and determine our concepts of the external world', by which, indeed, we 'discover reality'. For 'in the crucible of his imagination', the artist 'dissolves the hard stuff of things . . . and the result of this process is the discovery of a new world of poetical, musical or plastic forms' (*ibid.* p. 164). The value, then, of a work of art will be to make 'durable and permanent' the moments of our especial penetration into reality. And in the experience of art, the mind will exercise its peculiarly human freedom, as a creator of symbols, consciously to dominate, even to organise, the world after its own design.[55]

With much, of course, of what Cassirer says, no one would disagree, who wished to demonstrate the importance of the arts in human affairs. At the same time the notion of truth involved in this philosophy will evidently be a peculiar one. Indeed, for Cassirer, truth is a matter not so much of accuracy, or of a proven adequacy in utterance, but rather of the coherence to which an utterance may attain. Thus Edgar Wind writes that, for Cassirer: 'The criterion of inner consistency guarantees the relative truth of every single system; while the value of absolute truth can be attributed only to the totality of all possible systems' ('Contemporary German Philosophy', *JP*, XXII (1925), 485.) And if this generally is the case, for every kind of symbolic creation, its significance is especially evident in respect of language. For, in Cassirer's system, the force of an utterance will reside, not in a simple quality of logic or unmediated rationality, but rather in a certain totemic power, whereby the form in which reality is defined, being itself entire and finished, is an epiphany or momentary consummation of the greater whole. Thus, as S. K. Langer writes, 'in the emotive or mythic phase of mentality' with which Cassirer is particularly concerned, 'the first dichotomy ... is not, as for discursive reason, the opposition of the 'yes' and 'no' ... or truth and falsity; the basic dichotomy is here between the sacred and profane' ('Cassirer's Theory of Language and Myth', in *The Philosophy of Ernst Cassirer*, ed. P. A. Schilpp (Evanston, 1949), pp. 387–8).

The objections to this are various. But even in matters of literature, where Cassirer's understanding might appear most appropriate, the source of complaint is not far to seek. For as H. Kuhn points out 'the concrete individual, living his own life and participating in the life of civilisation ...[56] will not be content with learning that [a] story exhibits certain features typical of "mythic" thought. He is interested in knowing whether, perchance, it prefigures a truth' ('Cassirer's Philosophy of Culture', *The Philosophy of Ernst Cassirer*, p. 573). The desire, that is, for a pronouncement more explicit and practicable than the oracle may deliver, will be hard sometimes to repress. And surely it is common enough to expect of an author at least a certain wisdom.

But such a suggestion is likely to encounter at once the best wrath of the modern critic. After all, for centuries it has been accepted that, in Sidney's phrase, 'the poet nothing affirmeth and therefore never lieth', and that consequently the poet should not, as Keats put it, concern himself with the 'irritable reaching after fact and reason'. It may indeed be argued that where the desire for practicable truth is irrepressible, one had better seek enlightenment not in the arts but elsewhere – in, say, religious or moral teaching. Dante, however, considered no retreat of this kind to be necessary. And one may observe that, for different reasons, in twentieth-century experience, it would appear scarcely any the more necessary, since the other activities which I mention themselves seem unlikely to furnish a more reliable statement than the arts might. This experience is, of course, accurately reflected in Cassirer's philosophy. And from two at least of its implications, I shall not, I think, be able to escape. For, firstly, it will be found that Dante himself allows a degree of relativity into human pronouncements, even at their surest. And secondly, the validity of his poetic word will continue to reside, if not in an 'organic' coherence, at least in a certain conceptual coherence.

Even so, is there no way in which a poem might more thoroughly satisfy Kuhn's 'concrete individual'? If he is to be satisfied, one thing, certainly, which he will demand is that the poet allow some test or trial to be made upon his pronouncements, so that apart from any formal cogency or 'sacred' strangeness which they might possess, they may receive, as the case may require, correction or confirmation. And to suggest anything of this sort is, again, all but absurd in the light of modern criticism. Certainly, one looks in vain at this point for support of the kind that Calogero and della Volpe earlier supplied. Yet Dante, I think, is willing to countenance such a trial. And if he does not precisely suggest that his word will submit to proof, nonetheless he formulates it, in the *Paradiso*, in such a way as to acknowledge the possibility of agreement and disagreement. Calling into play the freedom, not of creative consciousness, but of discourse, he invites the very 'yes and no' which Cassirer appropriates to the most sophisticated phases of thought.[57] Thus in the *Paradiso* Cacciaguida demands of the poet:

> Ma nondimen, rimossa ogne menzogna,
> tutta tua visïon fa manifesta;
> e lascia pur grattar dov' è la rogna.

(But nonetheless, all lying put aside,/ make clear the whole of your vision,/ and then let them scratch where the itch is.)

(*Par.* XVII 127–9)

And recently, Salvatore Battaglia has devised an entire interpretation of Dante as 'il poeta dell'antagonismo', (*Esemplarità e antagonismo nel pensiero di Dante* (Naples, 1966), esp. pp. 242–8). It is, of course, true that in the lines I refer to here the challenge that Dante offers so 'antagonistically' is directed not only to the intellect of his reader but also to his moral and perhaps to his political being. Yet clearly, in responding to the 'rogna', one is called upon to decide whether Dante's understanding has any bearing upon one's own position, and, accordingly, to accept or deny the force of his utterance. The implications of this will concern me closely in Chapters One and Four.

However, as I have said, the question that Cassirer raises cannot be separated from questions of style and psychology. And to see the problem in its totality one may turn finally to Terracini.

Now Terracini whose field of study is stylistics rather than philosophy is greatly interested, like many a student of style, in the capacity of language for innovation and for the refreshment of regular usage.[58] But for Terracini the freedom which possibilities such as these reveal is not merely a linguistic freedom, but equally a freedom of human consciousness. Thus, with an acknowledgement to Cassirer, he argues, in *Lingua libera e libertà linguistica* (new edition (Turin, 1970)) at p. 61, that the 'enemy' of linguistic liberty is not, as traditionally was supposed, the system of linguistic law, but rather the subjectivity of the speaker himself, who in speaking must seek constantly a way to escape from the enclosure of his own individuality. In language, then, as in every other form of culture, we observe the 'aspiration of the individual towards universality', and, properly, linguistic activity is to be understood as a continual effort, on the part of the individual, to make himself known by means of and through this universality (*un continuo sforzo dell'individuo per manifestare se stesso attraverso questa universalità* (*ibid.*)). More particularly, there arises an antinomy or dialogue between the creative moment and the moment of social adaptation (*fra il momento creativo e il momento di sociale adattamento* (*ibid.* p. 94)). For the speaker, precisely by submitting to 'processes that belong universally to the human psyche', comprehends and expresses himself, affirming, at the same time, his own historical presence (*ibid.* p. 61).

The especial freedom, then, which is revealed in creative speech and to a high degree in poetry consists in the speaker's conscious discovery of himself, and in the definite establishment of himself in relation with his audience. But in this, too, there lies the 'truth' of an utterance. For in and through his words, the appreciable reality of the individual comes to be acknowledged, and the universal pattern, within which the knowledge of the individual is contained, is likewise given voice.[59]

As to the formal product of such freedom, Terracini proposes, of course, to locate it in the symbolic phase of utterance. For, following Cassirer, it is through the creation of symbols – which he takes to be the moments of living speech – that the individual enters the common world of speech, bringing to bear upon its grammatical structures his personal consciousness. Thus in an important passage of *Analisi stilistica: teoria, storia, problemi* (Milan, 1966, pp. 41–2), distinguishing between symbol and sign, he asserts that in the sign, the significate is pre-existent to the significant, and that the value of the significant is determined by a structure of shifting, reciprocal relationships (*mobili relazioni reciproche*), in short by a scheme of grammar. On the other hand, in the symbol there exists neither significate nor significant, but purely a moment of activity which is formal in character (*soltanto un momento attivo, di natura formale*). Indeed 'symbolic activity' can be understood and analysed only as a part of actual speech, where utterance is governed, not by a grammatical scheme but by some particular and definite tonality (*secondo una tonalità determinata, senza la quale . . . non è concepibile un discorso umano*).

In the symbol, then, by the peculiar emphasis and intonation that he gives to his words, the speaker actualises language, endowing it with an expressive tonality and recreating it by exercising once again the vital responsiveness of speech to circumstance and impulse. In the effort towards expression, 'significato' and 'significante' will be fused. For the formal adaptation which the expressive utterance requires will tell as clearly of the author's meaning as the conceptual statement itself. Thus in poetry, where the creative moment is most clearly in evidence, the elements of discourse will, he argues (*ibid.* p. 19), present themselves as the symbolic reflection of a particular state of mind (*come riflesso simbolico di un particolare stato di animo*), as the reflection of an emotion that would remain ineffable if it were not embodied in the pattern of these elements (*che sarebbe ineffabile se in essi non si configurasse*). [60]

Now it happens that to support his position Terracini draws heavily upon passages in Dante's own writing which I would turn to an altogether different purpose. And I shall note the more important cases of disagreement as they occur. There is, however, one instance which must be acknowledged openly. For it is in the *Paradiso* that Terracini himself finds the very type of the activity he is attempting to describe. Thus Dante, he declares, retaining an intangibly dreamlike sense of ultimate beatitude, must seek in the poetry of the *Paradiso*, both to stimulate afresh and to define his awareness of the experience (*cerca, destandosene, di fissarne 'la passione impressa'* (*ibid.* p. 33)). But since the experience of beatitude is, logically, ineffable, one is to suppose that Dante in speaking of it will seek to fashion for his reader not statements merely but valid and creative symbols, and by these to display anew 'la passione impressa'. This view accords, as will be seen, with a common interpretation of the canticle. Yet I cannot believe it to be accurate. And the questions which it raises are the subject, largely, of the following chapter.

Of my theoretical objections to Terracini's point, I would only say, extending my argument against an emphasis upon the synthetic mode of utterance, that one must be ready now to renounce the expectation of an organic connection of 'significato' and 'significante' in poetry. Indeed, to revert to Terracini's own distinction of sign and symbol, one must ask whether a poet might not in fact grant primacy to the 'significato'. Might he not, so far from drawing upon the generative energies of the symbol, exercise a discursive estimate of the means of signification, choosing from the canon of linguistic signs, a structure to facilitate a thorough and particular comprehension of what he, as a particular thinker, has considered it worth his while to say?

To allow this is to allow, as few twentieth-century critics are inclined to, the importance in poetry of a regular grammatical structure. And equally it is to allow into poetic language, as no expressionist or 'panaesthetist' emphasising the adequacy of word to intuition could, the arbitrariness of grammatical structure. Yet Dante himself encourages this departure. And if one should object that a shift of this kind will deprive us of the imaginative 'sforzo' which Terracini especially attaches to artistic experience, I would answer that only if one does relinquish this will one begin to approach, in at least the *Paradiso*, the core of its author's personal presence and the truth that he means to offer us.

To see, however, more clearly the nature of the truth which a poet might thus reveal, and the procedures he might employ to guarantee it, one must turn directly to the text of the *Paradiso*.

I

THE 'MODEST VOICE' AND THE *PARADISO*

What, then, is the character of the truth that the *Paradiso* presents? And what procedures are employed in the pursuit of it? I will not pretend that Dante supplies an explicit answer. However, in the episode of the Sun, which is, of course, the Heaven of Christian Philosophy, there is much to suggest what his view might have been. And no part of this episode touches more closely on my argument than Aquinas's speech about distinction.[1]

Thus, in Canto Thirteen, Aquinas, answering Dante's perplexity over the phrase 'non surse il secondo', concludes:

> E questo ti sia sempre piombo a' piedi,
> per farti mover lento com' uom lasso
> e al sì e al no che tu non vedi:
> ché quelli è tra li stolti bene a basso,
> che sanza distinzione afferma e nega
> ne l'un così come ne l'altro passo;
> perch' elli 'ncontra che più volte piega
> l'oppiniön corrente in falsa parte,
> e poi l'affetto l'intelletto lega.

(And for you let this always be lead upon your feet/ to make you move slowly like a tired man/ both to the yes and to the no that you do not see:/ for that man is really low among the fools/ who, without distinguishing affirms or denies/ in the one case [*of the 'yes'*] as in the other [*the 'no'*]./ For it happens that often opinion bends –/ when rushing – in a false direction,/ and then the affections bind the intellect.)

(*Par.* XIII 112–20)

From the discussion preceding this, one has learnt how King Solomon may, without contradiction, be regarded as a man of unparalleled sagacity. This is undoubtedly an important matter. Yet in his final emphasis, it is not to Solomon's wisdom, but to his own, as exemplified in the method of the foregoing argument, that Aquinas points. The understanding of Solomon's wisdom was achieved by a scrupulous attention to the 'surse' (*he rose*). And from this, the poet is himself to learn how he, too, in his pursuit of truth should be painstakingly attentive to words and to their meanings.

That the art of distinguishing is taught here by so authoritative a figure as Aquinas, and that its application guides one to the truth about King Solomon, are indications plainly of the value which Dante placed upon it. However, to understand how crucial he considered the art to be, one must follow Aquinas to the end of his speech, where at lines 121–9, he speaks not of the rewards of 'leaden-footedness', but of the hazards one encounters in disregarding it. Thus Parmenides, Melissus and Bryson, among the pagan philosophers, have, by the very hastiness which Aquinas seeks to moderate in his disciple, surrendered themselves to blind and wayward error. Similarly, through inaccurate scholarship, the Christians, Sabellius and Arius, have fallen into heresy – a failing which in Dante's eyes would imperil not only the spirit of the heretic himself, but the spirit also of those who might read his work.[2] To judge from these unhappy instances, a leaden-footed caution is imperative to the health of philosophical discourse.

Here, too, one senses the 'punta' of Aquinas's teaching. For Dante, whether or not he considered himself a professional philosopher, must certainly have realised, as he wrote these lines, that his ambitions in the *Paradiso* were of a kind with those of Sabellius and Arius, and quite as likely to lead him astray. Is it not probable, then, that Aquinas in recommending caution reveals one, at least, of the considerations which weighed with Dante when composing the work? Of course, Aquinas's point, in its particular context, is itself not altogether a surprising one. Yet Dante's own emphasis upon it remains impressive. And there is, I believe, evidence, to which I shall return, to suggest that his procedure, in style and psychology, was indeed consistent with Aquinas's teaching.

However, as to the immediate question of what, for Dante, might be needed in a true statement, consider how Aquinas's position, in Canto Thirteen, is developed, particularly at the final terzina:

> Non creda donna Berta e ser Martino,
> per vedere un furare, altro offerere,
> vederli dentro al consiglio divino;
> ché quel può surgere, e quel può cadere.

(Let not Donna Berta and Ser Martino suppose/ on seeing one man steal, another man make offering/ that they see them [*as they are seen*] in divine counsel;/ for that one can rise up and the other one can fall.)

Here, the scope of Aquinas's argument is considerably extended, so that it applies not only to the doings of the scholar but even to the most humble manifestations of intellectual activity. In church-door gossip no less than in academic debate, a speaker must pause and ponder on what he is saying. And in these last lines, the reason why he should is far more clearly stated than before. For where earlier Aquinas required merely that one should be cautious at those particular places where one does not 'see' clearly (*ibid.* 114), we are now told that, to human eyes, there is a prevailing obscurity around 'divine counsel' itself, and this, too, must be a check upon our pronouncements. Thus, as Aquinas extends his theme so he touches more nearly upon the relation of man, as a creature, to the mind of his Creator. And such, it appears, is the status of humanity in creation, as represented in the typical 'ser Martino', that a certain darkness must always surround man's speaking. Indeed, even the order of nature, as a manifestation of creative Providence, need not perpetually accommodate itself, so Aquinas reminds us, to the conceptions which men have formed about it.[3] Thus:

> Non sien le genti, ancor, troppo sicure
> a giudicar, sì come quel che stima
> le biade in campo pria che sien mature;
> ch'i' ho veduto tutto 'l verno prima
> lo prun mostrarsi rigido e feroce,
> poscia portar la rosa in su la cima...

(Again, let not people have too much confidence/ in judging, like those who weigh up/ the crops in the field before they are ripe;/ for I have seen all spring at first/ the thorn display itself stiff and fierce/ and afterwards bear the rose upon its height.)

(*ibid.* 130–5)

Throughout the canto, then, the poet insists upon the difficulty of reliable statement, tracing this to the very condition of human existence. He does not, of course, suggest that reliable statement is impossible. For his demand is only that men should be not 'too' secure. At the same time, one must conclude, if only from the treatment of ser Martino, that where a speaker has disregarded his existential condition, his utterance, in Dante's view, will, at the least, be suspect. And to ask that we be not too secure is to ask that our words should evince, let us say, a certain mediocrity of confidence, as, certainly, Aquinas's words do by their leaden-footedness.[4]

But precisely this mediocrity, I maintain, may come to constitute a criterion, if not exactly for 'truth', then at least for a speaker's truthfulness. And that Dante himself would have been satisfied by such truthfulness, and indeed have felt competent to test it, may firstly be seen if one examines the importance of the Aquinas speech in the context of the Sun episode.

For the curious fact is that, even though the episode is dedicated to Christian philosophy, Aquinas's speech (with the possible exception of Solomon's in Canto Fifteen) is the one conspicuously successful piece of reasoning that the poet here presents. Furthermore, in the course of these cantos, several types of reasoning more familiar than Aquinas's process of distinction are deliberately brought into disrepute. Thus, at the worst, there is the situation of which Dante speaks at the beginning of Canto Eleven, where he denounces the pettifoggery and self-interested anxiety by which rational argumentation may be turned to improper ends:

> O insensata cura de' mortali,
> quanto son difettivi silogismi
> quei che ti fanno in basso batter l'ali!
> Chi dietro a *iura* e chi ad amforismi
> sen giva, e chi seguendo sacerdozio,
> e chi regnar per forza o per sofismi,
> e chi rubare e chi civil negozio,
> chi nel diletto de la carne involto
> s'affaticava e chi si dava a l'ozio...

(O mindless concern of mortals/ how many are the fallacious arguments/ that make you downwards beat your wings!/ Some in the pursuit of law, others of the 'Aphorisms'/ have been moving, others following priesthood,/ and others ruling by force or fraudulent subtlety,/ some in thieving and some in public busyness/ and some, wrapped up in delights of the flesh,/ have been wasting themselves, and others have been surrendering themselves to idleness.)

(*Par.* XI 1–9)

Then again, though less fiercely, when in Canto Thirteen Dante differentiates the wisdom of Solomon and the preoccupations of the schoolmen, he deliberately parodies, Contini suggests,[5] the terms of scholastic questioning, the 'necesse' and the

> se del mezzo cerchio far si puote
> trïangol sì ch'un retto non avesse.

(whether in a semicircle, there can be made/ a triangle so that it would not have a right angle.)

(*Par.* XIII 101–2)

If, then, rational discussion can be perverted by selfishness, speculative thought may also incur, if not a charge of corruption, then ridicule, by pretending to the solution of inappropriate questions. And to these two instances one might add the case of Siger, who, for all his heroic rationality, is still somewhat a sower of discord, with his 'invidiosi veri' (*invidious truths*),[6] and even, perhaps, the case of Dante himself. For in Canto Thirteen, Dante, in one of those retractions which are so important a feature of the *Paradiso*, corrects an emphasis which earlier he reached by honest and systematic effort in the *Convivio*.[7] However, the most important illustration appears in the representation of the Franciscans and Dominicans.

In one respect, the dominant issue of the Sun episode is the conduct of the religious life. The two great Orders of Friar are shown both as, ideally, they should be, and as actually they are in the world. But in actuality, the behaviour of most of their members manifests exactly the fret and error to which the human intellect seems naturally prone.[8] Among them, there are those who would rather tamper with the Rule than obey it, and others who depart from it entirely. Many a member of the flock of Dominic 'di nova vivanda/ è fatto ghiotto' (for new kinds of food/ has become greedy) (*Par.* XI 124). One party of the Franciscans, seeks unduly to relax its obligations, another prefers to straighten them too fiercely (*Par.* XIII 124–6). To these particular failings one may add the bickering and the mutual acrimony which exists between the Orders. The poet, to be sure, does not mention it. Yet the very concord which reigns in Heaven between Aquinas and Bonaventure is a reproach to their earthly fellows.

The picture then which emerges from these cantos shows rational effort to be a source of continual friction and distress. Even at its best in, say, Siger, the argumentative pursuit of truth, is it seems, vitiated by a 'tiredness unto death' (*Par.* X 135). The obvious conclusion to be drawn from this, of course, is that in Dante's view perfect certainty and concord might only be achieved after death in Paradise. But this cannot be entirely accurate, at least for the Franciscans and Dominicans. For as one sees at *Paradiso* Canto Eleven lines 28–36, it is precisely God's will that the concord displayed by Aquinas and Bonaventure should be attained on earth. Each Order as established by Providence is a distinct principle, invested with its own characteristic truth. And if each is to serve God's historical purpose, in the Church, it is bound to act in unison with the other, acknowledging the truth of which the other is possessed. To fail in this is to thwart God's counsel and to contradict the reason of its own historical existence.

But if this is so, one may now understand why the processes of thought which Aquinas exemplifies should be so significant.[9] For it is precisely by applying these that the Orders might rediscover their true role in the world. Thus if each of the Orders would only let be its fruitless curiosity and intellectual aggression, returning, as the mystery of its institution requires, to the word and spirit of the original authority, it would, in finding again its own peculiar truth, find also, as Aquinas and Bonaventure do, the kindliness and courtesy in which the Orders might together promote the word of God. In the face of the unsearchable wisdom which ordained their existence, each Order must turn again to a punctilious and responsible consideration of the words which have been given them to uphold. Thus, St Bonaventure, describing the Franciscan community significantly as 'our volume' (*Par.* XII 122), speaks of the signature of the true Franciscan as 'I' mi son quel ch'i' soglio' (*I am that which I used to be*) (*ibid.* 123). By this surely he intends to indicate the need for an act of deliberate and considered conformity, such as an indiscreet speaker could never achieve. Even more importantly, we find that Aquinas in criticising the Dominican Order thrice repeats, as a deliberate puzzle, the phrase

u' ben s'impingua ...

(where one fattens well.)

(*Par.* X 96; XI 25 and 139)

And one may safely say that if others were to approach the phrase with the patience and respect that Aquinas, for Dante's benefit, accords to it, they, too, would quickly return to what they 'used to be'.

One may conclude, then, that the process of distinguishing, when understood in the way that the Sun episode demands it should be understood, as an unremitting carefulness in utterance, is of value precisely because it introduces into the nerve of an affirmation the spirit of St Francis and St Dominic.[10] Thus to ask of ser Martino that he should recognise his standing in relation to Divine Counsel is to ask nothing but an obedience to the example of St Francis, whose espousal of poverty represents a loving acceptance of his destiny in creation. Likewise the foolhardiness of a Sabellius or Arius would have been subdued by an attention to the way of St Dominic, who, as the 'sacred athlete' (*Par.* XIII 56) and the 'farm-hand' of Christ (*ibid.* 71), is pre-eminent for his intellectual dexterity and persistence. An awareness of one's limitations in existence and a perseverance of application – together, these will enable one accurately to understand the value of what another speaker might say, and no less to speak in such a way that one's own affirmations may truthfully embody one's relation to reality.[11]

From the Aquinas passage, then, and its context, there emerges the pattern for a certain kind of truthfulness; a truthfulness to which the poet will I suggest himself aspire in the *Paradiso*. One will see in later chapters how consistent this aspiration is with Dante's theoretical conception of his art.[12] Here, however, it would be as well, following the arguments of the introduction, to translate the implications of the Sun episode into a more general form – though this, I think, is not the place to conduct a philosophical defence, nor, perhaps, would Dante himself have consented to the terms of the translation.[13]

Firstly, then, one must emphasise that the notion of truthfulness which I propose involves the acceptance, in intellectual affairs, of a certain relativity.[14] Dante himself offers a justification for this. For rational argumentation, it appears, may very easily be led astray. Even observation may sometimes prove mistaken, or even malign, as when the crops and ventures of which Aquinas speaks turn treacherous. Certainly the truthfulness of the honest Franciscan or Dominican will be relative not only in respect of transcendent counsel but equally, being the statement of a peculiarly personal commitment, in respect of every other man's truthful word. This, however, is not to say that the validity which an utterance of this kind owns will be purely subjective.

For there is a test to which it may be put. It is true, of course, that this test cannot, in any normal sense, be regarded as a method of proof, since that, as I take it, would imply a conclusive appraisal of the information which a speaker offers. Yet, in circumstances where information can never be 'too' securely assessed, it seems proper to ask, if only as a preliminary, that a speaker should manifest an awareness of the conditions under which his words are produced. And judging from the Aquinas speech, the impress of that awareness would for Dante have been an evident caution in the use and interpretation of words. It is this certainty which appears, in Dante's view, to have guaranteed the pronouncements of his most important mentors. For not only is Aquinas applauded for his own leaden-footedness, but King Solomon himself, who is, in all likelihood, the 'modest voice' of Canto Fourteen line 35, is commended by Aquinas for the humility of his request to God (*Par.* XIII 91–102). Even Vergil in whom one might expect to see, at its purest, the power of rational proof, is shown to possess fundamentally an unfaltering awareness of the conditions which govern his existence. Indeed, the first words which he utters express the tragically accurate distinction:

Non omo, omo già fui.

(Not man, man once I was.)

(*Inf.* I 67)

To someone as overwrought as the pilgrim, this might seem a pedantic response. But in its selflessly leaden-footed way, it is reliable. And from it there derives the subdued and purposeful progress which, at the end of Canto One, replaces the panic of the opening.[15]

Still, what in the end would be the status of such an utterance? The danger throughout, of course, is that its validity should appear a matter only of rhetoric. Yet the very submissiveness of which I have spoken so often, will forbid the author to angle, so to say, for the attention of his audience. And, in a particular sense, one might well speak of the 'authority' to which such an utterance would lay claim. For as Contini suggests, emphasising the lapidary and essentially memorable qualities of Dante's phrasing:[16]

Dante is a producer of *auctoritates*. Culturally, he is a man of the Middle Ages, for whom (even leaving aside revealed truth), the 'sentence', the saying in which human wisdom is deposited, is a source of knowledge no less important than (and in any case prior to) reasoning and direct experience.

('Un'interpretazione di Dante' in *Varianti e altra linguistica* pp. 375–6)

Somewhat similarly, then, I would conclude that where a speaker, in confronting issues which transcend our normal powers of assessment, has displayed a proper humility and discipline, one should on that account be ready to receive him as an 'authority'. And in the circumstances of the *Paradiso* where so many things of which the poet speaks do indeed exceed our ordinary range, an authoritative word would seem especially to be called for. But why a modesty of proceeding should be appropriate to the canticle is the question I have now to consider in detail.

Why is it, then, that a modesty of speech should be appropriate in the *Paradiso*? One need not after all doubt the reality or the liveliness of Dante's heavenly experience. And it might be supposed that, above all things, he would desire in his poetry to exhaust that experience. But natural as that desire might seem, there is reason here to tread carefully.

For, in the first place, the experience of beatitude itself is, as Dante knows, by no means without its limitations.[17] A fear of the

Lord, even in Paradise, is still the beginning of wisdom. Then again while many things in Paradise are revealed to Dante which exceed his normal comprehension, there remain, for all that, many things which are not and cannot be revealed to him. In the Jupiter episode for example, the poet learns that, precisely in a state of grace, the true answer to certain questions is simply that the question itself ought never to have been put. The 'why' of predestination is obscure to the eyes even of the Justice Eagle, who declares nonetheless that his very ignorance is a sweetness to him (*Par.* xx. 136–8). The consequences of this, for men, are drawn in phrases which at *Paradiso* xx 133–4 echo exactly the earlier words of Aquinas:

> E voi, mortali, tenetevi stretti
> a giudicar...

(And you mortals, hold yourselves in check/ in judging.)

And if at this point the Eagle does behave as Aquinas himself might have done, a further reason is that like all the souls in Paradise, the just souls await, with awe if not with terror, the Day of Judgement – when God will finally reveal himself – and the Resurrection of the Body.[18]

In Paradise itself, then, a limit is set upon experience by the transcendence of Divine Counsel and by the promise of Resurrection. But if an understanding of this is necessary even in Paradise, a still more acute understanding of it will be necessary in the conditions of time. It is to earth that the poet must return, after his vision; it is here, too, that the record of his vision is to be written.[19] Nothing could demonstrate more clearly the poet's awareness of this than the recurrence in the *Paradiso* of the ineffability topic.

This, of course, is that very frequent device, whereby the poet confesses an inability to comprehend, in verse, the height of his experience. In the past, it is true, the inexpressibility topic has generally been regarded as evidence, not of modesty, but of an invigorating 'struggle with the unsayable' or dramatic rebellion against the ordinary confines of speech.[20] Recently, however, two essays have appeared, one by Francesco Tateo, the other by Angelo Jacomuzzi, which present these highly characteristic sequences in a different light. Thus Jacomuzzi, citing a number of the passages which I shall consider, writes:

> In these passages, in which the structure of the period is clearly marked by causal propositions, it is easy to see that the explicit sense of ineffability is not based upon nor articulated around the matter of the

vision, but around the nature and limits of the mind, of the memory, of the imagination and of speech.

('Il "topos" dell'ineffabile nel *Paradiso*', *L' imago al cerchio* (Milan, 1968), p. 119)

In the ineffability topic, then, we are to observe not so much the pressure that the poet's material exerts upon him, but his awareness of the mental limitations to which, in transcribing his material, he is naturally subject. Again where other critics would emphasise the expressive effort which the passages reveal, Jacomuzzi, one should note, draws attention to their grammar and the prevalent 'causal propositions'. This I would take to be an important point especially if one is to see the significance of the Aquinas lesson. For it is in the grammar of the ineffability sequences that one finds the surest indication of how restrained and careful Dante's words may be when approaching the inexpressible.[21]

Let me, then, consider in detail a number of these passages, beginning with the following from Canto Fourteen, where the connection with the Aquinas episode will be most clearly apparent:

Qui vince la memoria mia lo 'ngegno:
ché quella croce lampeggiava Cristo,
sì ch'io non so trovare essempro degno;
ma chi prendre sua croce e segue Cristo,
ancor mi scuserà di quel ch'io lasso,
vedendo in quell' albor balenar Cristo.

(Here my memory overcomes my wit:/ for that cross so flashed forth Christ,/ that I do not know how to find a fit comparison;/ but whoever takes up his own cross and follows Christ,/ will again excuse me for that which I abandon/ seeing in that luminosity Christ lightning.)

(*Par.* XIV 103–8)

This passage marks the transition from the Heaven of the Sun to the Heaven of Mars. In the episodes which precede and follow it, the common theme is the theme of sacrifice and spiritual poverty.[22] One has already noted this theme in the Sun sequence. And in the Mars sequence the images of martyrdom and of heroic asceticism in ancient Florence demonstrate how obedience and the acknowledgement of poverty pertain as well to the layman's life as to the life of the religious.

With this in mind, however, it seems likely, when Dante at the transition declares 'he does not know how to find a fit comparison' that his purpose is not to indicate an extremity or urgency of emotion, but to acknowledge rather an instance of his own peculiar poverty and to manifest precisely his acceptance of this condition. No word or analogy is adequate to his remembrance. Yet, poet though he is, Dante does not repine. Nor, most remarkably, does he lament even the lack of detail in his description of Christ. On the contrary, his principal concern, as one sees in the second terzina, is merely whether his own action in interrupting the narrative is an 'excusable' one or not.[23] The reason for his concern bears closely on my argument. For at this point – as, more generally, in an existential sense – the poverty of the poet is intrinsic to the reality he enjoys. He is 'poor', paradoxically enough, only because his experience of Christ is rare and great. If, then, with a submissiveness he might have learnt as well from Cacciaguida as from Aquinas, he chooses here to be silent, his object, I suggest, is to display an honest awareness of that paradox – the paradox that the reality of Christ, by its very presence, is unutterable. And no one who blames him for his action is likely to appreciate how real the vision is to him.[24]

The principal features, then, of the Aquinas canto are reflected in this passage. Where the word cannot command, the poet, acknowledging his particular poverty, will hazard no word at all. This finally will prove a protection to the authority of the little that he can say. There is, however, at least one difference between the Canto Fourteen passage and the Aquinas speeches which needs to be emphasised. For where in Canto Thirteen, it is the incalculable mystery of God which quiets the voice, here it is rather the brilliance of his presence. And this suggests two important developments of the original notion.

In the first place, it would seem that the very presence of truth is not enough to justify a man in speaking of what he knows. For even when the truth is present to him, there may still arise a disproportion between his experience and his powers, so that in regard to one aspect of his nature, particularly his power of speech, another aspect may effectively be as inapproachable as the transcendent wisdom of God. And the most important consequence of this is that in many of the 'inexpressibility' passages, the decision as to what may or may not admit of verbal definition is made to depend upon an exact examination, in point of scope and capacity, of the constituent faculties of the intellectual being.[25] So here, to speak is one thing, to remember quite another. Though speech may be possible only where memory is active, the action of the memory cannot, it seems, automatically ensure that speech should follow.[26]

But this, in the second place, is a matter of significance not only to the question of truthfulness but also to the questions of poetic psychology and form. For to argue in this way is to argue that, in composing his poem, Dante would feel unable to rely upon any direct or immediate connection of word and experience. In that case the justification of an utterance must clearly depend upon no simple relation which it might bear to a state of things, but rather to a demonstrable integrity in the introspection of the speaker. A certain self-knowledge, then, – the grounds of which are, for Dante, defined in Canto Fourteen – will be an essential component of reliable utterance. And in that case, too, it will plainly be inappropriate to expect in the style or behaviour of the poet any simple spontaneity of delivery. The force, however, of this conclusion, in respect of psychology and form, may best be seen from a further instance of the inexpressibility topic.

This is the passage in the final canto which begins:

> Da quinci innanzi il mio veder fu maggio
> che 'l parlar mostra, ch'a tal vista cede,
> e cede la memoria a tanto oltraggio.

(From that point on, my seeing was greater/ than my speaking – which yields before that sight – displays/ and memory yields at so great an outrage.)

(*Par.* XXXIII 55–7)

Now the reason in this instance why Dante cannot speak of his experiences is almost the exact contrary of his reason in the Mars passage. For where the vision of Christ in the Cross is firm and essential to him still, here only the 'sweetness' of the actual moment remains (*ibid.* 63). All that he knows apart from this is that his memory is outraged and overborne by the vision. Yet strikingly the very reality of the ravishment is itself taken as a point of reference, so that again one finds the poet measuring and assessing the conditions of his experience, and deciding, on the strength of this assessment, what he can and cannot say. Thus, in the phrase 'Da quinci innanzi . . .', he displays no desire to surrender himself to the memory. Rather, remembering how, at a certain moment his vision began to magnify, the poet surveys and defines the plan of his canto, and predicts, for the benefit of his reader, the relation in which his words will stand to the actuality of the experience. The lines, then, are evidence of an act of calculation. Certainly there can be no suggestion that in writing the canto the poet expects any wholly adequate word spontaneously to present itself.

From the point of view of modern poetic theory, few things, of course, would appear more restrictive than this. Yet the principle is not, I think, a restrictive one. For precisely through his reliance at such moments upon calculation, the poet affirms the value of merely human sense, and announces without exaggeration a confidence in the conventions of the intellect. It is, indeed, one of the finest and most abiding characteristics of Dante's thought that he should acknowledge, as a force which men are bound to suffer, the reality of God in its most terrible aspect, and yet insist upon the right of the human intellect to adjust itself towards this power in its own, albeit inadequate, terms. This certainly may be seen here.

So, with the 'maggio', where an exquisitely superlative colouring might have been expected, one finds rather a true comparative. For in the conventions of human judgement, the vision, however much it may exceed the word, may still be placed in a relation of 'more' to 'less'. And in the same way, the apparent baldness of:

Da quinci innanzi il mio veder fu maggio

is to be seen as an indication of a healthy and humane temperance, upholding the value of the words and the concepts – conventional as they may be – by which we commonly interpret our experiences. At this point one may well agree with Fubini, who suggests that the more rarefied Dante's experience here becomes, so much the more precise and scientific his language becomes ('L'ultimo canto del Paradiso', *Il peccato di Ulisse*, p. 124).

As to psychology, then, the ineffability topic illustrates the importance of introspection; as to form, the value of a reliance upon the normal conventions of speech and judgement. With this in mind, one may return to the first occasion of its appearance, in *Paradiso* Canto One.

From the lengthy exordium, consider the following two passages:

> Nel ciel che più de la sua luce prende
> fu' io, e vidi cose che ridire
> né sa né può chi di là sù discende;
> perché appressando sé al suo disire,
> nostro intelletto si profonda tanto,
> che dietro la memoria non può ire.

(In the heaven that most receives of his light/ I have been, and seen things that, to tell again,/ he that descends from up there neither knows how nor can; for drawing near to the object of its desire, our intellect plunges in so much,/ that behind it the memory cannot go.)

(*Par.* I 3–9)

O divina virtù, se mi ti presti
tanto che l'ombra del beato regno
segnato nel mio capo io manifesti,
vedra'mi al piè del tuo diletto legno
venire, e coronarmi de le foglie
che la materia e tu mi farai degno.

(O divine power, if you lend yourself to me/ so much that the shadow of the blessed realm,/ marked in my head, I may show forth,/ you will see me come to your favoured tree and crown myself with the leaves/ of which the subject [*of the Paradiso*] and you will make me worthy.)

(*ibid.* 22–7)

Dante's purpose in these passages, one might say, is to establish the psychological and the existential considerations which will govern him in the writing of the canticle. Certainly in the first of the passages one sees, without question, how rigorous are the limitations to which the poet is subject. Simply, there are many things in his vision which, on his return to earth, Dante neither 'knows how nor can retell'. And there is not the slightest suggestion that he desires to violate the boundaries of his condition. Rather, he speaks of the general law to which all who 'descend from up there' must agree. His own attitude to the law is apparent in the second terzina, 'perché appressando sé . . .', where so far from implying that it is at all irksome to him, he offers a reasoned account of its consequences, as if to signify an intelligent acquiescence. His intention, clearly, is to offer neither an exhaustive account of beatitude, nor a reconstruction of his experience, but rather to achieve, at the expense, even, of what his vision contained, the vital proposition of a part of it.

In that case, though, how is one to interpret the second of the passages? Does not the invocation of divine assistance, here as elsewhere, imply that after all the ambition of the poet *is* to say more than language normally would allow? The objection is an important one. But the poet defines his need for such assistance in a sense which must defeat it. What he asks for, in fact, is no access of suprahuman ability, but only as much assistance as may help him to win the laurel, and triumphant recognition from his fellows.[27] This ambition, which appears in a variety of forms throughout the *Paradiso,* is itself a great and taxing one. And in Dante's view, as will be seen, it is by no means inconsistent with the consummation of his own Christianity. Here, however, one need only emphasise how fully the passage suggests the poet's allegiance to the world of time. It is to this world that he addresses himself, hoping, by its supreme standard, to make his work accessible and satisfactory to his fellows.

In the same passage, finally, one may see something of how this ambition may affect his way of writing. For in its syntax, and particularly in the treatment of the word 'ombra', the passage demonstrates at once how rigorously, within the conventions of ordinary understanding, the poet demanded of himself a clarity of statement. One has only to remove the 'ombra' from its context to see how easily the word might be taken to suggest an unresolved even ambiguous yearning. It is indeed quite usual to suppose that Dante intended to express by 'ombra' something like 'merely the shadow', or 'unhappily no more than the shadow'.[28] Yet this interpretation is hardly permissible. For, in the first place, 'ombra', as used here, is technical in value, signifying, without any necessary appeal to sense or emotion, a self-sufficient, if minor, degree of the real, the reality of the 'immagine'.[29] And, what is more important, it is precisely the syntax of the terzina which insists upon this reading. For Dante writes '. . . se mi ti presti/ *tanto che* l'ombra del beato regno/ segnata nel mio capo io manifesti . . .'. Here, as even more obviously in the preceding 'si profounda *tanto*/ *che* dietro la memoria . . .', the 'tanto che' is a central and emphatic feature, establishing a logical connection, in respect of proportion and consequence, between the three entities, 'ti', 'ombra' and the laurel-crown that Dante expects to win. When in a certain way the three are conjoined, then, Dante judges, his triumph will be assured. Merely, then, to play its part in the formula of the poet's judgement, the 'ombra' has evidently to be taken as something definite and calculable. Any emphasis upon its emotional and sensuous connotations would prevent this. Yet such an emphasis is possible only if one overlooks the steady progress of meaning designated in the syntactical plan.

Here, then, in establishing the conceptual simplicity of 'ombra', the poet employs the commonsense logic of syntax, analysing his meaning in terms of syntactical convention in much the same way that he does elsewhere in terms of the 'more' and 'less'. It is with this that one returns to the lesson of Aquinas. For syntax, when so deliberately used, is a very intimate and pervasive agent of discrimination. And certainly it is to the syntax of the *Paradiso*, which will prove throughout to be especially stringent, that one must look if one is to find linguistic evidence of Dante's own 'leaden-footedness'.

Lest it be supposed, however, that this is a formula only for efficiency in thought, consider lastly the passage where the soul of Saint Peter encircles Beatrice:

> con un canto tanto divo.
> che la mia fantasia nol mi ridice.

(with a song so divine/ that my imaginative power does not repeat it to me.)

and where Dante concludes:

> Però salta la penna e non lo scrivo:
> ché l'immagine nostra a cotai pieghe,
> non che 'l parlare, e troppo color vivo.

(Therefore my pen leaps and I do not write it:/ for our imagination, as well as our speech,/ is much too vividly coloured for such folds.)
(*Par.* XXIV 23–7)

What is especially notable in this case is the decisiveness, even the pride that one hears in the 'e non lo scrivo'. The heavenly song, to be sure, is infinite in subtlety. But since there can be no question of his echoing it, the poet, with no negative unwillingness, stands down from the attempt. The significance of the decision is various. In the first place, precisely by his unwillingness to compromise its splendour, the poet holds out an earnest of how real and valuable he knows the song to be. One may add, however, that, in the Examination sequence from which the passage is taken, such caution is especially fitting. For here, certainly, the poet cannot afford the blunderings of a Sabellius or Arius. At the same time, the value of his caution resides not only in the reverence it displays, but equally in the dignity and the self-possession which the poet, by his very silence, secures for himself. Unashamedly, he will say nothing nor strain himself beyond the powers he naturally has. On the honesty of that decision there rests, as the poet would seem confidently to realise, his own authority among his fellows.

To certain of the inexpressibility passages, I shall return in later chapters, where I shall also consider the implications of the author's 'leaden-footedness' for the reader's reception of the work. However, there is by this time at least one important objection which must, I think, have presented itself. For the *Paradiso*, surely, cannot be as consistently 'leaden-footed' as hitherto my argument may have suggested. To be sure a certain modesty of procedure has long been reckoned among the most valuable attributes of the poet's style.[30] And my own concern with principle and theory will, of course, lead me to give an especial prominence to it. Considering, however, that even in Canto Thirteen of the *Paradiso*, there occur such passages as that beginning 'Lì si cantò non Bacco, non Peana . . .' at line 25, I would agree very willingly that the concept of leaden-footedness cannot, as I have presented it so far, be wholly appropriate to the canticle. From the first lines of the canticle, one senses unmistakably the joy that inspires the poet in his 'ultimo lavoro'. Nor could any reading of the *Paradiso* be at all satisfactory if it ignored a canto like the Twenty Third – to which I shall return in my final chapter – where Dante responds to the vision of Christ's triumph with a miraculous vivacity of image and effect.

Even so, it is important to emphasise that the joy which Dante so fully displays in the canticle is itself inseparably connected with the confidence he has in his own understanding of the Christian faith. His purpose here is, after all, to declare finally the principles of his belief, and, no less to display, through his presentation of Beatrice, the true centre of his essential being. And joyous though this declaration will naturally be, there is every reason to expect, since it is indeed a declaration of his faith, that the poet's joy will be compatible with a carefulness and discipline of procedure. In fact I would suggest that, in the particular case of the *Paradiso*, the very leaden-footedness of the poet is itself the ground from which his exhilaration securely rises.

To illustrate this, one may turn here to the visual imagery of the canticle. Certainly to any reader of the *Paradiso* the visual imagery is itself likely to be a principal source of pleasure. And there are other reasons, too, why I should consider it.

For in the first place, the images of the canticle which typically assume the pattern of 'come ma non così' (*like this but not thus*) may be regarded quite satisfactorily as recurrent instances of the inexpressibility topic, pointing as they so frequently do, to the intrinsic limitation of the poet's word.[31] In the second place, it is, of course, to the imagery of the canticle that modern critics, both as historians and aestheticians, have given most of their attention. Indeed in one interpretation, Dante's imagery has commonly been regarded as an alternative to the normal language of concepts. Thus Battaglia argues that just as in the physical universe of mediaeval man, all objects reflected the significance of the spiritual world, so too the images of the *Commedia* represent concepts directly, and are consequently to be regarded no longer merely as utterances but as, in their own right, 'things' ('Linguaggio reale e linguaggio figurato' *ACNSD* (1962), 34–5).

This type of reading, though it runs counter alike to my theoretical and to my stylistic argument, is undoubtedly a compelling one, in explaining not only the vivacity of the *Paradiso*, but also its 'truthfulness'. Yet it has, I believe, its weaknesses.[32] And in discussing these, I shall, I hope, be able to show how the imagery of the canticle, which does, to be sure, reveal a great brilliance of perception, may still not be inconsistent with the deliberateness of which I have been speaking.

The critic whose work I wish to concentrate on is Joseph Mazzeo. Mazzeo's position is not identical with Battaglia's. Rather, he is the representative of a school which latterly has sought to interpret Dante's poetry in the light of Platonic or Platonising doctrine.[33] Still, Mazzeo is as deeply concerned as Battaglia with the force of Dante's imagery, and as eager as I am to represent the *Paradiso*, especially in its relation to the ineffable, as, in some way, the utterance of a truth.

The essential argument, then, which Mazzeo proposes is that Dante's utterances are to be taken as the *dicta* of inspiration, even, in a more or less technical sense, as those of a mystagogue, conducting the reader to an ever deeper awareness of the ideal. The truth, therefore, which the *Paradiso* offers is to be acknowledged under a condition of increasing enlightenment, whereby the enthusiasm of the poet and the enthusiasm of the reader correspond, thanks to the power of poetic utterance, in a gradual comprehension of a final whole. Thus, arguing that, in Dante's view, imagination is the direct recipient of divine inspiration, Mazzeo attributes to the poet an ability, in imagination, to triumph over the ineffable, and quotes with approval J. D. Sinclair's comment upon *Purgatorio* Canto Eighteen, lines 13 *et seq.*:[34] 'poetry is the utterance of the truth in terms of the imagination which cannot otherwise be known or told'.

It will at once be apparent that Mazzeo's view carries with it an understanding of Dante's style which, if his position were accurate, would gravely undermine the argument I am pursuing. For his contention is that, quite apart from the importance of Dante's explicit statements, his images act, in sequence, as the 'symbolic representation of a particular reality bringing us closer to what that reality is in itself' (*Structure and Thought*, p. 49). In this way Dante's images are to be compared with those of which Dionysius speaks in the Ninth Epistle, – figures which 'not only help us to understand what we have grasped of reality, but lead us to that reality' (*ibid.* p. 44). Consequently, at those moments when he encounters the ineffable, Dante may be said to 'leap' from one image to another in the process of accommodating himself 'to a reality which the individual images both hide and disclose' (*ibid.* p. 48). In the end Mazzeo is prepared to maintain that Dante, in the manner of Dionysius, resorted to paradox and ambiguity in his imagery, since – to paraphrase Dionysius – 'only paradoxical terms can be used to describe the luminous and more than luminous dark, which terms both *hide* and *reveal* the divine mysteries' (*ibid.* p. 43).[35]

Now, as analysis will show, there is little evidence in the text itself to indicate any extensive reliance upon paradox.[36] However, in principle, the difficulties of Mazzeo's position may best be overcome if one returns to the question of inspiration. For in the Sun episode there are indications of what Dante did consider inspiration to be. And these do not consort with the notion of vatic rapture. I refer in particular to the evidence of the Solomon figure, who speaks some of the most elevated poetry of the whole canticle, and who, as Aquinas describes him, at the moment of his great request, is shown to be in direct communion with God – which is surely to say in a state of inspiration.[37]

The significance of Solomon in the *Paradiso* is highly complex. Still whatever else he signifies, he must, as the author of the *Song of Songs*, be regarded essentially as a type at once of the human lover, and the lover of wisdom. Nothing would appear more Platonic, even Socratic, than this. Yet in two respects the intelligence of Dante's Solomon is wholly at odds with the spirit of Platonism.

In the first place, it is through Solomon, in Canto Fourteen, that Dante promulgates his belief in the Resurrection of the Body.[38] And there can be little doubt that Dante here is speaking of a true body, and not of an idealised or spiritualised substance.[39] Then, in the second place, in Canto Thirteen the exemplary value of Solomon's behaviour at the moment of inspiration is to be found, as Aquinas shows, in the restraint with which he asks for wisdom only

> acciò che re sufficiente fosse.
>
> (so as to be a satisfactory king.)
>
> (*Par.* XIII 96)

The especial virtue of this request is that, simultaneously, it recognises the transcendence of God – who will not yield himself to the inquiries of the metaphysicians – and no less makes clear the worthiness of the human sphere of creation, which merits, in God's eyes, the sincere attention of a just king.

The character, then, of Solomon's inspiration is profoundly consistent with his acknowledgement of the Resurrection in Canto Fourteen. For it is this inspiration which leads him, in contradiction of a mystical Platonism, to appreciate firstly, that the physical and natural orders of existence are worthy in themselves of a high regard, and secondly, that the ultimate reality of God, in one aspect, is entirely unreachable. So even those who see beyond the present world, are required, as it were, to return to it, recognising the world as no mere shadow, but as a reality for which God has prepared a final glory. Even (or especially) the wisest of men, in their prayers, will approach their God not only as an illuminating spirit, but equally as a transcendent power on whom the mysterious creation and the recreation of the world depend. It is right, therefore, that the condition in which the truths of inspiration are accepted should be a condition of modesty. Rapture there may be at the moment when they are conceived. Nonetheless the voice of inspiration is the 'voce modesta'. For the accent of modesty is an accent in which one's love of the world and one's reverence for its creator may both be made manifest.[40]

Evidently, then, the Solomon sequence will lead one to a view of truth and of intellectual propriety very similar to that which I have associated with the Aquinas sequence.[41] And for the interpretation of Dante's imagery in the *Paradiso* the importance of Solomon, the earthly king and herald of Resurrection, is as great as the importance of Aquinas for the understanding of the poet's intellectual procedure. For, by the promise of Resurrection, the facts of the physical world are sanctioned and dignified, as, indeed, they are by the present glory of God which:

> per l'universo penetra, e risplende
> in una parte più e meno altrove.

(through the universe penetrates, and shines back/ in one place more and less elsewhere.)

(*Par.* I 2–3)[42]

But, knowing that, the poet would surely seek, not to force these facts into the speculative conjunctions of metaphor and symbol, but rather, with a positive recognition of their value, to describe them as precisely as he may. The facts of the world may themselves relate an adequate reality – the reality to which the 'sempiternal flames' of the philosophers are longing to return (*Par.* XIV 61–6). And a man has only to acknowledge, as Solomon and the philosophers do, that the sphere of physical nature, properly, is his, for the meaning of it to reveal itself. So the souls of the Just, who are quick to understand how immeasurably the deity exceeds 'ogni minor natura' (*every lesser nature*) (*Par.* XIX 49), at once establish the value of the 'minor natura' when, taking upon themselves the character of natural birds, they proclaim and celebrate the great sentence of Solomon: *Diligite Iustitiam* (*Par.* XVIII 91–6). The 'just' meaning of the physical world is written in the existence of its creatures, and those who approach it justly may read it there. But the consequence of this must be that the poet, in transcribing the images of nature, will manifest the greatest reverence for the integrity of his 'text'. And, in point of style, the form which this reverence takes is, as will be seen, a lucid, even scientific particularity of description.

But a particularity of this sort, though very different from the intuitive particularity of the modern image, is, of course, entirely compatible, in its scientific tenor, with the discipline which Aquinas demands. Indeed the Justice Eagle itself, in writing out the *Diligite Iustitiam* with fine ceremony across the sky displays something very like the carefulness which Aquinas requires of the human speaker. Again, at the opening of Canto Thirteen, there occurs a passage which, if not in all respects a typical one, does largely illustrate what the reconciliation of King Solomon and Aquinas might imply for the style of the *Paradiso*:

> Imagini, chi bene intender cupe
> quel ch'i' or vidi – e ritegna l'image,
> mentre ch'io dico, come ferma rupe –,
> quindici stelle che 'n diverse plage
> lo cielo avvivan di tanto sereno
> che soperchia de l'aere ogne compage;
> imagini quel carro a cu' il seno
> basta del nostro cielo e notte e giorno,
> sì ch'al volger del temo non vien meno . . .

(Let him imagine, whoever wishes truly to understand/ that which now I saw, – and let him retain the image/ while I speak, like a solid rock –/ fifteen stars that in various regions/ enliven the sky with such a clearness/ that it overcomes all density in the air;/ let him imagine that Wain to which the bosom of our heaven/ is sufficient both night and day, so that with the turning of its pole it does not fail)

and so on through image after image, until:

> e avrà quasi l'ombra de la vera
> costellazione e de la doppia danza
> che circulava il punto dov' io era.

(and he will have almost the shadow of the true/ constellation, and of the twofold dance/ that circled the point at which I was.)

(*Par.* XIII 1–21)

It will be apparent at once that imagination here is called upon to act in no creative way.[43] Rather, one finds what Coleridge would have called the operation of the fancy. The realities of the world, that is to say, are subjected merely to a certain rearrangement – – though a rearrangement such as this could be countenanced only by a mind impassioned with astronomy. And where, say, the sublimities of the *Inferno* and the delicately vital images of the *Purgatorio* do indeed lead the reader, 'creatively', into modes of experience which might otherwise be unattainable, these lines, elaborate though they are, are intended to serve simply as a 'rock', a steady and comprehensible point of reference, where, lacking the power to proceed any further, the mind may naturally settle itself.

The value of such an image is twofold. Firstly, as in the case of the syntax which accompanies the inexpressibility topic, the poet establishes with his descriptions the conventions by which he may best define his understanding of beatitude. It remains true that he cannot speak directly of what he saw in Paradise. Yet confident by virtue of his vision of the reality of God, he may also be confident of the scheme which God has prepared for man.[44] And assured of his own right-mindedness in the eyes of God, he may proceed to establish, from the images of the world, a token, or, so to say, an authorised coin, to stand for what he has experienced. In receiving that, the reader may expect, if no sudden insight into his own beatitude, then a reliable understanding of how one man, 'figurando il paradiso', might, in the normal terms of humanity, grasp and comprehend his own experience.

Secondly, as well as the careful application of the mind which the passage so clearly demonstrates, there is to be found in it another quality, a quality, I mean, of solemn and ceremonious joy. It is this which may compensate for the tension of ecstasy which Mazzeo would have one feel. For the very fact that these images are, in the end, only a convention for the truth, encourages one to approach them as the enacting of an intellectual *ludus*.[45] To be sure, the distance between the human mind and absolute truth may impose an extreme discipline upon a speaker. Equally, however, it may prove a liberation, in that once a man has whole-heartedly consented to the Rule, its convention may become for him the counters of an intelligent play. Thus the Souls in Jupiter not only take the greatest care over the phrase *Diligite Iustitiam*, but also, by their action decorate and embellish it. Thus, too, when Aquinas concludes with:

e poi l'affetto l'intelletto lega

his words certainly are as well articulated as one might expect. Yet in their superb balance, and in the rhyming of the ' – etto', there is also a flourish of triumphant and conscious artistry as the argument reaches its clear, unwavering climax. Lastly, in the present passage, a moment occurs of the purest and most liberated play when after twenty lines of rigorous concentration, Dante informs us that now we might have 'quasi l'ombra da la vera/ costellazione'. Still only 'almost', and even then, almost 'the image'. But the dance of word and astronomical description has for the reader been itself a reality, and one will, I suggest, touch upon the poet's own mind more nearly if one enters with him, willingly, in this dance than if one supposes the 'quasi' to signify a tension or fictive 'ansietà'. For to Dante, whether one shares his outlook or not, the *Paradiso* is the ultimate formulation of a life-long belief.[46] And in the solemn freedom of his triumph no less than in the rigour of this final statement, one may actually hear the poet, if one respects his enterprise, as he himself would wish to be heard, and see what he has decided one ought to see.

2

DANTE'S CONCEPTION OF POETIC DISCIPLINE

In a number of ways, I believe, the principles I have associated with the notion of intellectual modesty are consistently foreshadowed in Dante's own pronouncements upon his art. My intention therefore in the following two chapters is to examine, partially at least, what Dante himself has to say about the literary act, so that in the light of his theoretical writings one may recognise a general application in relation to the *Paradiso*.

In the present chapter I shall consider particularly the spirit and psychology of poetic discourse, in the next, the form which a 'modest' piece of writing might be expected to possess. Throughout, however, the feature of Dante's theory which evidently must be of greatest interest, pursuing the argument of the preceding chapters, is the emphasis which the poet places upon the moral and intellectual potentialities of literary culture.

In one respect such an emphasis is not at all remarkable. For, to the theoretician of Dante's era, literature was pre-eminently didactic in its purport and significance. As to its creation, the principles which governed it were assumed regularly to be those by which the mind proceeded in every other responsible engagement.[1] Nor can one doubt that Dante would largely have assented to these notions. Indeed, his awareness, throughout his writing, of a responsibility towards his reader appears to have been quite exceptionally acute.

Yet it is not sufficient, or even, at the last, entirely accurate in considering what for Dante was the intellectual importance of poetry to speak of poetry only as a didactic influence. For what is remarkable is the consistency with which, in Dante's view, every aspect of literature, be it a matter of form or of procedure, is related to the moral and intellectual virtue of its author. Thus, as will be seen, the right-mindedness of an author will for Dante reveal itself not merely in the explicit purposes of his work, but also in the most intimate manifestations of his technique and style. The responsibilities of an author, so far from being those only of a teacher to his disciple, are represented likewise among the vital responsibilities of his spiritual existence. As Mario Casella has suggested every linguistic question will resolve itself for the poet into an urgent investigation of his own being ('Il "Volgare Illustre" di Dante', *GCI*, I (1925), 37). Contini, too, declares that for Dante technical method is precisely a means for the investigation of the inner self (introduction to the second edition of the *Rime* (Turin, 1970), p. XI).[2] And P. V. Mengaldo, in his invaluable edition of the *De Vulgari Eloquentia* (Padua, 1968), locates the originality of Dante's theory in 'an interiorization of the norms of poetic art' (p. XLVIII).

Two consequences of this view particularly concern me. For firstly, where the procedures of composition themselves possess so inward a significance, it will be seen that decisions as to the form and structure of a work, which now one might think of as literary or aesthetic in character, are to be understood rather as the product of a deliberate and regulative introspection. So that, in judging even the formal or linguistic detail of a text, Dante would encourage one to expect an appreciable demonstration of its author's philosophical conscience.

From this already certain resemblances may be apparent between Dante's theory and his procedure in the *Paradiso*. However, let me concentrate for the moment only upon the discipline to which, in such a conception of his art, the poet will have to answer, considering in particular three passages, the first from the close of *Convivio* Book One, the second from *De Vulgari Eloquentia* Book Two, chapter four, the third, the Bonagiunta episode – from a sequence of the *Purgatorio* in which the poet conducts an oblique but nonetheless coherent investigation of poetic principle.[3]

In each of these instances, one will observe not only what the poet might have demanded of himself in composition, but also how in the light of his principles he was accustomed to assess the behaviour of other writers. Thus in *Convivio* I v *et seq.* Dante offers, firstly, an explanation of why he should have written the work in the vernacular rather than in Latin. The decision to do so, while of cardinal importance in his literary development, was in part no doubt dictated to him by reasons of didactic expediency and artistic inclination.[4] Yet Dante himself is at pains to represent his choice as a matter of philosophic and deeply spiritual propriety. And in this regard nothing is more revealing than his assault upon those Italians who, where he would have chosen the vernacular, persist in their preference for Latin.

Thus with a vehemence which would be wholly disproportionate if the issue were less than vital, Dante assails 'li abominevoli cattivi d'Italia che hanno a vile questo prezioso volgare' (*the detestable wretches of Italy who hold this precious vernacular cheap*) (*Con.* I xi 21). Within what appears a literary lack of grace, Dante discerns a very perilous corruption of the spirit. For pride itself is the failing of those who, while they accept the vernacular, do so apologetically, in the hope that, blaming their own shortcomings upon the medium, they may still be acknowledged as 'masters' (*ibid.* 11–12). On the other hand, the evil may appear as envy, moving a man to deride in others the language which he himself is incapable of using correctly. For:

> Intra li uomini d'una lingua è la paritade del volgare; e perché l'uno quella non sa usare come l'altro, nasce invidia.
>
> (Among the speakers of one language, there exists equality in respect of the vernacular, so that when one man knows how to use that language less well than another, there arises envy.)
>
> (*ibid.* 17)

And to pride and *invidia* there may promptly be added, among other vices, cupidity and avarice. For 'la terza setta contr' a nostro volgare si far per cupiditate di vanagloria' (*the third party against our vernacular is formed out of a lust for vainglory*) (*ibid.* 15). Already in fact in chapter nine Dante has spoken wrathfully of those who, again, rejecting the vernacular for the more professional Latin, prostitute the intellect to wealth and pomp:

> E a vituperio di loro dico che non si deono chiamare litterati, però che non acquistano la lettera per lo suo uso, ma in quanto per quella guadagnano denari o dignitate.
>
> (I say to their grievous shame that these ought not to be known as men of learning. For they acquire learning not for the sake of learning itself but only inasmuch as they gain by it money or status.)
>
> (*ibid.* ix 3)

Pride, *invidia* and avarice – these of course are the very evils which at *Inferno* VI line 74, XV line 68 and throughout the Cacciaguida sequence Dante identifies as the triune cause of civic disaster. But for Dante, it appears, they are as likely to be present in literary behaviour as in any other civic or social or personal undertaking, so that even the form of language which an author favours may tell in the reckoning of his virtue.[5]

The converse of this must clearly be that Dante himself, in adopting the vernacular, was moved not by practicality and sentiment alone, but as well by a desire to signify his own avoidance of the corruption which affects the 'evil men of Italy' (*ibid.* xi 1). It is to this, too, that his insistence upon the 'pronta liberalitade' of the vernacular points (*ibid.* viii *et seq.*) For liberality itself, being specifically the opposite of pernicious greed, is a social and personal attribute of the highest order, the exercise of which as D. Consoli suggests 'implies a sense of responsibility and a rectitude of spiritual disposition' (*ED* III, p. 639). In this sense, indeed, liberality is a form of just behaviour,[6] and will depend, one may add, like every other mode of justice in Dante's system, upon the willingness of the individual to practise patience and self-denial.[7] Certainly, against the avaricious, Dante asserts that literature must be approached 'per lo suo uso' (*for its own sake*) (*ibid.* ix 3–4), and not for any benefit it may bestow upon its author. Maintaining, curiously, that the vernacular in the *Convivio* is to be regarded as a 'gift' (*ibid.* viii), Dante claims for his choice of language the value of a free act (*ibid.* viii 14), governed by clear purpose and honest intention.[8] Precisely, then, as the gift of a liberal mind, the vernacular, it seems, will betoken the merit of its devotee.

Now the *Convivio* is a work which in every aspect is dominated by a conception of the ethical and even political purposes of existence. It is not, therefore, surprising that literature, too, should be required to answer to the norms of justice. Yet the same principle, with some modification, is sustained with equal force in the poetic theories of the *De Vulgari Eloquentia* and in the *Purgatorio*.

Consider the fourth chapter of the *De Vulgari Eloquentia* Book Two. The chapter is constructed around an interpretation of the Horatian tag 'Sumite materiam', and a passionate evocation of the *Aeneid* Book Six. Thus of 'Sumite materiam', Dante writes:[9]

Ante omnia ergo dicimus unumquenque debere materie pondus propriis humeris coequare, ne forte humerorum nimio gravata virtute in cenum cespitare necesse sit: hoc est quod Magister noster Oratius precepit cum in principio Poetrie 'Sumite materiam' dicit.

(Above all, therefore, we declare that each poet should balance the weight of his subject against the strength of his own shoulder, lest being borne down by a burden too great for his powers, he is brought to stumble in the mire. It is this that our Master Horace counsels when at the opening of the *Art of Poetry*, he says 'Choose your subject'.)

(*D.V.E.* II iv 4)

It is to the forceful imagery of 'pondus humeris coequare' that I would draw attention. For Dante himself returns to it at the end of the chapter where, defining the characteristics of the tragic poet, whose theme will be the three 'Magnalia', he writes of the 'opus' and the 'labor' to which such a poet must submit:

Caveat ergo quilibet et discernat ea que dicimus, et quando pure hec tria cantare intendit, vel que ad ea directe ac pure secuntur, prius Elicone potatus, tensis fidibus ad supremum, secure plectrum tum movere incipiat. Sed cautionem atque discretionem hanc accipere, sicut decet, hic opus et labor est...

(Let everyone pay attention, then, and clearly understand what I say, and when he means to sing of these three subjects directly or in their consequences, he should first drink deep of Helicon and tighten his strings to their perfect pitch, then after begin firmly to move his plectrum. But to learn, as is right, discretion and caution, that is the real task and the real labour.)

(*ibid.* 9–10)

In both of these passages, Dante's purpose must partly be to enunciate a principle of technical procedure. Yet in neither would any purely literary interpretation exhaust his emphasis. For Dante's intention surely is to direct the author not merely to the canons of correct usage, but also to a moral assessment of his own particular worth and fitness.[10] And in each case one sees, as in the emphasis upon liberality, an insistence upon the need in literature for a disinterested application and strenuously disciplined commitment. So, in the 'Sumite materiam' passage a moment of self-appraisal is made an essential preliminary if the poet is not in the end to be broken by his work, besmirching both his own dignity and the dignity of his enterprise. Similarly in the second passage, the poet is required to ask at all times whether in aptitude and perseverance, he is equipped to execute his original design. I need not emphasise that in proposing this regimen, Dante is establishing a rule to which he himself will respond in the ineffability passages of the *Paradiso*. Indeed, as Jacomuzzi notes ('Il "topos" dell'ineffabile nel *Paradiso*', *L'imago al cerchio*, pp. 122–3), the imagery of the 'shoulder' is exactly reflected in one of the greatest instances of the ineffability topic, at *Paradiso* XXIII 64–6:

Ma chi pensasse il ponderoso tema
e l'omero mortal che se ne carca,
nol biasmerebbe se sott' esso trema.

(But whoever were to think of the weighty theme/ and of the mortal shoulder that loads itself with it,/ would not blame it if it trembles under it.)

If, however, one is to appreciate how deep the similarity is between the *Convivio* and the *De Vulgari Eloquentia*, one must turn to the continuation of the second passage, where, in phrases which recall Dante's own situation as he rises from the remembrance of Hell and Purgatory to the celestial vision of Paradise, the poet designates the 'opus' and the 'labor' as qualities of the 'fili*us* deorum:

Et hii sunt quos Poeta Eneidorum sexto Dei dilectos et ab ardente virtute sublimatos ad ethera deorumque filios vocat...

(It is these whom in the sixth book of the *Aeneid* the poet calls the chosen ones of God, those who are raised to the heavens by their burning virtue, the sons of the gods.)

(*ibid.* 10)

But in these lines the sons of the gods, who achieve by their virtue a return to the upper air, are most notably represented by Aeneas, to whom in the *Aeneid*, the Sybil addresses the verses that Dante here adapts.[11] May one not say, then, that in associating the tragic poet with the 'filii deorum', Dante is proposing, as a principle of his labours, a tenacity of the kind upon which the Roman patriarch himself relied? Marigo certainly would support this view in his note on the passage (ed. and comm., p. 196), and the interpretation appears to be confirmed by the final section of the chapter, where with a sarcasm equivalent to the ire of his attack upon the 'malvagi uomini', Dante derides the poetic 'geese' who are either unwilling or unable to imitate the eagle, emblem of Roman culture:[12]

Et ideo confutetur illorum stultitia qui, arte scientiaque immunes, de solo ingenio confidentes, ad summa summe canenda prorumpunt; et a tanta presumptuositate desistant; et si anseres natura vel desidia sunt, nolint astripetam aquilam imitari.

(And on that account let the stupidity be silenced of those who, innocent alike of art and learning, burst forth boldly, trusting only to their talents, upon subjects that are appropriate to the noblest poetry. And let them abandon their excessive presumption. If they are geese by nature or by laziness, let them not seek to imitate the star-seeking eagle.)

(*ibid.* 11)

To be sure, the imitation which Dante recommends may, in a particular sense, mean the literary imitation of classical authorities. As will be seen, the discipline of the 'opus' and the 'labor' is certainly connected with a respect for the Latin model. At the same time, I suggest that as in the *Convivio* so here the poet is called upon to exhibit a selflessness and essential justice, after the fashion of the antique Roman. And if, like the 'geese', he should decline the heroism of the 'opus' and the 'labor', the very quality of his achievement may in some way stand to suffer. I shall presently offer an example of such a failing.

Firstly, though, one should note that in one respect *De Vulgari* II iv offers an advance upon the *Convivio*. For the analogy between Aeneas and the tragic poet, while revealing the ethical character of poetic composition, as Dante saw it, indicates also Dante's interest in the poet as a figure of destiny, and as a recipient of divine revelation. This suggestion, of course, is one which easily accords with the notion of poetry as a prophetic or enthusiastic activity.[13] Yet in context the emphasis upon revelation and destiny, though important, in no way overbears the theme of 'caution' and 'discretion'. Furthermore, one has only to pursue the comparison of the poet to Aeneas to see that revelation itself, by its very seriousness, may impose upon the visionary a most binding discipline.[14] Thus, to prove himself worthy of what he has been given, or of the eminence to which he is elected, the poet on his own account will prepare himself for labour. Service will again coincide with self-possession. The significance of this, however, in terms applicable to Dante's own poetry, may best be seen from the *Purgatorio*.

Now throughout the *Purgatorio*, there is much to suggest that Dante envisaged a specific relationship between artistic activity and the patient spirituality of the purgatorial life.[15] The manifestations of this are various. But around the central sequences of the canticle, with Vergil's discourse upon love and the appearance of Statius, the interest in poetry itself becomes peculiarly strong.[16] This section of the work prepares one gradually for the Cornices of Greed and Lust, where every important character is, in some measure, a poet. Here certainly Dante seems to attribute to the poet an especial talent for the disciplines of Purgatory. And it is not difficult to appreciate why he should.

For these cantos are dominated by a sense of how near the advent is of Beatrice; and though in Beatrice one sees primarily the consummation of the penitential life, it is through his love for Beatrice, of course, that the poet simultaneously fulfils his poetic destiny. In fact the courtly devotion of the poet to his Lady would demand of him, as Purgatory itself does, obedience to a just imperative and an utter purity of purpose. Certainly it is this which Beatrice requires of Dante in the Earthly Paradise. So, by drawing attention to the courtly or amatory inclinations of the poet, Dante again emphasises in the poetic psyche a capacity for endurance and disinterested discipline. Here even a poor poet such as Bonagiunta centres his penance around the name of the enigmatic Gentucca while the comedian Forese now reverences the name of Nella his wife.[17]

It should, however, be noted that the principles of courtly rectitude and the principles of civic or political rectitude, though compatible,[18] are nevertheless not identical in scope. For where in the ideal morality of Rome, the predominant consideration is the relationship of the individual to his society, in the morality of the courtly code – as one sees especially in its philosophical development – the cardinal factor is rather the relationship of the individual to himself.[19] For through his love of the Lady, the courtly poet will find in himself a value to be served as zealously as the Roman serves his country. His own merit, in the eyes of the Lady, will itself become the object of his devotion.[20] If, then, for Dante an author should acknowledge certain civic responsibilities, he will also, it seems, bear towards his own being an equal responsibility. And it is this which is visualised in the Bonagiunta episode, as the setting for Dante's pronouncement 'I' mi son un . . .'.

Thus, in the first place, the sin which Bonagiunta is called upon to expiate in Purgatory is the sin of gluttony. In this he is the very kinsman of the 'evil men of Italy' who in the *Convivio* stand condemned for their avarice. But gluttony, in the largest terms, is the vice which most seriously interrupts the justice of society.[21] In the courtly ethic, too, it is gluttony which presents the vilest impediment to the integrity and worth of the individual.[22] So in the *Inferno* one sees how the 'manshape' of Ciacco is ruined by an unrepentant greediness, leaving him to wallow, with malice alone for comfort, in the slime of the most disgusting circle of Hell. But unlike Ciacco, Bonagiunta manifests a spirit inclined, however dimly, to justice. And the first indication of this is the '*OMO*' which he, like all his fellows on this cornice, carries upon his brow. No recognisable feature, to be sure, remains.[23] Yet his willingness to bear this mark is itself an acknowledgement of his submission to the general laws which regulate mankind. In this there lies the rationality of the Roman discipline. But as well as his conformity to the general law, Bonagiunta evinces a profoundly inward and introspective sense of rectitude. For as Dante first encounters him, he is meditating the mysterious Gentucca, 'in the place where he was feeling the stroke of justice' (*Purg*. XXIV 38–9), as though in his purgation, he could hearten and direct his spirit by a cleaving to the Lady and her Law.

In the light, then, of themes concerning, so deeply, discipline and personal integrity, one turns to the central terzina:

E io a lui: 'I' mi son un che, quando
Amor mi spira, noto, e a quel modo
ch'e' ditta dentro vo significando'.

(And I to him 'I am one who, when/ Love breathes in me, take note, and in the manner/ in which he inwardly tells, go spelling out its meaning.)

(*Purg.* XXIV 52–4)

Considering its context, it is impossible to suppose that Dante is recommending here any simple reliance upon inspiration or impulse. Rather, as Bosco and Luciana Cocito have argued, the passage displays an insistence upon control in composition precisely similar to that of the 'Sumite materiam' passage, and likewise advocates a self-possessing and self-critical introspection.[24] In this way the phrase 'quando Amor mi spira noto . . .' indicates, not the simultaneity of expression and intuition, but rather two quite distinct moments, the first of which may indeed be described as a moment of intuition, the second of which, however, is a moment of deliberation and well-disciplined attention. Love breathes in the poet, as it does in the penitent. But like the penitent, the poet has a responsibility of his own to 'spell out' the inner dictate. Though, of course, these two moments will in no way be discordant, Dante's phrasing of the theme brings the inspiration and the 'noting' into firm contradistinction. Likewise, when Bonagiunta, proving his willingness to hear, paraphrases Dante's speech, he shows himself to have learnt that, however strictly the poet may pursue his inspiration, he will move nonetheless 'behind' it (*ibid.* 58–60).[25] The psychological pattern, then, presented in these verses is exactly comparable to that which appeared earlier in the 'astripetam aquilam' passage. For if 'Amor' inspires him, the poet may rightly know himself to be the son of God. But this does not absolve him from the 'opus' and the 'labor'. On the contrary, in responding to the knowledge of his own peculiar gifts, the need for him to demonstrate a seriousness of commitment will only be the more acute. And in this same episode, there is a significant illustration of how a failure in this regard may influence even the finer detail of a style.

For Bonagiunta, speaking of the courteous and liberal Lady of Lucca 'who will make my city pleasing to you' (*Purg.* XXIV 43–4), employs not the courtly 'donna', but the mere 'femmina':[26]

Femmina è nata, e non porta ancor benda . . .

(A woman is born and does not as yet wear the wimple.)

(*ibid.* 43)

This surely suggests that Bonagiunta, although sensitive now to the values of the courtly world, has still not learned wholly to govern himself in the contemplation and acknowledgement of a worthy object. The 'femmina' is at once a lapse of style and a moral lapse. The corrective to it is the calm, introspective consideration of words which Dante has proposed throughout.

It will be apparent by now how far one has travelled from the poetic psychology of which I spoke in the introduction. In the Bonagiunta passage especially, there occurs a crucial rejection of any identity between aesthetic intuition and expression. The lesson, to be sure, which Dante teaches is a lesson in spontaneity. Yet few things are more common than the poet who, lacking a purposeful sense of his own meaning, descends, with spontaneity as his excuse, to a 'knotty' elaboration of phrase.[27] And the artificial phrasing of the Guittonians, from which Dante releases Bonagiunta, might reasonably be a consequence not of too little zeal, but of an intoxicated excess, where the excitements of the happy conceit are mistaken for accurate and penetrating statement.[28] Judgement and self-control are as well able to generate fluency as nervous excitement.

More importantly, however, as the discipline which Dante requires of the poet differs from any imaginative discipline, so, too, the disinterestedness which this discipline involves will differ, clearly, from any imaginative or aesthetic disinterestedness. At this point, my argument returns to one of the major proposals of the introduction. For there, referring to Calogero, one saw how important it might be, when a poet was approaching the images he had conceived, for him to exercise, as it were, an ascetic self-control. And Dante, it appears, would likewise demand that the poet exercise upon the truths he finds within himself a persistently moral and intellectual intention. By now, however, one has arrived at an extension of this original point. For the peculiar duty of the poet, one may now say, in his extraordinary self-awareness, will be to present, with an honesty like Dante's own in the inexpressibility topic, his personal being and the truth that it contains as worthy of regard. This ambition, as one sees, determined even Dante's choice of the vernacular in the *Convivio*. And in such a view, it is not the form or 'making' of the poem, but the poet himself, as the proponent of a truth, that will stand before one, in the frame of his art, as a distinctive object of contemplation.

That such a presentation of the self will differ, say, from the assertiveness of emotion that typifies certain Romantic poets will at once be apparent. For clearly what Dante would have one appreciate is the poet's own exemplification of integrity and perseverance.[29] And it will prove that this is best realised not through an emotional or imaginative sympathy, but rather, so to say, through a philosophical admiration – of a kind which Dante himself, at times, appears to have paid to human achievement.[30] However there are questions here, which so far I have not considered, concerning not the disciplines of composition, but rather the reception of the poem, and the influence it might exert upon its audience. These questions are vital. And while from the point of view of the *Paradiso* I shall not discuss them until Chapter Four, an answer in theoretical terms will emerge if one considers, in one of its aspects at least, Dante's conception of the Volgare Illustre.

For, as is now recognised, the creation of the Volgare Illustre was, in Dante's view, the proper concern of the tragic poet.[31] Moreover, the theory of the Volgare Illustre is all but inseparably connected with Dante's political and social ideals, as Mengaldo, for instance, recognises when he sees in the *De Vulgari Eloquentia* an attempt to redefine the role and significance of the intellectual in Italian society ('De Vulgari Eloquentia', *ED*, II, pp. 407–9).[32] It is this aspect of the *De Vulgari Eloquentia* that I, too, shall be concerned with. I am aware that this is only one aspect of the work, and not, perhaps, the most important one. Yet the conclusion to which, I believe, it points is that precisely through the creation of the Volgare Illustre, the tragic poet may stimulate between man and man a sense of the virtue to which an individual might attain, and, thence, in the respect and regard which would reign between individuals, restore society itself to health and order.

An early indication of what was to be for Dante an especial virtue of the Volgare Illustre occurs in the first book of the *Convivio*, as a part of the discussion – from which I have already quoted – in which the poet justifies his use of a vernacular, and not a Latin commentary. Drawing to the climax of this argument, Dante speaks forcefully of the love he bears towards the vernacular and seeks to persuade his reader of how appropriate this great affection is. The vernacular, he claims, has itself been instrumental in producing for him the two most profound perfections of human existence:

Onde, con ciò sia cosa che due perfezioni abbia l'uomo, una prima e una seconda (la prima lo fa essere, la seconda, lo fa essere buono), se la propria loquela m'è stata cagione e de l'una e de l'altra, grandissimo beneficio da lei ho ricevuto... Questo mio volgare fu congiugnitore de li miei generanti, che con esso parlavano, sì come 'l fuoco è disponitore del ferro al fabbro che fa lo coltello; per che manifesto è lui essere concorso a la mia generazione, e così essere alcuna cagione del mio essere. Ancora: questo mio volgare fu introduttore di me ne la via di scienza, che è ultima perfezione, in quanto con esso io entrai ne lo latino e con esso mi fu mostrato; lo quale latino poi mi fu via a più innanzi andare . . .

(So, since man possesses two perfections, a primary perfection and a secondary perfection, – the first brings him into being, the second into being good – if my own tongue has been the cause in me of both the one and the other, then indeed I have received the greatest benefit from it . . . My own vernacular was the initial bond between my parents, who spoke to each other in that tongue – just as the fire makes the iron ready for the smith who is crafting a knife. Clearly, then, the vernacular had an active part in my begetting, and is thus in some measure a cause of my existence. Then again, it was the vernacular that I myself speak that led me first to the way of knowledge – knowledge being our final perfection. For through the vernacular I entered upon Latin; Latin was explained to me in the vernacular. And Latin was then the means for me to make yet further progress.)

(*Con.* I xiii 3–5)

Now nothing could be clearer than the sense in this passage of a most intimate connection between the vernacular, even in its unsophisticated form, and the perfection of the individual. Dante indeed would have us suppose that, were it not for the vernacular, he would never even have existed at all. For it was this language that first led his mother and father to an understanding. Then again (and in a less Shandean vein), Dante accredits to the vernacular his introduction to the intellectual life, since only after studying in the vernacular was he ready to advance to the full rigour of the Latin corpus. The vernacular thus stands at the root both of his natural and of his intellectual being, as a cause and as a source of nourishment. One may indeed agree readily with Gustavo Vinay who, commenting on the passage I have quoted, concludes that, in Dante's view, 'we mature as individuals to our earliest conscious awareness and to our first relationships as human being through the possession of the vernacular' ('Ricerche sul *De Vulgari Eloquentia*', *GSLI*, CXXXVI (1959), 240–1).

Notable, however, as the *Convivio* passage is, the issues that it raises, in their bearing especially upon the social function of the vernacular, may best be understood if one touches briefly upon the differences that existed in Dante's understanding of it between the force of the vernacular and the force of Latin 'grammar'. This, of course, is to raise questions of a highly controversial kind. But Vinay may again be of assistance. For crisply, though with something of a simplification, Vinay asserts that as Dante saw it Latin is necessary if one is to be a learned man, but to be a man at all one needs the vernacular (*ibid.* 241). This distinction is an important one and certainly would seem to be consistent with the poet's own practice. For wherever Dante's concern is with a learned or strictly technical matter, he is inclined to use Latin, even where his purpose, as in the *De Vulgari Eloquentia* itself, is to vindicate the vernacular. Conversely, where his purpose, as in the *Convivio* (or, perhaps, in the ode 'Tre Donne'), is to justify himself as a man or to repair his own reputation in the eyes of his fellows, then he relies upon the vernacular.[33]

At the same time, the distinction may, I think, be taken a little further than Vinay has taken it. As to Latin, certainly, it is inadequate to consider the language solely as the language of doctrine. For equally, as Dante himself uses it, Latin is the language of Law, and the language, too, of ceremony and ritual. Thus in the *Monarchy* or in the Epistles, where Dante affirms the principles of the Law, he elects to write in Latin. In the *Commedia*, moreover, the language is regularly employed to indicate moments of liturgical solemnity, as in the very impressive case of the Cacciaguida sequence, to which I shall shortly return. Latin, therefore, appears to touch on every aspect of life in which an effort of communal understanding or of communal celebration or of communal regulation is required. In this light, it is clear surely that the language is one that is appropriate not to learning alone, but to all the rational generalities that apply in human life.[34] Nor need one look further than the figure of Vergil to illustrate this. For if Vergil is supremely the teacher of Dante, he is also the interpreter of the Law, and no less the celebrant in the great rituals of Purgatory.

But if this extension is admissible in regard to Latin, may not an equivalent extension be called for in regard to the vernacular? Where Latin speaks of mankind's general destiny, may not the vernacular speak rather of the intimate, even existential ambitions of the individual himself?

I believe that it may, and that Dante himself sanctions this interpretation precisely in the view he takes of the highest form of vernacular speech, the Volgare Illustre. Indeed the very name of the Volgare Illustre, in Dante's own definition, indicates that a specific quality of this form of the language is to bestow a lustre of glory and honour upon those who cultivate it. Thus at *De Vulgari Eloquentia*, I xvii 2, Dante writes:

Per hoc quoque quod illustre dicimus, intelligimus quid illuminans et illuminatum prefulgens ... Et vulgare de quo loquimur et sublimatum est magistratu et potestate, et suos honore sublimat et gloria.

(By that, then, which we call illustrious, we understand something that illuminates, and being itself illuminated casts forth its light ... And this vernacular of which we speak is raised aloft in authority and power and raises its own followers in honour and in glory.)

Somewhat similarly at *De Vulgari Eloquentia* II iii 7 Dante, having already argued that the canzone is itself the form most compatible with the Volgare Illustre, goes on to claim that the writing of a canzone will bring particular honour to its author.

Now it would not surely be wrong to detect in these two passages a note of pathos, a reflection even of the predicament in which Dante, as an exile, found himself throughout his maturity. Urgently seeking, as Mengaldo suggests, a role in society as an intellectual, Dante himself had perforce to rely upon his own eloquence and the brilliance of his linguistic powers to impress upon the world at large – as he did so successfully – his claim to honour. To this deeply personal motive in his theory I shall shortly return. Here, however, there are two further passages to consider, which show particularly clearly the development in the *De Vulgari Eloquentia* of the position that Dante suggested in the last chapters of *Convivio* Book One.

The first of these occurs at *De Vulgari Eloquentia* II i 5–8, where Dante insists that so excellent a form of language as the Volgare Illustre

Excellentes ingenio et scientia querit

(seeks out men who are excellent in natural intelligence and learning)

and substantiates this by arguing:

Nam quicquid nobis convenit, vel gratia generis, vel speciei, vel individui convenit, ut sentire, ridere, militare. Sed hoc non convenit nobis gratia generis, quia etiam brutis conveniret; nec gratia speciei, quia cunctis hominibus esset conveniens, de quo nulla questio est – nemo enim montaninis rusticana tractantibus hoc dicet esse conveniens –: convenit ergo individui gratia. Sed nichil individuo convenit nisi per proprias dignitates ...

(For whatever appropriately belongs to us, belongs to us by virtue either of our genus (as does perception by the senses), or of our species (as does laughing), or of our individuality (as does soldiership). But this [*the Volgare Illustre*] cannot belong to us by virtue of genus. For in that case it would belong even to brute beasts. Nor by virtue of species. For in that case it would be a language appropriate to everyman. And there can be no question of that. For no one would allow that it suited mountain people in their country dealings. It belongs to us, therefore, by virtue of individuality. Yet nothing belongs to an individual save in respect of his personal standing.)

Emphatically, then, the excellence that the Volgare Illustre requires is not to be achieved by every man nor even by every Italian poet. On the contrary, the development and use of the form must rest with the individual, and particularly with the individual who is appropriately gifted in point of *ingenio* and *scientia*. Thus there appears in this passage, as in Dante's definition of the tragic poet, the markedly aristocratic inclination that characterises his thinking in the *De Vulgari Eloquentia* as a whole.[35] It is, however, especially important to note that Dante's exclusiveness is grounded not upon a notion of mere refinement or elegance, but rather, as the phrase 'ingenio et scientia' indicates, upon a principle of philosophical strength and self-possession. If, then, the simple vernacular introduces men to their first experience of the intellectual life, the vernacular in its sophisticated form would appear to stand as a peculiar product and a token of the individual thinker at the highest pitch of his powers.

But, as we saw in the *Convivio*, Dante's interest in the vernacular arose as much from its bearing upon his actual existence as upon his intellectual progress. And in the *De Vulgari Eloquentia*, too, there are indications that he found in the Volgare Illustre a form that might demonstrate the existential as well as the intellectual perfection of the individual. The indications of this are particularly strong in *De Vulgari Eloquentia* II ii, where Dante argues that the themes proper to the Volgare Illustre are 'salus', 'venus', and 'virtus'. These are the three 'magnalia', which Marigo defines as 'the supreme ends (*finalità*) great and wonderful in themselves that have been placed by God in the human soul' (commentary, p. 176).[36] As Dante himself explains, these magnalia are related to the very structure of the human person in its threefold constitution, as vegetative, animal and rational:

Ad quorum evidentiam sciendum est quod sicut homo tripliciter spiritatus est, videlicet vegetabili, animali et rationali, triplex iter perambulat. Nam secundum quod vegetabile quid est, utile querit, in quo cum plantis comunicat; secundum quod animale delectabile, in quo cum brutis; secundum quod rationale, honestum querit . . .

(For a clear understanding of these things [*the subjects that are appropriate to the Volgare Illustre*], it is necessary to know that man is sustained in life in three ways, – that is, by a vegetative soul, by an animal soul and by a rational soul – and proceeds according to these three modes. So, in accordance with his vegetative being, he seeks, in common with plants, what is useful to him, in accordance with his animal soul, he seeks, as beasts do, what is pleasing to his appetite, and in accordance with his rational soul, he seeks what is virtuous and honourable.)

(*D.V.E.* II ii 6)

As ordained, then, by God, man, in his vegetative aspect will naturally be interested in those things which defend or usefully sustain his existence. In his animal aspect, he will seek naturally the proper satisfaction of his appetites. In his rational aspect he will naturally pursue a virtuous rectitude. If, therefore, a poet seeks the noblest subjects – as he must where he intends to write in the noblest form – he will write of war, since in war man seeks supremely his own defence, of love, since love is the supreme expression of his appetite and of moral rectitude, since that is a matter that supremely concerns his rational being. These themes, then, by expressing the constitution that God himself has designed for man, will indeed be the greatest and most 'wonderful' that a poet can attempt. The poet, precisely showing forth these themes, the Magnalia, in his work, will also declare his responsiveness to the incidence, in his personal being, of creative glory. Thus where the simple vernacular embodied certain, at least, of the forces that sustained the poet's temporal existence, the Volgare Illustre, it appears, will rather display the wonder of the author's participation, as a creation of God, in the ultimate order of the universe.

Other arguments in the *De Vulgari Eloquentia* and elsewhere lead, I think, to a similar conclusion. And to these I shall return. But let me here digress a little. For by now a connection will have emerged between my present theme and those passages in the previous section where I spoke of the importance to poetry of the social ethic and the introspective ethic of courtly love. The differences in function between Latin and the Volgare Illustre closely reflect the differences between the two systems of discipline. And finally, I think, these differences themselves, in language and discipline, are to be seen, in a way which directly concerns the reception of the Volgare Illustre, as the manifestation of two distinct phases in the providential history of the world.

For in the ages before the redemption of the individual through Christ, the best of human effort was devoted to the commonwealth and to the observance of regulatory principle. But any goodness that the individual might personally possess was fated to be, as one knows from the plight of Vergil, fruitless and waste. With the Incarnation, however, there begins a new era,[37] in which, by the baptism which the Roman himself so painfully lacked, the personal and particular merit of a man may at last be validated. It is this new dispensation that the courtly life triumphantly incorporates, and it is this that appears in the relation of Dante and Beatrice. For from the moment of their meeting in the Earthly Paradise the love between Dante and Beatrice expresses precisely the capacity of the individual to participate, through intelligence and grace, in a life of literally divine courtesy. A supreme illustration of this is the Twenty Third Canto of the *Paradiso*, to which I shall return.

But if Latin, as the language of Law, of learning and of ritual is a language proper to the ordinances of common and corporate existence, the vernacular, which as early as the *Vita Nuova* (*cap.* xxv), was associated with the reign of Love, is a language in which the new dispensation may actively be proclaimed.[38] In the *Purgatorio*, where this order is dynamically in evidence, there is an episode which illustrates this very clearly.

I refer to the Sordello episode, which recently has been cited by Cecil Grayson in relation to Dante's linguistic theory.[39] The verse which particularly interests Grayson is:

> 'O gloria di Latin', disse, 'per cui
> mostrò ciò che potea la lingua nostra,
> o pregio etterno del loco ond' io fui,
> qual merito o qual grazia mi ti mostra?'

('O glory of the Latins', he said, 'through whom/ our tongue displayed what it was capable of/ what merit or what favour shows you to me?')
(*Purg.* VII 16–19)

From this he seeks to show, against a position which Vinay adopts, that Latin and the vernacular may rightly co-exist, and that at various moments in history a new enactment of linguistic potentiality may be entirely possible. This argument is not irrelevant to my present concern.[40] But it is the context rather than the verse itself that concerns me, above all the representation of Sordello's behaviour towards Vergil, and subsequently, the conduct of the two poets, one to another.

For Sordello, who, as well as being a lover and courtly poet is an upholder of political rectitude, not only recognises in Vergil the great exemplar of 'our language', but also behaves with the utmost reverence towards his name and person.[41] Indeed even before he knows precisely whom he addresses, he is moved to embrace the man, not from any general sympathy for his fellows, (for Sordello, at his first appearance, is 'altera e disdegnosa', and altogether remote, one supposes, from regular affection) but on the strength, solely, of the word 'Mantua'. He recognises, that is to say, a kinship of a most particular and penetrating kind, and testifies to the strength of it in a way which the true Roman, proud only of his allegiance to the citizenship of Rome, might never have done. This is not to suggest that Sordello's ultimate recognition of Vergil as a Roman is unimportant.[42] It would nonetheless seem evident that, as well as demonstrating the Imperial ideal, Dante here wishes to represent another, in which the individuality of person and of native place is expressly acknowledged.[43] A certain courtesy, emanating from Sordello's unexpected deference, inspires the whole tableau. And the most remarkable consequence of this is to be seen in Vergil's own speeches.

For Vergil, availing himself of the respect which Sordello extends to him, presents, in a most acutely personal way, the true condition of his own individual existence. So in reply to Sordello's:

dimmi se vien d'inferno, e di qual chiostra...

(Tell me if you come from Hell, and from what enclosure)

(*Purg.* VII 21)

where the opprobrium of Hell is smoothed away in the mannerly interest of the tone, Vergil confronts, unflinchingly, the facts of his own existence, and trusting to the benevolence of his audience is able momentarily to claim for himself the merit which is truly his:

quivi sto io con quei che le tre sante
virtù non si vestiro, e sanza vizio
conobber l'altre e seguir tutte quante.

(There I remain with those who with the three holy/ virtues did not clothe themselves, and without sin/ knew the others and followed them all entirely.)

(*ibid.* 34–6)

In this lovely and very subtle presentation of Vergil, there is, as it were, the dawn breeze of what the tragic poet and the Volgare Illustre, in their fullness, are to be. It is a pattern which Dante himself has foreshadowed in the *Convivio* where, to repudiate the charges which have been laid against the canzoni of the Donna Gentile, he recommends himself, by his adoption of the vernacular, to the good will of his nearest countrymen. It is this pattern, too, that one discerns, at *Purgatorio* XXVI 140–9, in the final and supreme presentation of penitential discipline. For here Arnaut Daniel, expressing whole-heartedly his submission to due penance, is dignified by the use of his native tongue:

> Ieu sui Arnaut, que plor e vau cantan;
> consiros vei la passada folor,
> e vei jausen lo joi qu'esper, denan

(I am Arnaut, who weep and go my way singing/ I remember grievingly the folly of my past/ and I see joyfully the day for which I long ahead) (*Purg.* XXVI 142–4)

Why, though, for a speech that so aptly summarises the substance of the *Purgatorio*, should Dante give such prominence to the vernacular of Provence? The answer must, I suggest, be that allowing to the 'miglior fabbro del parlar materno' the use of his own illustrious vernacular, Dante meant us to see in such a language a mode in which one might properly celebrate the wholeness of identity to which the Christian confession had at the last led.[44]

It should, however, be emphasised that, while Dante may indeed see in the forms of elevated language a means to the sustaining of personal reputation, there are matters of wider consequence, in such a view, than the affirmation only of individual merit. Thus, explaining the language of the Arnaut Daniel episode, Glauco Cambon suggests that by his peculiar presentation of Arnaut, Dante wished to show that at last the great confusion that befell mankind at the time of Babel had been healed (*Dante's Craft* (Minneapolis, 1969), p. 44). Multiplicity of speech need no longer signify anarchy. Indeed, the cacophony of Babel, with its implications of an utter disruption in the social world, has now given way, as Cambon argues, to an ordered polyphony, in which each tongue may possess its own proper place and importance. Of Babel and linguistic confusion there will be a little more to say in the next chapter. But in the Sordello episode, Dante himself is quick to draw from the image that he establishes of harmony between the two poets of Mantua a conclusion which suggests how aware he is of its broadly social and political implications.

For it is against the background of the embrace between the two Mantuans, that Dante enters upon his great digression 'Ahi serva Italia'. Yet in these lines, though the saddle of the Empire is riderless, it is not the convulsion of the world in general that Dante emphasises, but rather the inner strife and civic self-destruction which arises where the individual, be it the Emperor Albert or the 'many' who 'rifiutan lo commune incarco' (*refuses the common burden*) (*Purg.* VI 133), prove irresponsible and vicious. The possibilities and the duties which are revealed to individuals in the Christian order of history, are ignored.[45] And where there should be a courtly fulfilment, one sees only the restlessness of 'quella inferma/ che non può trovar posa in su la piume' (*that sick woman who can find no ease on her feather-bed*) (*ibid.* 149–50). Italy, where courtesy might triumph, is now:

non donna di provincie, ma bordello.
(no mistress of provinces but of the brothel.)

(*ibid.* 79)

In the *Commedia* itself, then, Dante plainly envisages a central position for the poet of proven capacity in the order that he himself so urgently longed to see re-established in the world. Nor is it easy, returning to the *De Vulgari Eloquentia*, to avoid the conclusion that Dante's vision of this order is a vital inspiration in this work, too. For the language of the Volgare Illustre is there shown clearly to be the language of men who in their art have proved themselves personally fitted to participate, alongside the honest rulers of the political world, in the reign of courtesy.

For instance, speaking of the honour among men that the Volgare Illustre confers, Dante writes:

Quod autem honore sublimet, in promptu est. Nonne domestici sui reges, marchiones, comites et magnates quoslibet fama vincunt? Minime hoc probatione indiget. Quantum veros suos familiares gloriosos efficiat, nos ipsi novimus, qui huius dulcedine glorie nostrum exilium postergamus.

(That it may elevate in honour is at once apparent. For do not its servants exceed in repute any king, marquis, count or baron at all? It is hardly necessary to argue this. For I myself know how renowned it makes its followers, I who, because of the sweetness of that renown, make light of my exile.)

(*D.V.E.* I xvii 5–6)

From this passage it is evident that, as Mengaldo emphasises, Dante did recognise in the excellent use of language a testimony to the aristocratic spirit.[46] The dignity, indeed, that the Volgare Illustre carries with it may be greater even than that which attaches to men of the most imposing social rank. However, the especially striking feature of this passage is its tone. For in that – which is a poignant harmony of pride and gratitude – one does indeed sense the poet's own awareness of a power in the Volgare Illustre to establish a world of justice and courtly order. It appears that precisely as a servant of the Volgare Illustre, Dante has assumed the place that, in his own estimation, he rightfully deserves among the rulers of the world. The pride he takes in his own achievement rings out forcefully in support of this implication. Yet, as well as pride, the passage unmistakably evinces the gratitude and the relief that the poet feels, on receiving, despite his exile, that just appreciation of his merit that his native Florence so painfully withholds. In this respect, the passage has much in common with a sequence of the *Paradiso* to which I shall return – the great 'Se mai continga' in Canto Twenty Five – where the hopes of the poet for an accurate assessment of his character do again repose upon the acknowledgement of his poetic prowess.

In the *De Vulgari Eloquentia* itself, however, the most direct evidence of how, for Dante, the Volgare Illustre might give rise to an order in which the individual would receive just recognition emerges from the discussion that Dante offers of the courtliness of the Volgare Illustre.

In Dante's view, then, to describe the Volgare Illustre as a courtly language cannot mean (or cannot only mean) that it is a form of language that is spoken in the centres of Italian sophistication. For in divided Italy, it would be mistaken to suppose, as Dante allows at *De Vulgari Eloquentia* I xviii 5, that there existed, in physical reality, any particular centre at which a courtly language might have been developed. If, however, there is no physical court in Italy, there are nonetheless individuals throughout the land who do respond to the ideal of Italian courtliness:

Nam licet curia, secundum quod unita accipitur, ut curia regis Alamannie, in Ytalia non sit, membra tamen eius non desunt; et sicut membra illius uno Principe uniuntur, sic membra huius gratioso lumine rationis unita sunt. Quare falsum esset dicere curia carere Ytalos, quanquam Principe careamus, quoniam curiam habemus, licet corporaliter sit dispersa.

(For granted that there exists in Italy no court in the sense of a single and unified court like that of the King of Germany, nonetheless the members of a court are not lacking and just as the members of a court are united around a single Prince, so the members of this are united by the gracious light of reason. Thus, although we do not have a sovereign, it would be false to say that we do not have an Italian court. For we have a court, though its members are scattered.)

(*D.V.E.* I xviii 5)

The life, then, of Italian courtesy depends upon men who, scattered though they are, devote themselves single-mindedly to the principles of reason. And the Volgare Illustre is a courtly language precisely in proclaiming to the world at large the existence of such devotion. For in defining the 'curialitas' of the Volgare Illustre – which as Renzo lo Cascio shows is precisely the quality of courtliness – Dante writes:[47]

Est etiam merito curiale dicendum, quia curialitas nil aliud est quam librata regula eorum que peragenda sunt.

(It [*the Volgare Illustre*] is rightly called curial, for 'curiality' is nothing other than a balanced measure for things that one should properly do.)
(*ibid.* I xviii 4)

Evidently, then, the Volgare Illustre, bearing within it the mark of carefulness and rational consideration, will announce precisely the possibility of a communion between those individuals who are themselves capable of intelligent and well-regulated behaviour.

By now, it will, I think, be apparent how deeply Dante's own experience of exile, and his own sense of a self-lacerating Italy, influenced his conception of the Volgare Illustre. Indeed it is notable, in view of Dante's own impoverished wanderings that he should speak of the Volgare Illustre, too, as a wanderer and an exile:

hinc etiam est quod nostrum illustre velut acola peregrinatur et in humilibus hospitatur asilis.

(thus it is that our illustrious vernacular wanders like an outcast and lodges itself in humble places of refuge.)
(*ibid.* I xviii 3)

Nor is this image an incidental one. For in the canzoni, too, – the language of which Dante takes to be an exemplar of the Volgare Illustre – the poet not infrequently personifies the canzone itself as a lady of virtue wandering from one Italian city to another. But precisely by the nobility of their presence these poetic ladies, like the Volgare Illustre, may be expected to stimulate in any man of virtue whom they meet the very depths of courtesy, and thus arouse that deference of like to like that the meeting of Sordello and Vergil has illustrated so forcefully. Hence in the first congedo of 'Tre Donne', after counselling sternness to the 'Lady' Dante writes:

Ma s' elli avvien che tu alcun mai truovi
amico di virtù, ed e' ti priega,
fatti di color novi,
poi li ti mostra; e 'l fior, ch'é bel di fori,
fa' disïar ne li amorosi cori.

(But if ever it happens that you find someone/ who is a friend to virtue, and if he asks you,/ put on new colours/ then show yourself to him; and make the flower which has beauty outwardly/ to be desired in loving hearts.)

Here, as Fubini has suggested, speaking of the effect that generally Dante achieves in his canzoni, the artist stands alone before his public to whom his art, in its most sophisticated form, presents the essential conclusions of his philosophical inquiries (*Metrica e poesia*, vol. I, p. 99). To this, however, our response as readers must clearly be the response of the 'friend of truth', who attends courteously to the offering that the author makes of his own considered meaning.

The conclusion, then, to which the passages I have discussed appear to point is that the Volgare Illustre, in its effects, is especially intended to direct the minds of men in admiration towards the qualities and being of its exponent, and in doing this to foster between men of good will the institution of a rule of philosophical courtesy.[48]

There remain, however, two further questions to be considered. For as yet one has to see the bearing of the notions I have presented here upon the *Paradiso* itself, and equally to suggest the significance they possess for the general understanding of poetic experience. In neither case do I wish to say that the theory which Dante develops in the *Convivio* and *De Vulgari Eloquentia* is relevant in all its detail. That plainly would be absurd. For while Dante's argument is indeed passionately rooted in his sense of poetry, it is also, in places, undeniably wire-drawn.

Nevertheless considering firstly its importance to the *Paradiso*, it may already be apparent that a similarity exists between the world of philosophical courtesy to which Dante looks in his theoretical writings and the condition of mutual reverence that he depicts ideally in the relationship between the Franciscan and Dominican philosophers. In each instance, the response to intellectual achievement that Dante wishes to define is one that involves a willing but alert admiration between thinker and thinker. And, as I shall argue in Chapter Four, it is this kind of admiration that Dante specifically claims of his own reader in the *Paradiso*.

More generally, there are passages in the *Paradiso* itself, notably the Cacciaguida sequence and the Venus sequence, which forcefully suggest that Dante did have in mind his earlier theory at the time he composed the final canticle. To these I shall return in the present chapter and the next. Yet it would hardly be surprising if Dante had, when he approached the *Paradiso*, brought to mind the principles that he envisaged in his earlier theory. For, as one has seen, the great themes that the tragic poet is called upon to deal with in the Volgare Illustre are the themes of Salus, Amor and Virtus. Yet precisely these themes, in their highest sense, are the themes of the *Paradiso*, where Dante speaks of man's ultimate salvation, of his supreme desires, and of the most exalted forms of rectitude.[49] One might reasonably expect, then, that in writing the canticle Dante would have been concerned to create, if not exactly a Volgare Illustre, then at least a form of language in which his final comprehension of the absolute Magnalia did stand signally forth.

The second matter to be settled here concerns the relation between the present discussion and the theoretical argument that I began in the introduction. For how, in the end, is it possible to adapt the position that Dante has developed to any modern conception of poetic experience? Even, indeed, apart from any incidental difficulty of detail, is not the poet's emphasis upon courtliness itself too intimately a part of his own experience to apply beyond its sphere? I do not think so. To be sure, it may not at once be apparent how one might speak now at all comfortably of 'courtesy' in literary dealings. Yet precisely in the notion of courtliness, a living English poet, Donald Davie, has already discovered a model which, in his view, the modern poet would do well to cultivate. Thus in Chapter Six of *Purity of Diction in English Verse*, pp. 87–8, Davie, referring both to the poetry of Samuel Johnson and to the *De Vulgari Eloquentia*, quotes I xviii 2–3 of Dante's work and concludes that 'Dante's "courtliness" is our "urbanity". And . . . for Dante too the question was of a spiritual quality, "urbanity" as opposed to "provincialism", not of any actual metropolis or any actual provinces in the sense of the geographer.' But this very urbanity of language is the quality that Davie sought to uphold, when he first wrote, against the eccentricity and excess that in his view marred the English poetry of the early 1950s (*ibid*. p. 199).

However, to equate courtliness, as Davie does, with urbanity or the tone of the centre cannot in the light of the argument I have offered be entirely adequate. For throughout one has seen that true courtliness arises between poet and reader, not merely from the community of taste and judgement, but from the recognition on the reader's part of a discipline in the poet, and a certain gravity of demeanour. The extension, however, which this implies of Davie's position is one which Davie himself would not perhaps be unwilling to accept.

For writing a postscript in 1966 to the second edition of his work, he declares:

If I were now writing *Purity of Diction in English Verse* I should need to take greater pains than I did in 1952, to distinguish the literary styles I was analysing from what passes for style in the hectic circles that invent or exploit or tamely follow the dictates of the 'with it'. I could not now take it for granted so much as I did then, that the only elegance worth bothering with, in life or in art, is that which is heartfelt.

Yet is it not exactly this heartfelt elegance that Dante too would have one look for? Davie himself, in fact, all but recognises this when, citing the definition of 'curialitas' that I quoted earlier, he concludes: 'that the passage seems to be Dante's way of insisting that to attain this pure diction is a moral achievement, a product of integrity and equilibrium in the poet...' It is, then, unfortunate that Davie expressly refuses to pursue the implications of this passage, since, for the reasons that he so clearly presents, these implications continue to possess a considerable importance in the conditions of modern poetry.

There is, however, a further reason why it is timely now to return to Dante's thought. For in modern poetic theory, particularly of the kind I have exemplified from T. S. Eliot's writing, there is an evident reluctance to admit of any immediate connection between the personal experience of the poet and the personal interest of the reader. Reacting, no doubt, against the egotistical sublimity of his immediate predecessors, the modern theorist has tended to give especial emphasis to the impersonality of aesthetic experience. Yet it remains natural enough in reading poetry to prize the peculiar sensitivity or the exceptional merit of the author. What Dante allows one to understand, in the works I have discussed, is that a bond may exist between poet and reader which has no more to do with Romantic indulgence than with classical frigidity. For in the courtesy that may arise between poet and reader as Dante depicts it, there lies in fact the possibility of a very direct encounter. To be sure, the encounter will be one that is founded upon an intellectual communication.[50] However it is not for that reason any the less profoundly a meeting of individuals. Indeed in the Sordello sequence, one has already seen how very vital such a meeting might be. A more impressive instance still, however, is to be found throughout the first two canticles of the *Commedia* in the relationship that Dante portrays between himself and the poet Vergil. Here indeed we do see, in an intensely dramatic form, how literature may permit, in spite of the limitations of time and place, the most intimate engagement of one individual to another. In the companionship of Dante and Vergil, we see in fact something of what W. B. Yeats may have seen when, lamenting the disappearance of a great age of courtesy, he writes of

> The intellectual sweetness of those lines
> That cut through time and cross it withershins.
> (*Coole Park*, 1929)

In concluding this chapter, let me return briefly to the *Commedia* itself, to see what evidence it contains of Dante's prevailing interest in the issues that he raises in his theoretical writing. Three sequences in particular concern me, the Cacciaguida episode, the episode of Vergil's disappearance in the Earthly Paradise, and the 'Se mai continga' passage of *Paradiso* Canto Twenty Five.

Now, as to the Cacciaguida episode, set in the Heaven of Mars, André Pézard has clearly shown how concerned Dante is throughout the sequence with questions of linguistic procedure. Indeed, it is the seventeenth canto of the *Paradiso* that leads him to remark that while the *Commedia* in its entirety may not be written in the Volgare Illustre, there are nonetheless moments at which the tone of the work is consistent with the ideals of such a form ('Les trois langues de Cacciaguida', *Revue des études italiennes*, XIII (1967), 232). Pézard, to be sure, licenses no particular adaptation of the Volgare Illustre to the *Paradiso*. Yet undoubtedly the Cacciaguida sequence does suggest a certain correspondence between the linguistic repertoire of the canticle and the canon of the *De Vulgari Eloquentia*. There is an unmistakable elevation of style here, including latinisms and refinements[51] such as 'magno' (XV 50), 'verbo' (XVIII 1), '*robbio*' (XIV 94), 'avaccio' (XVI 70), 'pandi' (XV 60), and the Roman 'voi', which occasions Beatrice's mirth at XVI 10. Also one should note the very courtly manner in which Dante addresses Cacciaguida at XV 73 *et seq.*, the imagery, too, of flight in Cacciaguida's 'mercé di colei/ ch'a l'alto volo ti vestì le piume' (*thanks to her/ who clothed you with wings for the high flight*) (XV 53–4) – which recalls Dante's discussion of the tragic poet in the *De Vulgari Eloquentia* – and finally an explicit acknowledgement of at least the moral influence of Vergil at XVII 19. These instances are, however, less interesting than instances I shall examine later from Cantos Eight and Nine, and it is in the themes and action of the Cacciaguida sequence that Dante's preoccupation with language is at its most illuminating.

As to the significance of the vernacular itself, the most striking passage is:

L'una vegghiava a studio de la culla,
e, consolando, usava l'idïoma
che prima i padri e le madri trastulla;
l'altra, traendo a la rocca la chioma,
favoleggiava con la sua famiglia
d'i Troiani, di Fiesole e di Roma.

(One would keep watch, attending to the cradle/ and, in calming, made use of the tongue/ that first delights fathers and mothers;/ another drawing the strands from the distaff,/ told tales with her family/ of the Trojans, of Fiesole and of Rome.)

(*Par.* xv 121–6)

These lines, of course, recall the very definition of the vernacular which Dante offers at *De Vulgari Eloquentia* I i 2:

vulgarem locutionem appellamus eam qua
infantes assuefiunt ab assistentibus cum
primitus distinguere voces incipiunt

(What I call vernacular speech is that to which babies are made accustomed by those around them when first they begin to make sense of speech.)

But the image they present is also consistent with the themes I have been discussing. Thus one sees here the security which a society may enjoy when it is truly attentive to the principles of personal discipline and sobriety. If the domestic happiness that the passage represents is the outcome of such principles, it is the vernacular which in turn propagates an understanding of what these principles are. For the stories which the mothers tell to their children – speaking doubtless in the vernacular – are stories of Troy, Fiesole and Rome. These are the legends of Florentine heroism, and to relate them in the native tongue is to reveal and corroborate at the very roots of life the historical destiny of Florence. Nor can the significance of this motif be incidental in a sequence which portrays the meeting of the poet and his forebear as a parallel to the meeting of Anchises and Aeneas. Indeed, turning to the dialogue itself, one sees not only how the vernacular may promote in the individual a sense of destiny, but also how in this regard the vernacular will differ from the grammar. Once more one discovers that the language of the new Rome is not identical in scope and purpose with the language of the old.

The dialogue, then, begins with a verse which conflates two allusions, the first from *Aeneid* VI 835, where Anchises announces the history of Rome, the second from the second epistle to the

Corinthians, Chapter Nine, where Saint Paul concerns himself with the destiny of God's people in the Church:[52]

> 'O sanguis meus, o superinfusa
> gratïa deï, sicut tibi cui
> bis unquam celi ianüa reclusa?'

('O blood of mine, o exceeding/ grace of God poured forth, for whom, as for you,/ was the gate of Heaven ever opened twice?'.)

(*Par.* XV 28–30)

It will be at once apparent that Latin is being used here, as earlier I suggested it might be, as a language of ceremony to bring to mind the universal fate of man in time and eternity. Yet this, as it emerges, is not a language which suits the particular purposes of the meeting between the two Florentines. To actuate that personal union of morals, of spirituality and, no less, of blood which so inspires his offspring, Cacciaguida is obliged to descend to the vernacular, touching more precisely upon the cynosure of the human intellect (*ibid.* 43–5). Between one man and another, a language more humble than eternal Latin will be of greater value.

Proceeding from this, the episode continues, in two ways, to exemplify the principal themes of Dante's theory. And firstly one notes how urgently the poet calls to mind the importance of linguistic discipline. Even the restraint which Cacciaguida displays in the opening moments is, broadly, in keeping with Dante's own procedure in the inexpressibility topic. And when in Canto Seventeen, Cacciaguida speaks of Dante's mission in the human world, one sees again how profoundly the poet did connect the discipline of language and the disciplines of the moral and intellectual life.

Thus the heroic Cacciaguida – who not only sacrificed himself to the service of the Cross, but also embodies the tradition of Florentine asceticism – makes known to Dante how severe his coming life will be, renewing with precise information the determination of his descendant to stand 'ben tetragono ai colpi di ventura' (*really square to the blows of fortune*) *Par.* XVII 24. There is no discrepancy at all between this lesson and the lesson in poetic conduct which Cacciaguida goes on to teach. Dante, being no 'timid friend to the truth' (*ibid.* 118), must hold hard to what he has seen, and, removing from himself all obscurity and falsehood, proclaim the truth of his vision as vigorously and clearly as he may:

> Ma nondimen, rimossa ogni menzogna,
> tutta tua visïon fa manifesta;
> e lascia pur grattar dov' è la rogna.

(But nonetheless, all lying put aside,/ make clear the whole of your vision,/ and then let them scratch where the itch is.)

(*ibid.* 127–9)

The courage, then, of a martyr and an unswerving clarity of speech are both required of the poet. And even in point of clarity, Cacciaguida's example is good. For, as Dante emphasises, Cacciaguida, though a prophetic spirit, does not speak, even so, in enigma:

> Né per ambage, in che la gente folle
> già s'inviscava pria che fosse anciso
> l'Agnel di Dio che le peccata tolle,
> ma per chiare parole e con preciso
> latin . . .

(Not with cryptic utterances, in which the foolish people were entrammelled, before He was slain –/ the Lamb of God who takes away sin –/ but with clear words and with precise/ speech.)

(*ibid.* 31–6)

The new order of history, ushered in by the 'Agnel di Dio' demands of its prophets plain-speaking.[53]

But if the Cacciaguida episode is consistent with the *De Vulgari Eloquentia* on the question of poetic discipline, it is also consistent on the question of the influence which a disciplined poem might exert. Both works in fact adumbrate a new order of society in which the honest ruler and the honest poet may stand together upon their merits. For while, as Cacciaguida makes clear, Dante will owe his day-to-day existence to the liberality of his patron, Dante's own words, bitter as at first they may seem, may prove, in the end, a true return:

> Ché se la voce tua sarà molesta
> nel primo gusto, vital nodrimento
> lascerà poi, quando sarà digesta.

(For if your voice is upsetting/ at the first taste, vital nutriment/ afterwards will it leave, when it is digested.)

(*ibid.* 130–2)

The Cacciaguida episode, then, forcefully illustrates how both the linguistic and social interests that Dante had formulated in his conception of the Volgare Illustre continued to occupy his mind as he wrote the *Paradiso*. But why, one may ask, considering the general plan of the *Commedia*, should these issues have been given any particular prominence in the final canticle? An answer will, I think, suggest itself if one turns now to the Earthly Paradise episode.

A single verse, in fact, in this great episode is all that here concerns me, that which includes the last words that Dante addresses to his master Vergil:

conosco i segni de l'antica fiamma

(I recognise the signs of the ancient flame.)

(*Purg.* xxx 48)

Now, as R. Mercuri has shown, these seven words are among the most ore-laden in the whole *Commedia*.[54] Nor could anyone doubt, I think, that for Dante himself the line must have been an exceedingly crucial one – a line, indeed that, in respect of form and placing, he had meditated long and expectantly. It is, after all, precisely at this point that the transition begins from the mode of the first two canticles to the mode of the last. For the verse marks simultaneously the disappearance of Dante's original guide, Vergil, and the Pilgrim's first realisation of Beatrice's presence. Moreover, the form of the verse is itself designed, so it appears, to attract one's attention. For Dante here offers, in the vernacular, a painstakingly exact translation of a line from Book Four of Vergil's *Aeneid*:

agnosco veteris vestigia flammae.

The speaker of this line in the *Aeneid* is, of course, Dido. But to remember that is to realise yet again how remarkable the line is. For it is surely strange that Dante, speaking of his sanctified love for Beatrice, should deliberately evoke the memory of so fabled a sinner. Why is it, then, that at the instant of his triumph the poet should decide upon such words as these, and choose at the climax of the second canticle to translate so obviously from the Latin text?

One general but not irrelevant answer is that the urgent desire of Dante, in his role as pilgrim, must be to define his great experience in terms that will be readily comprehensible to his guide. Until now, his habit has naturally been to do this, turning to Vergil at moments of doubt or trepidation so as to strengthen himself in the knowledge of the other's comprehension.[55] The line, then, represents a dramatic appeal of the pilgrim to his mentor, and indeed calls to mind for a last time the character of the relationship that has prevailed between the two men. For the foundation of this relationship has never been one of simple rationality, but has consisted rather of the many and various bonds that rational intercourse can foster. These at one extreme include certainly the disciplined communion of master and pupil. Equally, however, they include the sophisticated sympathy that arises where two minds respond alike to the same piece of art.

At this final moment Dante's emphasis falls upon the delicate rationality of this latter type.

The point of critical importance, however, is that, be it as a teacher or as a friend, Vergil is no longer at hand to hear what Dante says to him. Nor is it appropriate that he should be there. For the experience in fact that the poet seeks to articulate is one that can no longer be shared in any directly rational communication or governed by general principle. The most impressive indication of this is that Dante, precisely in seeking a civilised definition of his feelings, should be constrained by the quotation he offers to class himself with Dido. In *Inferno* Canto Five, one remembers, Dido did represent a category of sinner, becoming, in name, a means to define the distractions of lust. But whatever guilt the poet himself has here to acknowledge before Beatrice, can no longer be interpreted by reference to a mean or a generality. His sins, as a Christian, are as much his own as his accomplishments will be, and must consequently be confessed to the very roots of his being, the being that at *Purgatorio* XXX, line 55 is called upon so dramatically to answer in its given name, Dante.

In one aspect, then the 'conosco' verse identifies the inadequacy of a relationship which until this moment has been of surpassing importance. It is thus a studied preparation for the scourging even of Dante's rational 'prodigality' which Beatrice proceeds to administer in Cantos Thirty and Thirty One.[56] Yet this is by no means the whole of its significance.

For the same verse, by its very form, is also a sign and a promise of how, henceforth, the poet intends to conduct himself. It is, as I say, a vernacular imitation of the Latin original. That Dante should begin, at such a moment, to exercise the vernacular with such manifest deliberation on the pattern of a classical authority is consistent, I think, with the argument I am pursuing. For Dante, in the presence of Beatrice, is at last obliged to make himself known in the fullness and depth of his personal being. One has seen already in Arnaut, the 'miglior fabbro', how the disciplined vernacular may for Dante affirm an author's self-hood. Now Dante, too, encountering most acutely the forces and limitations of his proper nature, transposes the noble Latin, which is the very pattern of a disciplined language, into a mode which, humble as it may be, is indeed his own. B. Terracini in fact has discovered in 'conosco i segni', the 'tonality of the instinctive language of childhood' ('L' aureo trecento', GSLI, CXXXIV (1957), p. 24).[57] But this is perhaps to underestimate the earnestness with which Dante, as an artist, shapes his line to the

Vergilian model. Having, as it were, over the space of two canticles, been obedient to the example of his master, he has now to demonstrate on his own account the independent virtue of his art. In this second aspect, 'conosco i segni' is the seed of that supremely confident Latinity which flowers, as Paratore has shown, in the opening verses of the *Paradiso* itself.[58]

From the evidence, then, of this transitional passage, I would suggest that the poet, arriving at the *Paradiso*, discerned the need for a style which might display, in guilt and grace, his personal being to the full; and, theoretically, he had already countenanced such a style in the Volgare Illustre.[59] One should note, however, that any such development here would concern not only the style of Dante's poetry, but also the response which he desired for his work. For, as one sees in the disappearance of Vergil, the thought of the poet is now too self-involved to admit, in any normal sense, of rational debate. And this, for any reader of the *Paradiso*, is a point of consequence, which I shall consider at length in Chapter Four. For Dante himself, however, the significance of it may roughly be understood – though I intend no hard and fast distinction – if one compares, at last, the poet's relationship with, on the one hand, Vergil and, on the other, Cacciaguida.

For where in the main the relationship of the poet with Vergil is built, as one sees, upon rational co-operation, his relationship with Cacciaguida – though it involves an extreme of moral bravery – is a matter rather of challenge and example. So while Cacciaguida is indeed the poet's kinsman, Dante is asked to emulate, in his own way, his ancestor's accomplishment rather than to learn from him or defer to him. In austerity, heroism, and even in boldness of speech, the old crusader has erected a standard to which Dante the poet, on his own very different crusade, must determine independently to rise. Only then through his personal achievement, may the poet hope to consummate the expectations that his forebear has conceived for him.

Now my contention throughout is that Dante himself, in the *Paradiso*, means to offer to his reader a challenge very similar to that which Cacciaguida here delivers. The two final illustrations in the *Paradiso* which point to this conclusion occur in Canto Twenty Five, the first at the opening:

> Se mai continga che 'l poema sacro
> al quale ha posto mano e cielo e terra,
> sì che m'ha fatto per molti anni macro,
> vinca la crudeltà che fuor mi serra

del bello ovile ov' io dormi' agnello,
nimico ai lupi che li danno guerra;
con altra voce omai, con altro vello
ritornerò poeta, e in sul fonte
del mio battsmo prenderò 'l cappello.

(If it should ever chance that the sacred poem/ to which both heaven and earth have put their hand,/ so that for many years it has made me thin,/ defeats the cruelty which locks me out/ of the lovely sheep-fold where I slept, a lamb,/ enemy to the wolves that make war upon it;/ with another voice now, with another fleece/ I, as a poet, shall return, and at the font/ of my baptism I shall receive the chaplet.)

Here, then, in a canto that celebrates the final acknowledgement in Heaven itself of his Christian faith, the poet also examines the importance in the circumstances of time that may attach to his poetic achievement. Confidently, he recognises the exalted nature of the *Commedia*, claiming for it the title, 'sacro poema'. On the other hand, he vividly records how great a sacrifice his own commitment to the work has required of him. Over the years he has grown thin in the writing of it, acceding wholly in mind and body to the heroic martyrdom that Aeneas and Cacciaguida had taught him. Yet Dante's principal concern in the passage is evidently with the effects and consequences that his poem will have, as he looks poignantly forward to the day when, possibly, it will win for him the triumphant recognition of his fellow Florentines.[60]

What, then, for the poet himself will the triumph signify? That it cannot signify merely the confounding of his Florentine enemies will at once be apparent from the tone of the passage which, so far from being arrogant or exultant, is sober, even introspective in its estimate of the hurt that has been received. More positively, however, one should note the emphasis that Dante has given remarkably to the particular place in which his coronation as a poet will be solemnised. The laurel-crown, he insists, will come to him 'at the font of my baptism'. But the implication of this, as Boccaccio recognised very early, must plainly be that, as Dante envisaged it, the poetic triumph for which he longed was in its own fashion to be an equivalent of his Christian baptism. Nor is it difficult to see why he should think it so. For in their different ways both the baptism of the poet and his ultimate triumph are occasions which herald publicly the consecration of his self-hood. Thus, where at baptism, the guilt of his original sin had in the eyes of God been annulled, making it possible for his virtue as a man to come to fruition, so likewise his poetic triumph will mark the cleansing in the eyes of men of his slandered reputation and announce at last his return to that place in the world to which justly he belongs. Through the force of his art as once by the faith of his parents, Dante hopes again to be known for what he truly is.

But if, in the claiming of his name and fame, the example of heroic commitment that Aeneas or Cacciaguida presents has assisted him, so, too, will the wonder of Dante's ultimate triumph encourage in those who admire it a willingness, likewise, to submit to their own peculiar destinies. So in the same canto, St James requires that the poet should speak out confidently in the celebration of hope, so that others, too, may observe in him the power of hopefulness:

> sì che, veduto il ver di questa corte,
> la spene, che là giù bene innamora,
> in te e in altrui di ciò conforte,
> dì quel ch'ell' è dì come se ne 'nfiora
> la mente tua, e dì onde a te venne.

(so that, having seen the truth of this court,/ the hope – which below inspires true loving –,/ you may strengthen in yourself and in others,/ say what it is, say how there comes to flower with it/ your mind, and say whence it came to you.)

(*Par.* XXV 43–7)

The brilliance, then, of Dante's achievement is a clear and vital challenge to the spirit of Christian philosophy. Those who do respond to it will promote the restoration not only of the poet himself to honour, but also of a philosophical courtesy, where every man's attainment may again receive the honour it deserves. The sheep-fold – to return to the pastoral imagery of the 'Se mai continga' passage – will be restored once again to its natural condition of innocence and peace.

3

THE STABLE PHRASE

I have now to consider how the disciplines of which I have been speaking may, as Dante understands them, influence the linguistic form of a poem, and how the modesty of mind and the courtliness, which are the root and the flowering of such discipline, may be incorporated in a poetic style. The question bears directly upon the matter of textual analysis, and I shall in fact be able to begin in this chapter a detailed analysis of the style of the *Paradiso*. Firstly, however, there is a notion in Dante's theory of considerable importance to the analysis that I have yet to examine. This is the notion of stability.

The term 'stability' is one which Dante himself introduces in the great conclusion to *Convivio* Book One, where, concerning his own affection for the vernacular, he writes:

Ciascuna cosa studia naturalmente a la sua conservazione; onde, se lo volgare per sé studiare potesse, studierebbe a quella; e quella sarebbe acconciare sé a più stabilitade, e più stabilitade non potrebbe avere che in legar sé con numero e con rime. E questo medesimo studio è stato mio . . .

(Everything by nature is studious for its own preservation. If, therefore, the vernacular were able to study on its own account, it would study to that purpose, which would be to adapt itself to a greater stability. But a greater stability it could not have than by binding itself with metre and rhyme. And that same study has been mine.)

(*Con.* I xiii 6)

As a particular consequence, then, of that love for his native language that Dante so forcefully emphasises, the poet will seek to bestow upon the vernacular a permanence such as, by its nature, it is bound to lack. As to the exact character of this permanence I shall have more to say shortly, though it is as well to say at once that it does not imply the pursuit of an academic rigidity. For the moment, however, one should note that the permanence of which Dante speaks will reside in a certain 'binding' or quality of formal order. Still more importantly, the order that Dante envisages is one that will arise artificially, in the deliberate exercise of metre and rhyme. These are the primary instruments of the poet's craft, and for that reason the creation of stability in the vernacular may be regarded as a responsibility that belongs specifically to the poet. So we find that at *Convivio* Book Four, Chapter Six, Dante defines the very meaning of the word 'author', which he associates with 'authority', as one who can bind words harmoniously together. The argument itself is an exceedingly strange one, depending upon the visual image that the Latin word 'aueio' presents. But the sense which emerges, of the poet as a man whose particular function is to achieve a formal firmness in language, returns, as will be seen, at certain important moments of the *De Vulgari Eloquentia*.

Considering, however, only the passage from the *Convivio* that I have quoted, it will be apparent that the notion of stability touches on matters far wider in significance than the technical alone.[1] For to speak of stability in language implies at once a recognition of linguistic changefulness. From this there arises a problem which is to interest Dante throughout his career. Thus in the *De Vulgari Eloquentia* the problem of mutability in language is central to Dante's discussion of the Fall of Babel,[2] while in an altered but equally impressive form, it occurs again in Canto Twenty Six of the *Paradiso*, where Adam demonstrates that even before the confusion of Babel human languages were prone to change:[3]

> La lingua ch'io parlai fu tutta spenta
> innanzi che a l'ovra inconsummabile
> fosse la gente di Nembròt attenta:
> ché nullo effetto mai razïonabile,
> per lo piacere uman che rinovella
> seguendo il cielo, sempre fu durabile.
> Opera naturale è ch'uom favella;
> ma così o così, natura lascia
> poi fare a voi secondo che v'abbella.

(The language that I spoke was wholly extinguished/ before the work – impossible to finish –/ had been looked to by the people of Nimrod:/ for no creation of reason at all –/ because human preference is renewed/ following heavenly influence – was ever enduring./ It is a work of nature that man speaks;/ but whether thus or thus, nature leaves for you to do, according to what pleases you.)

(*Par.* XXVI 124–32)

In this perspective, the question of stability is related evidently to questions concerning the very structure of human speech. These questions, which have been discussed exhaustively in recent years and need not greatly occupy me here, are relevant nonetheless in two ways.

In the first place, Dante's approach to the concept of stability indicates again, as I have maintained throughout, that for him matters of style and language stand close to the very core of human existence. This may be seen in the connection he draws between the development of language and the loss both of Babel and of Paradise – though in the second case the connection is an implicit one. In the mutability of language, it appears, Dante sees an accurate reflection of the history of the human spirit in its relation to God. One may add that if, as in these two instances, the results of pride impinge so heavily upon the human word, it is understandable that Dante should insist upon the importance in speech of humility. Be that as it may, where speech and spirituality are so forcefully linked, it is apparent that any answer to linguistic mutability, in the form of a stable utterance, is likely to serve also as an answer to the larger preoccupations of the spiritual life. Stability, indeed, will be as much a spiritual as a linguistic accomplishment. Thus as Mario Pazzaglia has noted, pointing to the continual interchange in the *De Vulgari Eloquentia* between the terms of rhetoric and the terms of ordinary existence, the artistic construction in which stability inheres will manifest the order (*ordo*) which a person is called upon to actuate, in himself and in the world (*Il verso e l'arte*, p. 111). One has in fact already seen how the Latin grammar and the Volgare Illustre may each foster a certain kind of spiritual culture, each in its own way answering the corruption of Babel. And stability, as will be found, is a quality especially associated with the Volgare Illustre. However, even in the *Convivio* passage, where the desire for stability appears as an aspect of right-minded love, Dante envisages that same relation between form and spiritual intention which I am concerned here to pursue.

The second point of importance which the passages I have quoted suggest is, at first sight, of a different character. For what emerges very clearly out of Dante's concern with mutability is that the achievement of a stable utterance will be a positive response to the arbitrariness of language. That Dante did consider language to be arbitrary – even, approximately, in a modern sense of the phrase – has been demonstrated by Antonino Pagliaro in his important essay 'I "primissima signa" nella dottrina linguistica di Dante in *Nuovi saggi di critica semantica*'.[4] Certainly the alterations of language are not to be thought of as a matter only of corruption or decadence. For whether these changes are a divine punishment, as Dante suggests in the *De Vulgari Eloquentia*, or simply a feature of the Creator's dispensation in the world, they are still inherently and inevitably characteristic of language. Nor, one should emphasise, will stability itself in the vernacular represent any final or absolute modification of this condition, any more than a single instance of the Volgare Illustre, which is of value precisely for its relation to the individual speaker, will possess a universal validity. So Pazzaglia concludes that the poet, faced with the constant variation of language, will seek to arrive at a lasting structure, but will always be aware of something insecure in it (*ma avverte sempre in essa qualcosa di precario*) (*Il verso e l'arte*, p. 116). Yet the very sense, of course, of a 'continual variation' in his language is likely to sharpen the alertness and the circumspection of an author. Indeed, when rightly understood, as a natural challenge to the reason of the speaker, the arbitrariness of language may be as much a liberation as a restriction.[5] And from this one will see the bearing of the present argument upon preceding chapters. For in the inexpressibility topic, Dante displays a most acute, though untroubled, awareness of how, in respect of his experience, his words are arbitrary. One may also recall, from the introduction, that precisely such an awareness will find no explanation in any poetic theory which has chosen to emphasise a power of expressive 'adequacy' in the word.

What effect, though, will the awareness of mutability have upon the technical procedure of the poet? This is the principal question that I have to consider. Here at once there appears the relation between the notion of stability, as a spiritual product, and the sense of arbitrariness in language. For, in general, what Dante recommends to the poet who seeks the stability of the vernacular is an attentive imitation of Latin, as a 'grammatical' language. Consequently throughout his theoretical writings, he points to Latin as a permanent repository of the rules by which all languages are to be governed.[6] Clearly the technical control which the stable utterance will require is to be learnt firstly from an observation of the Latin model. Of the run, therefore, of vernacular poets Dante writes:

Differunt tamen a magnis poetis, hoc est regularibus, quia magni sermone et arte regulari poetati sunt, hii vero casu, ut dictum est. Idcirco accidit ut, quantum illos proximius imitemur, tantum rectius poetamur. Unde nos doctrine operi intendentes, doctrinatas eorum poetrias emulari oportet.

(They differ, however, from the great poets, that is from poets who are guided by rules. For the great poets wrote in a language and with an art that follows rule, while in fact these [*the vernacular poets*], as has been said, write in accordance with chance. It comes about, therefore, that the more closely we imitate these [*the great poets*], the more correctly we write poetry. Thus, when we intend to write learned works, it is proper that we should take as our model their learned poetic teachings.)

(*D.V.E.* II iv 3)

At the same time, – and this, in view of the arguments in Chapter Two, is not surprising – the poet may also be expected to acquire, from his study of the grammar, a certain understanding of the spirit which poetic discourse ought properly to manifest. Let it be said at once that neither in spirit nor in form will the 'imitation' of the grammar be a matter of mimicry or even of retrospective classicism. A profoundly original initiative, to which the stable utterance will itself bear witness, will still be required of the vernacular poet.[7] Yet in one essential respect, the prevailing genius of the Latin manner may still strengthen and encourage him. For, as Di Capua has forcefully demonstrated, the virtue above all others which Dante observed in the Latin grammar was a simplicity of utterance, born of 'discretion' – which is 'la potenza efficace di communicare agli altri' (*the power that makes communication with others possible*).[8] As will be seen shortly, Dante's own utterances, in form and spirit, do indicate the significance of this observation.

The importance, however, of discretion, in Di Capua's understanding of it, to the creation both of simplicity and in the end of stability cannot, I think, be over-emphasised. It is discretion, as Di Capua and Pazzaglia agree, which infuses the verbal construction with a sense both ethical and artistic of measure.[9] It is discretion, too, which teaches a poet the inherent rule of his medium, so that, acknowledging language to be labile, he may bring to bear upon it a rational and responsible governance. Simplicity is the product and reflection of such control. Pazzaglia emphasises this by applying to Dante's theory the mediaeval notion of music, which, he argues, is to be understood as a purity of rational organisation, capable of restoring in the soul the 'intimate harmony' that it lost through sin (*Il verso e l'arte*, p. 99; see also p. 17). One need not here consider why rhetoric and 'music' should be thought of in a similar way. But, as Pazzaglia shows very clearly, the phrase which manifests a rational or a 'musical' simplicity will also be a stable phrase, in opposing to the waywardness of spirit and tongue a most deliberate and conscious artistry.[10]

Coming now to the particular detail of style, it will be found that, in the stable utterance of the poets who have learnt to 'lean' upon the grammar, the simplicity of rational discretion will be evident above all in two features of the style, the rhetorical ornamentation and the control of syntax.[11] It is not, of course, difficult to see how a rational order may be sustained in the syntax of an utterance. For syntax, in any circumstances, will tend to reveal the logical conventions of a language. What, at first sight, is more remarkable is that the same kind of order should be expected to show itself in the embellishments which a poet employs. It is here after all that the modern critic seeks a demonstration of imaginative or expressive energy. Yet at *Inferno* Canto Two line 67, Vergil was called upon to exercise his 'parola ornata' in the interests precisely of morality and spiritual health. Indeed from an instance of Dante's own devising, one may see how far his similar purposes remove him from any modern concept of poetic decoration.

Thus, as a Latin exemplar of the 'gradum constructionis excellentissimum', Dante offers:

Eiecta maxima parte florum de sinu tuo, Florentia, nequicquam Trinacriam Totila secundus adivit.

(The greatest part of your flowers having been cast from your breast, O Florence, in vain the second Totila went on to Trinacria.)

(*D.V.E.* II vi 4)

Of this Roger Dragonetti, concentrating upon the balance which Dante erects around the central 'Florentia', has given an account which does in fact seek to apply the standards of modern criticism.[12] Dragonetti firstly notes the horror that the line expresses at the destruction of the flowers of Florence, but argues that the effect of this horror is 'mysteriously' assuaged by the formal unity of sentence itself. Dante's subject may arouse violent associations. Yet the simplicity and calm power (*la puissance simple et calme*) of the verbal structure contains and organises in its measured progress the sense of dissolution. So there arises a harmony of opposing forces (*une harmonie de forces contraires*) between the form and the content of the sentence. The tension out of which this harmony springs is itself the ground of a certain serene and vibrant immobility (*immobilité vibrante sereine*) which, for Dragonetti, is the peculiar characteristic of the classical style, and the characteristic, too, of the tragic mode of Dante's own art (*Aux frontières du langage poétique* (Ghent, 1961), p. 69).

To the extent that Dragonetti emphasises the strenuous order and the unity which this imposes upon experience in the passage, his comment is an accurate and useful one. Nonetheless, it is incorrect, I suggest, to suppose that the unity arises somehow from an intrinsic 'tension' of thought and emotion. Nor is this unity in any way an expression of violence or mystery. On the contrary, it arises from an analytical reflection upon the events and circumstances which the poet is depicting. And the rhetorical structure of the line, precisely as Dragonetti describes it, is the means which the poet employs to enforce this analysis.

Consider only the treatment of 'Florentia'. Placing the word at the central point of the phrase, the poet does indeed draw attention to the personification and to the etymological play on 'florum: Florentia'. Yet so far from producing a 'symbol rich in suggestion' (Dragonetti, *ibid.* p. 69), the etymology and the metaphor, when presented in this way to one's attention, assist in the establishing of at least one quite determinate concept, the concept of 'unnaturalness'. So, in the way that, as a flowering thing, Florentia would be ruined in its very nature by the dispersal of its flowers, so has the city been ruined, in respect of all that gave it its essential quality, by the exile of its most eminent citizens. Through the analogy, Dante presents not an emotion but a judgement, that by the banishing of its 'flower', the essential worth of Florence has been destroyed. And this judgement would not have appeared, at least so clearly, if the rhythmic disposition of the sentence had not induced one to investigate the relationship between its constituent parts. The stability of the lines inheres in the satisfyingly conscious sense of what these relationships are.

To read the passage in this way is certainly to paraphrase. Yet its structure is a positive invitation to paraphrase. Such a reading is not, I think, likely to injure the line, as undoubtedly it would injure a line which was expressive in character. Rather, in appreciating the analogy which is offered and made emphatic by the disposition of the rhythm, one approaches directly the assessment which the poet has himself arrived at of a certain situation. The organisation of the passage is, so to say, a guarantee of how the poet, personally and deliberately, has seen fit to organise his own experience. And the more clearly one appreciates that, the closer one will come to the working mind of the man himself.

Consider, also, the phrase 'nequicquam Trinacriam Totila secundus adivit'. Here again, in the antonomasia and the periphrasis Dante constructs his own judgement upon Charles de Valois, and also brings into account the occurrences which support his position, so that there can be no doubt of what the poet's opinion was or how he arrived at it. If, like Auerbach, one finds in these lines 'a striking clarity', it is because of, not, as Auerbach suggests, in spite of the ornamentation (*Dante, Poet of the Secular World*, p. 51). For the devices of rhetoric carry the very scheme of reference which the poet himself has employed to articulate his understanding. From the dominating presence of that scheme arises the simplicity of the phrase. And in that, too, there lies its stability.

The example I have given here is, of course, a piece of prose. However, it will be easy to show that the qualities I have found in it, depending as they do upon the co-operation of rhetoric and rhythmic disposition, may attain to an even greater force where an author has metrical emphasis at his command. Thus one has seen that in the *Convivio* passage Dante looked to the ordering effect of rhythm and rhyme as indispensable to the creation of stability. It is, of course, in the great canzone that one may expect to see the supreme demonstration of stability. Indeed, in the canzoni, which are the great exemplars of the Volgare Illustre and hence of a philosophical courtliness, Dante proposes that there should be a control so great that, in theme, 'nothing accidental should cheapen it' (*D.V.E.* II iv 8). And the very virtue of the canzone-form is that it should depend upon nothing extrinsic – such as music – for its effect. So Dante writes:

quicquid per se ipsum efficit illud ad quod factum est, nobilius esse videtur quam quod extrinseco indiget; sed cantiones per se totum quod debent efficiunt, quod ballate non faciunt – indigent enim plausoribus, ad quos edite sunt: ergo cantiones nobiliores ballatis esse sequitur extimandas . . .

(Whatever accomplishes that for which it was made by itself, is evidently more noble than that which depends upon things extrinsic to it. But canzoni achieve everything they have to achieve by themselves, which ballades do not. Ballades stand in need of people to beat time [*dancers*] – for whom they are intended. It follows, therefore, that canzoni are to be considered more noble than ballades.)

(*D.V.E.* II iii 5)

The structure of thought and word will itself be sufficient in a canzone to satisfy one's attention. As one might expect in a form whose language is defined, in a passage I have quoted before (*ibid.* I xviii 4) as remarkable for its 'curialitas', every feature of its style will be thoroughly weighed and well regulated.

Though I shall have no opportunity to examine any instance of the canzone, it will be found that many aspects of Dante's style in the *Paradiso* do answer to the description which he offers of the canzone in the passages I have referred to. On this score one may well agree with Dragonetti, who notes that the 'grammatical language' of the canzone is 'a remembrance of paradise lost' (*Aux frontières*, p. 77). However, before considering the application in verse of a 'stable' rhetoric, I have to return, briefly, to the matter of syntax, to show more precisely how syntax may promote the stability of a style.

For while it is true that syntax usually is, to some degree, an agent of deliberate organisation in sentence structure, one is bound to emphasise how intimately, in Dante's hands, it could signify and sustain the order which an author himself desired to impress upon his meaning. As Segre has shown so excitingly, the very development of Italian syntax, in which Dante had a cardinal role to play, was a matter rather of 'revolution than of evolution'.[13] And Dante's own syntax is no product merely of stylistic growth, but a conscious creation, designed – even perhaps programmatically designed – to expand the philosophical capacities of Italian writing. Thus his introduction, in the first instance, to the importance of syntax appears to have arisen from a penetrating engagement with the thought of his classical authorities, where endeavouring, precisely, to achieve a philosophical understanding, he was led to a 'struggle with the robust organism of the Latin period'.[14] Then again, his attention to syntax may be taken as a response to the exigencies of his own intellectual mission. Thus, acquiring, in the *Convivio*, what Terracini has called an outlook both 'scientific and critical', he also ensures that instead of – to quote Terracini again – the mere 'bundling together' (*affastellamento*) of notions that one finds in the *Vita Nuova*, the style of the *Convivio* is one in which doctrine and opinion are critically sifted and graded (*criticamente vagliata e graduata*) ('La forma interna del *Convivio*', *Pagine e appunti di linguistica storica* (Florence, 1957), p. 275).

In Terracini's comment, the important word, of course, is 'critically'. For while in any developed syntax notions may be qualified, emphasised and systematically established in their relations one to another, such syntax, when it is conscientiously handled, may also guarantee, as Dante demonstrates, the integrity of the poet's own intelligent control. Consequently syntax is to be regarded not as a means only to the mechanical or efficient ordering of thought, but also as a mode, so to say, of intention, by which an author may engrave upon his utterances a considered agreement and deliberate consent. The 'total attention to the structural force of syntax' which Segre sees in Dante's response to his didactic responsibilities may explain why his didacticism should ring to so intensely personal a note ('La sintassi' in *Lingua, stile e societa*, p. 231). It most certainly does explain, as Pazzaglia emphasises, the stability of the poet's word (*Il verso e l'arte*, pp. 202–4).

From the *Convivio* a single instance must here suffice to epitomise the value of Dante's procedure. Thus Mario Marti, in his excellent 'Aspetti stilistici di Dante traduttore', noting Dante's ability 'to give new significance to old words, to re-clothe, with a cultural sophistication, the rough but not unresponsive material of the vernacular',[15] emphasises the skill with which Dante translates the Latin ablative in:

> omnes homines natura scire desiderant
>
> (all men naturally desire to know)

with 'naturalmente' in:

> tutti gli uomini naturalmente desiderano
> di sapere.

The Latin paradigm is treated with the utmost respect. Yet through this, the vernacular is itself revitalised; the common adverb 'naturalmente' being charged, perhaps for the first time, with a 'philosophical intensity which is absolutely new' ('Aspetti stilistici', pp. 114–15). To appreciate the value of this, one has only to think how difficult it is, without a close attention to syntax, to use 'naturally' in English with anything save a most casual significance. Certainly in the present case, the stability of 'naturalmente' arises from Dante's intelligent control of syntactical convention.

From the *Convivio*, of course, one could multiply such examples indefinitely.[16] Finally, however, my concern here is to indicate a compatibility between the stable phrase and the self-sufficient authority that a well-distinguished utterance might encompass. And on this score one may return to Terracini, who speaking of the discriminating use which Dante makes of etymology, as in the play on 'gioventute: giovare' (*Con.* IV XXIV I), and 'idee: dee' (*ibid.* II IV 5–6), argues that just as Dante uses, in place of simply rational constructions, the comparisons and analogies that were commonplace in his day, so, too, in the *Convivio* he employs etymologies, glosses, and learned explanations in place, again, of pure reasoning (*in sede di puro ragionamento*) to establish clearly the particular relationships of which he is speaking ('Il lessico del Convivio', *Pagine e appunti di linguistica storica*, p. 282). Even in the *Convivio*, it appears, which depends far more than does the *Paradiso* upon a mode of investigatory and more or less syllogistic procedure, one finds that

Dante is developing, as an alternative to regular argumentation, a method by which his conscious art and rhetoric may fix, peremptorily, the meaning he has to offer.[17] In such cases, indeed, as in the play on 'flos: Florentia', judgement, rhetoric, rhythmic balance and syntax conspire to substantiate the position which an author has adopted. And recognising in such order the mindfulness of the poet, one will, I think, be ready to receive his utterances with an appropriate courtesy.

What now remains, however, is to show in practice how a syntactical stability may consort with poetic form. In the first instance, one may turn to the eighth and ninth cantos of the *Paradiso*, where Dante's intention, I suggest, is to offer something of an 'aggiornamento' of the themes he treated in the *Convivio* and the *De Vulgari Eloquentia*.

In the case of the Venus episode it is even easier than in the case of the Cacciaguida episode to see why Dante should have had in mind the questions which he raised in the *De Vulgari Eloquentia*. For the Heaven of Venus, as one learns at *Convivio*, II xiii 13–14, is the Heaven of Rhetoric.[18] It is true that Dante's most obvious interest in the sequence is with the themes of prophetic love and political regeneration. However it will be apparent from all I have said of the social function of the Volgare Illustre that these themes are by no means unconnected with the discussion of language. Certainly the principal figures of the episode are associated with the courtly world to which Dante, as a rhetorician, addresses himself. There is Folco, the warrior bishop who was himself once a troubadour, Cunizza, the courtly mistress of Sordello who in her declining years was renowned for her Christian liberality, and Charles Martell, who, as Dante suggests by alluding to his own great canzone 'Voi che 'ntendendo' (VIII 37), may first have brought home to the poet how, through his art, he might become the familiar of rulers and of princes. However, it is with the style of the episode that I am concerned here. For nothing could be more striking than the determination which Dante shows in these cantos to enhance and embellish his subject with devices of the highest dignity.

Merely to list, for the moment, the passages which concern me, there occurs at the very opening of the sequence a learned reference to the pagan cult of Venus, culminating in the highly ornate:

> e da costei ond' io principio piglio
> pigliavano il vocabol de la stella
> che 'l sol vagheggia or da coppa or da ciglio.

(and from her [*Venus*] whence I take my opening/ they took the word for the star/ that caressingly gazes upon the sun, now at the nape, now at the brow.)

(*Par.* VIII 10–12)

Then, as Carlo Martell begins to speak at line 49, his introduction of himself unrolls in a great geographical periphrasis, which is matched by those which in turn Cunizza and Folco employ at Canto Nine lines 25 and 82. To these very significant speeches I shall return more than once in what follows. In Carlo's speech itself, however, one may also note the lines beginning 'Fulgeami già in fronte la corona' (*already the crown shone on my brow*) (*ibid.* VIII 64), and the periphrastic description of Etna, which includes the locution 'Trinacria', that occurred in the *De Vulgari Eloquentia* in Dante's example of the highest style:

E la bella Trinacria, che caliga
tra Pachino e Peloro, sopra 'l golfo
che riceve da Euro maggior briga,
non per Tifeo ma per nascente solfo . . .

(And the beautiful Trinacria, that is foggy/ between Pachino and Peloro, on the gulf/ that receives from Eurus the greatest trouble,/ not through Typhon but through sulphur being generated.)

(*ibid.* 67–70)

In Canto Nine, apart from the periphrases which I have already mentioned, Dido is referred to indirectly as

la figlia di Belo

(*ibid.* IX 97)

And Ezzelino as:

una facella
che fece a la contrada un grande assalto.

(a firebrand/ that made a great assault upon the region around.)

(*ibid.* 29–30)

just as in Canto Eight, Daedalus has been characterised, not directly, but as:

quello
che, volando per l'aere, il figlio perse

(he/ who flying through the air lost his son.)

(*ibid.* VIII 125–6)

And Canto Nine draws to a close with a passage reminiscent of 'Eiecta maxima parte . . .':

> La tua città, che di colui è pianta
> che pria volse le spalle al suo fattore
> e di cui è la 'nvidia tanto pianta,
> produce e spande il maladetto fiore
> c' ha disvïate le pecore e li agni . . .

(Your city, which is a plant belonging to him/ who first turned his back upon his maker/ and from whose envy comes so much lamentation,/ produces and spreads abroad the evil flower/ which has misled the sheep and lambs.)

(*ibid.* IX 127–31)

To be sure, one may find in the same two cantos extraordinary or 'violent' formations, some of which might at first seem inconsistent with the standards of the *De Vulgari Eloquentia*, like 'malta', 'bigoncia', 'oncia', 'm'intuassi', 't'inmii' (*ibid.* IX, 54, 55, 57, 81) Phrases of this sort, of course, are precisely those which are most likely to appeal to modern poetic taste. Yet, as will be seen in Chapter Five from similar instances, even such extreme examples may conform to the principles of a rational stability. And certainly it will appear that the characteristic of the other passages, in point of syntax and rhetorical figure, is stability.

If, however, in these passages, the Venus episode does reflect the considerations of Dante's theory, it also reveals an unmistakable parallel to the thought which in Chapter One I associated with Aquinas and Solomon. Nor is this surprising. For the thought of the episode revolves around two points of doctrine, that of Providence, which is Aquinas's peculiar concern, and that of generation in the natural world, which is the sphere that Solomon is given to celebrate. The proper response to the mysteries both of Providence and of generation – which cannot, for Dante, be unconnected – [19] is suggested at Canto Nine line 4:

> Taci e lascia muover li anni
>
> (Be silent and let the years move on).

In the face of Providence, as it directs the natural world, silence is the true answer. Dante's poetic reaction involves equally the modesty of voice which Aquinas and Solomon exemplify, and the simplicity of the stable phrase.

Consider, then, the passage, quoted above, on the 'maladetto fiore' which now corrupts the Florentines. Biting as the lines may be, there is nothing in them of the unbridled anger that one finds, say, in:

> Ahi serva Italia, di dolore ostello,
> nave sanza nocchiere in gran tempesta,
> non donna di provincie, ma bordello!

(Oh, slave-like Italy, hostel of misery,/ ship without helmsman in a great tempest,/ no mistress of provinces but of the brothel.)

(*Purg.* VI 76–8)

Nor is there any great similarity in respect of style. For where in the *Purgatorio* speech the accumulation of disparate images has a fully expressive force, each phrase making its contribution to the effect of the whole, in the *Paradiso* passage the 'maladetto fiore'' is plainly a figure for the golden florin, inviting one to pause and paraphrase even more obviously than the 'Totila secundus' of 'Eiecta maxima parte . . .'. The spirit which governs the *Paradiso* passage is a spirit not of expressivity but of analysis. It is, indeed, recognisably the same spirit which in *Inferno* Canto Eleven classified usury as a form of unnaturalness and perverted growth. For within the compass of these five lines, the origin and function of the florin are traced, with a theological eye, to the moment at which the devil turned his back upon the creator of the natural universe. The unnatural flower is no opulently evil 'fleur du mal'. Nor does it possess any imaginative or independent resonance. It is a factor, simply, in the progress from Satanic rebellion to the dissemination of avarice. The figure, then, is used precisely to establish the poet's understanding of that progress. In the conscious definition which it carries the phrase is evidently not expressive but stable.[20]

An even more remarkable, though apparently less important instance, occurs with Dante's reference to Etna at *Paradiso*, Canto Eight, 67–70:

> E la bella Trinacria, che caliga
> tra Pachino e Peloro, sopra 'l golfo
> che riceve da Euro maggior briga,
> non per Tifeo ma per nascente solfo . . .

The passage is rich in rhetorical adornment. Yet the final line deliberately eliminates the mythic and imaginative explanation of how the volcano is fired, substituting for this, in its mention of sulphurous vapour, a plainly scientific account.[21] To modern eyes, of course, it is the mythic image that appears the more attractive. However, there is good reason for Dante to suppress its force. For, as Solomon might have taught him, the natural world is as wonderful a subject for contemplation as the world of ancient fable. Indeed, at the very beginning of the Venus sequence, the myths of Venus, by which men once interpreted their relation to the world, are associated with the 'peril' and the 'antico errore' of the pre-Christian era.[22] Throughout the episode the poet is concerned, more deeply perhaps than anywhere else in the *Commedia*, with the redemption and rejuvenation of natural phenomena. Through Christ, the world itself is made stable and simple. And the scientific stability of the Etna passage is a sign that the poet is aware of this.

At the same time, though the myths might in substance be rejected, they may nonetheless serve the poet as an ornament to his Christian theme. The play of rhetoric, when it manifests the rational control of the poet, need not be at loggerheads with a scientific consciousness. This may best be seen from the use which every character in the episode makes of learned periphrasis.[23] These characters themselves, of course, – and notably Cunizza – embody in their own persons the redemption of natural instinct, and through the periphrases, each in turn displays a sense both of geographical knowledge and of the ceremony to which the redeemed soul is now entitled. Nor is it surprising that, in style, these speeches should manifest a perfect co-operation of rhetorical and syntactic 'music'.

Consider, then, in point of theme as well as style, the lines which Dante gives to Folco:

> 'La maggior valle in che l'acqua spanda',
> incominciaro allor le sue parole,
> 'fuor di quel mar che la terra inghirlanda,
> tra ' discordanti liti contra 'l sole
> tanto sen va, che fa meridïano
> là dove l'orizzonte pria far suole.
> Di quella valle fu' io litorano . . .'

('The greatest valley into which water spreads', his words then began, 'apart from that sea that casts around the land a garland,/ between discordant shores against the sun/ goes so far that it makes the meridian there where before its horizon was./ Of that valley was I a shore-dweller.)
(*Par.* IX 82–8)

In theme, this extract, like many another in the episode, calls to mind very forcefully the present evil of human behaviour. The shores of the Mediterranean are 'discordanti'. This adjective, though its meaning is disputed, cannot fail to suggest the long centuries of antagonism between the natives of these shores, just as at line 93, Folco reminds one, with his reference to the massacre of Marseilles, of how once the very waters of the port were coloured with internecine blood. Yet the viciousness of men can in no way pollute the existential value of the world itself. The Judgement, which Dante anticipates in Paradise, will secure in the end the cleanliness of the human habitat. And of such security, the descriptive clearness and simplicity of Folco's speech is the verbal reflection.

Thus, the sea continues to 'garland' the earth, and the decorative metaphor at once offsets the menacing tonality of 'discordanti liti'. Folco, moreover, accepts without hesitation the designation 'litorano' – which he might have shunned as a mark of his own association with these broils – and proceeds, in the interest of a purely biographical exactitude, to indicate the whereabouts of his birth-place on these unhappy confines (*ibid.* 88–9).[24] Then, again, in the same line, the phrase, 'contra 'l sole', which, had it occurred in the *Inferno*, as in Ulysses' 'di retro al sol' (*Inf.* XXVI 117), might well have suggested a certain violence against the natural order, is here neither more nor less than a geographical bearing. The generation of any complex or ambiguous sense for 'sole' is positively inhibited, not, in this case, by the weight of metaphor, but by the structure of the syntax. For in the formula 'tanto . . . che' in 'tanto sen va che . . .', 'sole' is required to stand as one of the fixed references in Dante's geographical calculation, which it can only do if, like the 'ombra' I spoke of in Chapter One, it is regarded simply as the denotation of a physical fact. No passage could indicate more clearly Dante's interest in the organisation of the natural world, while throughout, his accuracy in the establishing of geographical or descriptive co-ordinates is possible only because of his sureness in the placing of defining clauses.[25]

In what way, however, does the style here differ from the descriptive style of, say, the *Purgatorio*? A single example must here suffice: Statius's account of the exotic, but for Dante, natural climate of the upper Purgatory, which is free from every ordinary change:

> Per che non pioggia, non grando, non neve,
> non rugiada, non brina più sù cade
> che la scaletta di tre gradi breve;
> nuvole spesse non paion né rade,
> né coruscar, né figlia di Taumante,
> che di là cangia sovente contrade . . .

(For neither rain nor hail nor snow/ nor dew nor frost falls any higher/ than the little stairway of three narrow steps;/ there appear neither dense clouds nor thin ones,/ neither lightning-flashes nor the daughter of Thaumas [*Iris*],/ who, beyond, often changes her region.)

(*Purg.* XXI 46–51)

In its entirety, this passage, as befits Statius, is highly decorated, even manneristic in character. But the rhetoric and the rhythmic pattern are truly expressive rather than 'stable'. The exquisite strangeness of Dante's intuition is perfectly realised in the lulling and diaphanous *occupatio*, 'non pioggia, non grando, non neve . . .'. Clearly there are forces here which no orderly progress of syntax could contain – the forces of that vital tremor which interfuses the natural world of Purgatory,[26] and of which Statius himself speaks in this same Canto:

> Trema forse più giù poco assai
>
> (It trembles perhaps further down a little or much)
>
> (*ibid.* 55)

and

> Tremaci quando alcuna anima monda
> sentesi . . .
>
> (It trembles here when any soul feels itself
> pure.)
>
> (*ibid.* 58–9)

To such mysterious vivacity an imaginative precision, in a sense that Eliot would have understood, is entirely appropriate. For this accuracy may indeed embody the creative penetration of the spirit and its environment. And this penetration is, in large measure, the subject of the *Purgatorio*.

But if, with the language of the *Purgatorio*, Dante investigates the sources and primary impulses of life, with the language of the *Paradiso*, he marks, so to say, the limit at which the man of goodwill will rest if he is to honour and enjoy the result of his investigations. To this mode the firmness and the self-possession that one finds in Folco's speech are the more appropriate.[27]

Stability, then, is a characteristic of the natural descriptions in Cantos Eight and Nine. More importantly, however, it is also to be seen in the presentation of dogma and of truth. At this point the comparison between the *Paradiso* and the *Purgatorio* becomes especially significant. Consider the following passages which, as one might show if there were time, are not dissimilar in theme and plan, the first being Carlo Martell's discussion of Providential creation, the second, Marco Lombardo's discussion of free will.

Thus, Carlo Martell:

> S'io posso
> mostrarti un vero, a quel che tu dimandi
> terrai lo viso come tien lo dosso.

Lo ben che tutto il regno che tu scandi
volge e contenta, fa esser virtute
sua provedenza in questi corpi grandi.
E non pur le nature provedute
sono in la mente ch'è da sé perfetta,
ma esse insieme con la lor salute:
per che quantunque quest' arco saetta
disposto cade a proveduto fine,
sì come cosa in suo segno diretta.
Se ciò non fosse, il ciel che tu cammine
producerebbe sì li suoi effetti,
che non sarebbero arti, ma ruine;
e ciò esser non può, se li 'ntelletti
che muovon queste stelle non son manchi,
e manco il primo, che non li ha perfetti.
Vuo' tu che questo ver più ti s'imbianchi?

(If I can/ show you a truth [*in response*] to what you ask/ you will hold your eyes where now you hold your back./ The Good that all the realm which you are traversing/ turns and contents, makes to be a virtuous strength/ its providence in these great bodies./ And not only are the natures [*of all things*] provided for/ in that mind, which of itself is perfect,/ but these natures together with their proper state of well-being:/ therefore, whatever this bow shoots forth/ falls disposed to a foreseen end,/ like something directed to its own mark./ If that were not so, the heaven that you journey through/ would so produce its effects that they would be not works of art but ruins;/ and that cannot be unless the intelligences/ that move these stars are deficient, and deficient, too, the Primal [*intelligence*], which has failed to bring these to perfection./ Do you wish me further to illuminate this truth?.)

(*Par.* VIII 94–111)

And thus Marco:

Alto sospir, che duolo strinse in 'uhi!',
mise fuor prima; e poi cominciò: 'Frate,
lo mondo è cieco, e tu vien ben da lui.
Voi che vivete ogne cagion recate
pur suso al cielo, pur come se tutto
movesse seco di necessitate.
Se così fosse, in voi fora distrutto
libero arbitrio, e non fora giustizia
per ben letizia, e per male aver lutto.
Lo cielo i vostri movimenti inizia;
non dico tutti, ma, posto ch 'i' 'l dica,
lume v'è dato a bene e a malizia,
e libero voler . . .'

(A deep sigh, which sorrow constrained to 'Alas',/ he uttered first; and then he began: 'Brother, the world is blind, and really you do come from it./ You who are living attribute every cause/ to Heaven alone, just as if it carried all things with it by necessity./ If it were thus, in you would be destroyed Free Will, and there would be no justice/ in having joy for goodness and woe for evil./ Heaven initiates your movements;/ I do not say all, but granted that I said so,/ a light is given you [*to see*] good and evil,/ and freedom of will.)

(*Purg*. XVI 64–76)

Now, to recall an earlier argument, the style of the Marco passage, I suggest, is exactly in keeping with those procedures of thought which Dante himself, uttering 'conosco i segni . . .' attempted to employ in the Earthly Paradise. Marco, with his aggressive and stimulating 'Frate', appeals directly if scoldingly to a latent brotherhood between himself and the pilgrim. In this respect, his opening words might also be compared to Vergil's gentle 'figliuol', at *Purgatorio* XVII 91–3:

Né creator né creatura mai',
cominciò el, 'figliuol, fu sanza amore,
o naturale a d'animo; e tu 'l sai.'

('Never creator nor creature',/ he began, 'dear son, was there without love,/ either natural or rational; and you know that.')

For the purpose, clearly, both of 'Frate' and of 'figliuol' is to arouse, in the enforcement of a reasoned and generally accessible argument, the gamut of common sympathies and emotions. If Vergil's address is to 'common sense', Marco's exhortation plays no less upon the intelligent nerve of Everyman. His purpose is at once to expound and to excite, so that, opening with 'uhi!' in a key of despairing amazement, even a word as stubbornly conceptual as 'necessitate' is bitten out with a sarcastic relish, its acrid consonants, 's' and 't', dramatically emphasised by the preceding 'movesse' and 'tutto'. More important still, in view of my present argument, the syntax of the passage is similarly an expressive syntax, carrying simultaneously a conceptual design, and the voice of Marco himself in all its challenging humanity. So the repeated 'pur' in 'pur suso al ciel, pur come se tutto . . .' (68), introduces, especially in conjunction with the conditional clause, an unmistakable note of disdain and astonishment. Likewise, in 'non dico tutti, ma posto ch'i 'l dica . . .' (74), the concessive 'posto che' not only refines the concept of human liberty, but also indicates the boldness and intellectual freedom of the speaker, as he allows himself confidently to beard the extremes of necessitarianism.

In the Marco argument, then, as in the Statius passage, there appears a rhythm of intuition and sensibility which exceeds and modifies the rhythm of syntactical logic. Thought here is 'felt' thought. This, perhaps, is the point at which to make clear the grounds of my disagreement with Getto. For in these lines one may indeed discern a 'vibration', of the kind which for Getto is an essential characteristic of the 'poesia dell'intelligenza'. In Getto's work, the concept of the 'vibration' is an exact one, which he defines most clearly in his excellent analysis of Vergil's 'State contenti' speech, showing how the sense of limitation which Vergil seeks to inculcate in his pupil is both a stimulus to him and a way to the achieving of equilibrium (*Aspetti della poesia di Dante*, p. 185). This sense, he argues, is reflected both as a balance and as a stimulus in the vivacity and steadiness of Dante's own writing.

Now there can, I think, be little doubt that Getto's position is highly appropriate to the *Purgatorio*. In this canticle, we tread, like Dryden in Johnson's phrase, upon 'the brink of meaning where light and darkness meet'. And the thrill of this condition animates every feature of thought and feeling. In the Marco episode, too, where the awareness of penitential discipline and purpose is exceptionally acute, the application of Getto's reading is again indisputable. Yet the full possession of truth, which the poet claims for himself in the *Paradiso*, imposes its own peculiar disciplines. And from these, I would suggest, no similar vibration will result.

So when Carlo speaks, he appeals neither to fraternal sympathy, nor, rhetorically, to the shame and sensitivity of his audience, nor even to the persuasive logicality of Vergil's 'Né creator né creatura mai . . .'. Rather, throughout the speech he takes wholly for granted the interest and intellectual resourcefulness of his questioner, as one who is independently qualified to understand him. And this certainly is appropriate. For as Carlo courteously acknowledges, it is Dante's privilege to traverse the fullness of Heaven (line 97), while the poet's receptivity towards, so to say, trans-rational truth has been tested as early as the Piccarda episode. Carlo, then, may speak to him as one philosopher to another, assuming the competence and willing attention of his listener.[28] Now the first consequence of this, in respect of procedure and style is that, liberated from any need to persuade or attract, the speaker himself is able to concentrate entirely upon the authoritative formulation of his theme. Thus Carlo declares:

S'io posso
mostrarti un vero, a quel che tu dimandi
terrai lo viso come tien lo dosso.

His whole endeavour, it appears, will be to establish and show forth the truth of which he himself is possessed, while to the listener he attributes an agility of mind sufficient to acknowledge this truth, when he sees it, in all its wonder and strangeness. From this initial attitude there arises the measured, unassertive and yet deeply committed stability of Carlo's address.

Carlo's speech, then, opens with no affective reverberation. Indeed, after the terzina which I have just quoted there is a notable pause in the rhythm of his speech. By these lines, it seems, he assures himself of the attention of his audience; then, but only then, does he enter with undivided concentration upon the statement of his theme. So in one rounded and articulate terzina, drawn with the virtuosity of a Giotto's 'O', he comprehensively formulates the principle upon which his entire manifesto will depend:

> Lo ben che tutto il regno che tu scandi
> volge e contenta, fa esser virtute
> sua provedenza in questi corpi grandi.

The totality of God's goodness, His action as the spur and satisfaction of life, His generosity in the 'delegation' of offices, His benevolence in making possible Dante's own ascent – these are the notions that the terzina brings to order. And to paraphrase in this way is instructive, since, like any other paraphrase, this is a misrepresentation of the original. However in the present case, the misrepresentation arises not from the dispelling of an imaginative effect, but rather from the tendentiousness – which prose so easily admits – of words like 'life', and images like 'spur' and 'offices'. The strength of Dante's own verse, on the other hand, resides in the pointed and conscious finality with which such phrases as 'fa esser virtute' are produced. Rhythm and syntax here co-operate to impress upon each component a terminological value, so that there can be little doubt that the poet has considered very thoroughly and satisfied himself, at least, about the meaning of such notions as 'making', 'being' and 'virtute'.[29] There are no abnormal emphases here nor even the balanced phrases by which Vergil sometimes brings a tension to his meaning. Even 'volge' and 'contenta' are not interactive but analytic. For each word possesses a separate force and function in the simple line of thought. Likewise, the word 'quantunque' in the phrase 'per che quantunque quest' arco saetta' at line 113, which in another context might have represented a merely expansive and excitative gesture, is here used calmly and plainly to signify the comprehensiveness of providential purpose. Finally note the phrase 'chè da sé perfetta' at line 111, before which there occurs a pause in rhythm which effectively isolates the defining clause. But precisely this pause is a mark of the deliberation, indeed the caution, which Carlo displays in the naming of a divine quality. And from such features as this arises the similarity between the stable and the well-distinguished phrase.

Returning, however, to the differences between Carlo's speech and Marco's speech, the most revealing lines are those beginning: 'Se ciò non fosse . . .' (116), which at first seem all but identical to Marco's: 'Se così fosse . . .' (70). Yet in Marco's words one cannot ignore the continuing effect of a vocal sarcasm, reinforced by the emphatic 's'. Indeed, even the use of the subjunctive in Marco's speech, though grammatically accurate, is interesting chiefly as a manifestation of that intellectual hardihood which earlier I noted in his 'posto che . . .'. Carlo's subjunctive, on the other hand, and the subsequent conditionals, show nothing save a strenuous determination to formulate within the conventions of human thought a notion of the virtual and impossible.[30] To make this and the concepts connected with it as luminous as he may has been the whole of Carlo's purpose. His final words are not, as Vergil's might have been, an inquiry about the response of his listener, or an exhortation (e.g. at *Purg.* XVIII 139), but an expression of concern as to whether or not the truth to which he himself is committed has been shown with sufficient lucidity:

Vuo' tu che questo ver più ti s'imbianchi?

Persuasiveness, then, and rhetorical cogency, have here given place to an accurate organisation of phrase and to an awareness that a speaker may best serve other men by presenting to them his own understanding as clearly and firmly as he can. Speculation, likewise, with its pursuit of probabilities and its prevailing 'ansietà', has found here a healthier counterpart in the simple and stable utterance of the truths by which an individual himself both thinks and lives. Even the tongue of the prophet is skilful now. For where Marco darkly proclaims:

Le leggi son, ma chi pon mano ad esse?
Nullo, però che 'l pastor che procede,
rugumar può, ma non ha l'unghie fesse

(Laws exist, but who is there who sets his hand to them?/ No one, for the shepherd that goes before them,/ can indeed ruminate but does not have a divided hoof.)

(*Purg.* XVI 97–9)

Folco at the end of the Venus episode speaks in the direct and normal tones of which Cacciaguida would have approved, firmly condemning the 'adulterous' love of riches that inspires the Princes of the Church:

> Ma Vaticano e l'altre parti elette
> di Roma che son state cimitero
> a la milizia che Pietro seguette,
> tosto libere fien de l'avoltero.

(But the Vatican and the other chosen parts/ of Rome that have been the burial ground/ of the army that followed Peter/ soon will be free of that adultery.)

(*Par.* IX 139–42)

4

INDEPENDENCE AND THE READER OF THE *PARADISO*

In the preceding chapters I have spoken not only of the discipline that Dante required of himself, as a poet, but also of the attention he might have expected from the reader of a disciplined work. It is this matter that I want to consider more fully now in respect of the *Paradiso*. But where, in regard to poetic discipline, my evidence came largely from the inexpressibility topic, here I shall discuss a number of Dante's 'addresses to the reader'. In these, I think, one may clearly see how a reader who means to benefit from the truthfulness of the canticle, is called upon to conduct himself. It will, however, be no surprise if the condition upon which the poet insists should be a carefulness equivalent to his own in composition, and a courteousness equivalent to his modesty.

Consider, then, the following lines from *Paradiso* Canto Two:

> O voi che siete in piccioletta barca,
> desiderosi d'ascoltar, seguiti
> dietro al mio legno che cantando varca,
> tornate a riveder li vostri liti:
> non vi mettete in pelago, ché forse,
> perdendo me, rimarreste smarriti.
> L'acqua ch'io prendo già mai non si corse;
> Minerva spira, e conducemi Appollo,
> e nove Muse mi dimostran l'Orse.
> Voialtri pochi che drizzaste il collo
> per tempo al pan de li angeli, del quale
> vivesi qui ma non sen vien satollo,
> metter potete ben per l'alto sale
> vostro navigio, servando mio solco
> dinanzi a l'acqua che ritorna equale.

(O you who in a little boat,/ eager to hear, have followed on/ behind my craft which as it makes its way is singing/ turn back to look again upon your shores:/ do not put out upon the open sea, for perhaps,/ in losing me, you would be left bewildered./ The waters that I take have never before been coursed;/ Minerva breathes, Apollo is my guide,/ and the nine Muses point out for me the Bears./ You other few who have straightened your necks/ in good time for the bread of angels, – on which/ one lives here, but with which one never comes away satisfied –/ you may indeed put out your ship upon the deep salt sea/ keeping faithfully to my furrow/ in advance of the water that returns to the level.)

(*Par.* II 1–15)

The poet, then, firmly discriminates between those of his readers who are in some way qualified to approach the *Paradiso*, and those who, sadly, are not. But on what grounds exactly does this discrimination rest? Why is it that, while some may rank with the 'altri pochi', so many must join the 'picciolletta barca'?

Of various interpretations that have been applied to this passage,[1] the simplest is offered by Ernst Curtius who, emphasising that Dante stands within the learned tradition of the Middle Ages, would have us believe that these verses in keeping with that tradition display a positive 'contempt' for the unlearned. Only the scholarly reader may attempt the *Paradiso*. All others, in their small boats, must be repelled indignantly (*European Literature and the Latin Middle Ages*, English translation (Princeton, 1967), p. 362). Now the difference in Dante's mind between the one group and the other was no doubt broadly a matter of intellectual grade. Yet to suppose, as Curtius does, that Dante is contemptuous towards the reader of lesser ability is, I suggest, to mistake very badly the tone of the passage. In failing to appreciate the bearing of the poet towards the 'piccioletta barca', Curtius implicitly distorts the qualification demanded of the 'altri pochi'. For one thing, it would surely be unfitting to a work as seriously Christian as the *Paradiso*, that its reader, superior as he may be, should at the outset look back in a mood of such disdain. Nor is there anything in Dante's words to suggest that he should.[2] On the contrary, the poet himself acknowledges that the crew of the 'piccioletta barca', who have already followed him through two of his canticles, are still 'desiderosi d'ascoltar'. Neither their devotion nor their accomplishment is belittled. The 'barca', to be sure, is 'piccioletta'. But the diminutive here is as much an endearment as a dismissal, and the prevailing attitude of the poet is one not of contempt but rather of counsel. Consequently if the 'piccioletta barca' should desist, it is precisely for its own benefit, 'ché forse,/ perdendo me, rimarreste smarriti'. Certainly no honour would accrue if, pursuing its desire, it extended itself beyond its capabilities. For 'smarriti', which at once recalls the opening canto of *Inferno*, will remind one that confusion may arise not only from insipidity and ignorance but as well from the over-taxing of one's powers, as when Dante himself in *Inferno* Canto One is driven back, for all his ill-directed endeavours, towards the pathless wood. The poet now seeks to alert his adherents to a similar danger.

What, though, is the relevance of this to the qualification of the 'altri pochi'? One should emphasise firstly that, declining to disparage the 'piccioletta barca', the poet inhibits in the chosen few any impulse to self-congratulation. This is of cardinal importance. For by this device, the emotional pressure, that could have arisen in the gauging of one's station, is at once allayed. There is here no moral subornation, but the opportunity, simply, for a decision. The reader has now to decide for himself whether or not he should continue. Dante, in cancelling the ignominy of a refusal, invites him plainly to be honest about his choice, as though the confession to a greater or lesser capability might be treated purely as a matter of fact. Such a choice, however, for the 'altri pochi' no less than for the 'piccioletta barca' must evidently imply a capacity for introspection. Supposing, then, that one should continue, one's confidence will be assured and tempered by the sense that one's superiority is neither more nor less than a fact.[3]

Now to require this, is, of course, to require of the reader a power of self-knowledge and equally a modest self-possession exactly comparable to the power which the poet himself displays in the inexpressibility topic, where what can and cannot be done is so often in question. However, the full significance of Dante's demand may perhaps best be understood from the interpretation of:

perdendo me, rimarreste smarriti

The implications here are twofold. In respect, firstly, of the 'piccioletta barca', the poet appears to recognise that, while until this point he has been able to accommodate the interests of these readers, he can now no longer undertake to do so. His address might indeed be regarded as a final act of concern, as he indicates the danger of their losing him. However, if that is so, then of the 'altri pochi' what the poet surely must require is not only a confidence but also a certain independence of motive, so that, without persuasion or assistance, they may support themselves where the poet himself is preoccupied. And this, I suggest, is borne out by the acclamation:

Voialtri pochi che drizzaste il collo
per tempo al pan de li angeli . . . ,

especially if one considers here the tense of 'drizzaste' and the phrase 'per tempo'. The 'altri pochi' are those who *have* in their own lives *already* (and at an early date), conceived an appetite for intellectual nutriment. Their philosophical powers must clearly be of long-standing. In Dante's view, they will have exercised these powers even before they came to the *Paradiso*. But these men precisely because of their acquaintance with the philosophical life will need no guidance from a teacher. Nor will they be dismayed, if their interlocutor should fail, as he does in so many crucial passages, to pursue his theme. For to them the *Paradiso* will be nothing more than an episode in the continuing saga of their own intellectual destinies. Consequently, they will seek from the work only as much as the author may competently offer them, having elsewhere the resource and energy to pursue whatever they may light upon.

Of the 'altri pochi', then, the poet would seem to require a temperate understanding of their own abilities and a certain initiative of intellectual inquiry. This reading, certainly, appears to be supported by other instances of the 'address'.

Consider firstly a passage from Canto Fourteen which I have already examined in Chapter One, particularly the terzina:

> ma chi prende sua croce e segue Cristo,
> ancor mi scuserà di quel ch'io lasso,
> vedendo in quell' albor balenar Cristo.

(But whoever takes up his own cross and follows Christ,/ will again excuse me for that which I abandon/ seeing in that luminosity Christ lightning.)

(*Par.* XIV 106–8)

Dante here clearly states that his action in arresting the narrative will be understood only by those who, as followers of Christ, have devoted themselves to the same reality as here so overwhelms him. But how is one to take this? Should the reader suppose that from his own experience he has now to supply the information which the poet cannot supply? The interpretation is a natural one. Yet Dante, one has seen, is exercised not primarily over the lack of detail in his description, but over the condemnation which his own behaviour in curtailing the description may attract. In fact, his purpose plainly is that the reader should properly understand his silence, or even perhaps should value it, as an instance of humility and right-mindedness.[4] If, however, this understanding is to arise, the reader, too, must know what it is to 'bear a cross'. This, as Dante's emphasis upon the act of 'bearing and following' makes clear, is to say that they will appreciate, precisely from their own enterprise, the conditions under which the poet proceeds, and therefore be able to estimate the virtue of his response to them. Dante then once more entrusts himself to the painstaking generosity of the mature philosopher.

From the addresses at Canto Ten lines 7–9 and 22–7, there follows an identical conclusion. However, at this point, an important distinction suggests itself. For from the imagery of the Canto Fourteen passage, it may at first be supposed that the initiative which the poet expected of his reader was a peculiarly Christian one. But while Dante evidently would have relied upon the Christianity of his audience, this alone cannot constitute a sufficient qualification for the canticle. For surely even the 'piccioletta barca' is a Christian ship. If yet more is required of the 'altri pochi' – Christian as they may be – this further requirement, I would suggest, is that they should also be men of philosophical good will and ability. This appears in the following passages:

> Or ti riman, lettor, sovra 'l tuo banco,
> dietro pensando a ciò che si preliba,
> s'esser vuoi lieto assai prima che stanco.
> Messo t'ho innanzi: omai per te ti ciba;
> ché a sé torce tutta la mia cura
> quella materia ond' io son fatto scriba.

(Now, reader, remain upon your bench,/ thinking back upon that of which you have been given a foretaste,/ if you wish to be greatly pleased before you are weary./ I have set [*the matter*] before you: now by yourself you must feed/ for all my own attention is drawn to itself/ by the theme of which I have been made the scribe.)

(*Par.* x 22–7)

and:

> Leva dunque, lettore, a l'alte rote
> meco la vista, dritto a quella parte
> dove l'un moto e l'altro si percuote . . .

(Raise, then, reader, to the lofty wheels/ with me your sight, fixing them upon that part/ where the one motion strikes upon the other.)

(*ibid.* 7–9)

From the first of these passages one at once recognises the independence which is required of the reader, who must now be prepared 'to feed himself'. Furthermore, the reason why he must, is here stated quite openly: the rigour of his subject demands a total attention of the poet, 'ché a sé torce tutta la mia cura/ quella materia . . .'. This of course is a pattern which has already appeared in the Venus episode, where a speaker, confident of the interest and ability of his audience, is free to devote to the formulation of his own thought an undistracted concentration. But with the 'Leva dunque . . .' verse there occurs a further resemblance, bearing directly upon my present argument. For these lines encourage the reader to contemplate with Dante himself the splendid manifestation of the natural order. Although this is entirely in keeping, as in the Venus episode, with a Christian acceptance of the redeemed world, it is equally an appeal to the philosophical spirit of wonder and admiration.[5] Nor is it difficult to see how those readers who are, philosophically, alert to the splendours of the world, will also be able to admire in Dante himself the evidence of God's glory, as, through his art, he brings his own existence to fruition. Hence, concluding his address to the 'altri pochi', Dante asserts:

> Que' gloriosi che passaro al Colco
> non s'ammiraron come voi farete,
> quando Iasòn vider fatto bifolco.

(Those glorious adventurers who made their way to Colchis/ did not marvel as you will do/ when they saw Jason made a ploughman.)
(*Par.* II 16–18)

What, then, is the relationship which Dante seeks to establish between himself and the reader? To Auerbach, the exhortations throughout the *Commedia*, express: 'a mixture, unique in its kind, of brotherliness and authority . . . The Reader is summoned, adjured and finally commanded to continue . . .' (*Literary Language and its Public*, p. 300). And this surely is an accurate interpretation for the addresses that Dante makes in the *Inferno* and *Purgatorio*. In the *Paradiso*, too, Dante does, I think, seek for himself the status of an authority, while the 'altri pochi', when seen as spiritual Argonauts, are clearly in some sense the 'brothers' of the poet. But, as in the relationship between Dante and Cacciaguida, so here the brotherhood, I suggest, is of a kind to foster in the individual rather an independence of activity than a reliance. If that is so, then Auerbach's insistence upon the magisterial imperative of Dante's tone might also require for the *Paradiso* a certain modification. For, precisely, Dante's address to the 'altri pochi' is not an imperative. It is the 'picciioletta barca' which he orders to return. To the other few he merely indicates that, upon certain conditions, they will be 'well able' to follow him, as though, possessing no special prerogative to command or guide, he intended the decision to be entirely theirs. Even in the 'Leva dunque . . .' passage, the imperative is softened by the 'meco' to a request not for submissiveness but rather for the urbane co-operation of equals.[6] The poet, after all, has no need to summon or stimulate since his audience in its own right will be competent and resolute. Still less need he enveigle their attention as, say, his own Ulysses does, in *Inferno* Canto Twenty Six, arousing in the 'compagna picciola' the clouded impulses of shame and audacity.

If, however, there is to be an urbanity here, it will, I repeat, be the existential urbanity which arises where the conditions of the intellectual life are fully understood. The Argosy is indeed a perilous one. That such perils, literally, imply a certain intellectual limitation, is apparent from the line:

vivesi qui ma non sen vien satollo . . .

An inadequacy, it appears, is intrinsic to the undertaking. But if, in the inexpressibility topic, the poet for his part demonstrates a thorough acceptance of this, the reader, it now appears, must acknowledge it with equal thoroughness. Thus, knowing from the first that the poet will be unable wholly to satisfy them, since no one can ever eat sufficiently of the bread of angels, they will retain throughout, as the 'piccioletta barca' could not, a certain critical reserve. As will be seen shortly, the very style of the canticle encourages such a remoteness. But precisely in repressing any exorbitant expectation, the reader will be able the more justly to prize the example which the poet, in formulating his own philosophical position, has offered them.

To speak of a certain remoteness about the *Paradiso*, is in one respect, to speak only of what many a reader has experienced on first turning to the canticle. Tarozzi, for instance, who refreshingly appears rather curious than reproachful about it, observes that at the opening of the *Paradiso* there disappear many of the links that have bound us until this point to the poet. We no longer feel, he continues, that an affinity exists between the emotional life of the poet and our own. There occurs in fact an interruption of that very correspondence and fellow-feeling (*consentaneità*) that hitherto has rendered the poet the interpreter of universal humanity (*Note di estetica sul Paradiso di Dante*, p. 4).

But it is precisely the interruption of 'consentaneità' that concerns me here. For the initial distance that Tarozzi notes between the poet and reader in the *Paradiso*, is, I believe, maintained throughout by the style of the work. The peculiar quality of Dante's writing is indeed to promote not only a chasteness of response, but also to demand continually a reaffirmation of that commitment which the 'altri pochi' were required to make in Canto Two. In defining this quality the notion of stability will reveal its importance. Here, too, one may appreciate most acutely Calogero's argument against 'panaestheticism'. For at all points the appeal of Dante's word in the *Paradiso* is to a conscious and determined respect, and not to any primitive or intrinsic capacity for artistic appreciation. There is indeed a sense in which the canticle might be regarded as deliberately gratuitous. For, having dismissed the 'piccioletta barca', Dante cannot have considered this section of his poem to be altogether essential for salvation or even for understanding. If it were, he could hardly admit so openly the choice that he does admit in Canto Two. And throughout, as I say, the work is apparently designed to offer a resistance to any approach that implies the support of an exigent sympathy between poet and reader.

In what ways, however, is this resistance reflected in Dante's language? I may, I think, for the moment best illustrate my point by a comparison of three passages: the opening of the *Paradiso* itself, the opening of *Inferno*, Canto Two, and, somewhat later, the concluding lines of the *Purgatorio*.

Consider, then, the following:

La gloria di colui che tutto move
per l'universo penetra, e risplende
in una parte più e meno altrove.
Nel ciel che più de la sua luce prende
fu' io, e vidi cose che ridire
né sa né può chi di là sù discende.

(The glory of him who all things moves/ penetrates the universe, and shines back/ in one part more and less elsewhere./ In the heaven that most receives of his light/ I have been, and seen things that, to tell again,/ he that descends from up there neither knows how nor can.)

(*Par.* I 1–6)

and

Lo giorno se n'andava, e l'aere bruno
toglieva li animai che sono in terra
da le fatiche loro; e io sol uno
m'apparechiava a sostener la guerra
sì del cammino e sì de la pietate,
che ritrarrà la mente che non erra.

(The day was departing, and the dark air/ was drawing the creatures that are on earth/ from their labours; and I – the only one – was preparing myself to sustain the strife/ of the journey and equally of the feeling/ which the memory which does not err will portray.)

(*Inf.* II 1–6)

Of the first passage the most impressive feature, even to those who might regard it finally as imaginative or stimulative in effect, is its thorough self-containedness.[7] Nothing 'accidental' cheapens it. No one word is important save for its dependence upon another. The movement of imagintaion and feeling is persistently subjected to a design which rhythm and the syntactical progress of meaning deliberately impose upon it. It is this design which constitutes a challenge to the tenacity of the reader's attention.

So for example the 'tutto', though it first appears perhaps with a fling of the heart, is allowed no disordinate emphasis. By the assonance of its first syllable with the 'u' in 'colui', the word is given a definite place in the pattern of the line. This pattern also is so constructed as to bring 'tutto' into a balanced relationship with the opening 'gloria'. But the balance itself prevents any disruptively emotional response. For in creating it, Dante clearly articulates his understanding of how for him the glory of God is the 'all' of creation. One would not of course want to say that there was no emotion at all behind these verses. On the contrary one might well allow that the emotion is very great indeed. But if it is great, it is still shaped and given focus by the concept which Dante here develops. And it is to the act of shaping that our attention is drawn by the poet's art, so that our response properly will be determined by our awareness of that and not by the emotion itself, nor even by the images that the passage may appear to offer.

Consider two further points. Firstly the pause, momentary as it may be, between the 'gloria' and the 'di colui' in:

La gloria di colui che tutto move.

The pause, which isolates the 'gloria', serves also to give prominence to the genitive construction, establishing that glory is an aspect of God, but distinct from God himself. This of course is an essential distinction, if Dante is to avoid the heresy of suggesting a pantheistic union of God and his creation. But a dextrous caesura maintains his orthodoxy. Secondly note the 'altrove' in the first terzina. Now if the imagination were allowed to linger upon this word, as it might in the *Purgatorio*, it could well appear as something of a dying fall, the brilliant affirmation of the 'gloria' descending to the foggy 'and less elsewhere'; as for instance, in the pathos of *Purgatorio* VI 120:

Son li giusti occhi tuoi rivolti altrove?

(are Thy just eyes turned elsewhere?)

Yet in the *Paradiso* passage there is no melancholy or tension. The word 'altrove' has an obviously conceptual function, in the defining of what Dante intends by 'gloria', 'tutto', 'universo' and so forth. The rhythm which, in co-operation with the syntax articulates the relation between these elements, holds the 'altrove' no less firmly than it does the preceding terms. From the rhyme on 'move' the word acquires a finality, in respect both of the formal design of the terzina, and of the sense which has evolved throughout the foregoing sentence. So conclusive a cadence is of course appropriate where the poet is attempting an ultimate definition of his thought. But the same cadence demands of the reader, too, a meticulous attention to each word as it presents itself.

In the *Inferno* there prevails an altogether different style of organisation and a different response is called for. So the rhythm in the *Inferno* passage tends to fall weightily upon single words such as 'giorno', 'bruno' and 'toglieva', while each element in the phrase 'io sol uno' stands somewhat separate from the simple line of meaning as it develops. The result, contrary to the exact and satisfying closes of the *Paradiso*, is that moral and emotional associations are aroused which cannot completely be organised within the structure of the sentence itself. Thus the rhythmic concentration upon 'giorno' wholly exceeds the emphasis it would normally receive in the denotation of time. This is why, correctly, one may seek for it a symbolic or an allegorical interpretation. To exhaust its significance one must organise the associations which the word arouses not merely by relating it to the other elements in the sentence, but also by referring to one's emotional sympathy or to a common principle of moral understanding. Similarly, the oxymoron 'aere bruno' may be supposed rightly to express the confusions and distraction of the reign of evil. For in this case, too, the realisation of the poet's meaning depends upon an appeal to a rational or imaginative communion, out of which a generalisation as to the reference of the words might be constructed. The tension of the word is indeed the tension of Dante's devoted struggle with the 'pity' of Hell.

What, then, of 'io sol uno', which has, one might think, a counterpart in the 'fu' io' of *Paradiso* I, 5. Of the complexity in 'io sol uno' there can be little doubt. For giving each word the emphasis which the rhythm requires, the phrase will generate overtones of pride, loneliness, effort and pain, which do certainly accord with the later part of the sentence, but which are most fully appreciated when one receives them in the isolation which the rhythm itself suggests. In the *Paradiso*, too, 'fu' io', standing at the opening of the line, is undoubtedly emphatic. But the effect of the phrase is by no means simply imaginative. Nor is it a moment of emotional exhilaration.[8] For the emphasis upon the phrase creates a balance between this and the 'gloria' – which is itself given exceptional weight by its position after the canticle break. And 'gloria' and 'io' are plainly the topic features of Dante's argument here. So the position of 'io' is dictated by simple clarity, while the two terzine, revolving around the two cardinal facts – the creative revelation of God in glory, and the poet's direct experience of this – are arranged in point of syntactical structure thoroughly to explicate the consequences and the character of the relationship between 'gloria' and 'fu' io', so that with 'perché appressando sé . . .' Dante may at once proceed to explain the possibilities and limitations which attend it. Both 'gloria' and 'fu' io', then, by the weight which the poet gives to them, participate in the over-arching development that leads to this explanation. And to suppose that Dante's emphasis were expressive of an exultant emotion would obscure in the end even the clear-headed pride which the poet takes in defining his experience of the 'gloria'.

Apart from this difference, there are others, particularly in the treatment of time and the treatment of light imagery, which also bear upon the manner of one's response. Thus, in the *Inferno* passage the dominant indication of time is the imperfect, the dusky air 'toglieva li animai . . .', the day 'se n'andava', while Dante himself 'm'apparechiava a sostener la guerra'. This is profoundly characteristic not only of the *Inferno* but also of the *Purgatorio*, where the poet's very exactitude in temporal reference frequently brings to notice the continual revolutions of the cosmic order.[9] But the effect of course of such imperfect constructions is to draw the reader, by the unfolding promise of the narrative, into the attractive and binding continuum of an action. A similar effect is to be found in the 'light' imagery of these earlier canticles. For generally speaking few categories of image are more likely to arouse the primal intuitions of the spirit than this.[10] In the *Inferno* one undoubtedly is drawn up into the battle of night and day and moved by the unresolved suggestiveness of 'L'aer bruno', mysteriously releasing the earthly spirit from its labours, as, likewise, in the *Purgatorio*, the various mythic personifications of night and dawn appeal at once to the child, the savage and the mage in the reader.[11]

But the light in the *Paradiso* is not the primitive light. It is the light as Dante has understood it in its final and factual relation to God. If in the opening lines of the *Paradiso* there is a complexity, it is the complexity not of an atavistic thrill but of an anatomy. So, appealing as the words 'penetra' and 'risplende' may appear at first blush, there is no strangeness in them but rather a sense of science, which is reflected, again, in the very form of the words and in their rhythmic arrangement. At 'risplende' for example any simple reaction to the image of splendour, is bound, in truth to Dante, to pause upon the significance of the prefix 'ri–'. For Dante, as a philosopher, is certain to be concerned with the conversion of glory *back* to God. It is this prefix which demands that the reader should carefully connect the notion of light to the whole analysis which the poet offers of glory in the universe. Similarly, the rhythmic disposition of 'penetra e risplende' prevents any isolating of the phrase, as an emotive or visual intensification. The second and third lines of the terzina are shaped to a chiasmus of prepositional phrase – verb: verb – prepositional phrase. Consequently, with 'risplende', there arises a pressure towards the completion of that pattern by 'in una parte più . . .'. The sense of repetition, which might have supported an affective emphasis, is destroyed as the words assume their station in the stable pattern of the whole.

Is there, however, nothing in the style of the *Paradiso* passage which might excite a direct communion between poet and reader? Consider again the impression of the 'gloria'. The word after all is as rich as any could be in its scriptural and liturgical associations.[12] Will not the reader, then, if he is a Christian, recognise in the 'gloria' a joyous reconciliation to the order of his belief? The attraction of the word would not in that case be as universal perhaps as the attraction of the phrasing in *Inferno* and *Purgatorio*. Nonetheless, an equivalent to imaginative pressure and to pregnant narrative might be found in a certain drama of liturgy.[13]

Even so, there is an evident alteration in style between these lines and the lines immediately preceding them in the *Purgatorio*, which are also in their way liturgical, since they vividly recreate a moment of baptismal refreshment:[14]

> Io ritornai da la santissima onda
> rifatto sì come piante novelle
> rinovellate di novella fronda,
> puro e disposto a salire a le stelle.

(I returned from the most sacred wave/ remade just as new plants/ renewed with new foliage,/ clean and ready to rise to the stars.)

(*Purg*. XXXIII 142–5)

These lines are organised around the characteristically tremulous intuition of the *Purgatorio*. Far exceeding in importance any grammatical progression is the unique synthesis of repeated sounds, of repeated concepts and images, and of a sensuous vivacity. Even the functional 'sì', by the repetition of the 's' out of 'santissima', vibrates with a resonance which quite outshines its grammatical force. Thus there grows in the imagination a clear sense of renewal both as physical and a spiritual power. But what is there of this in the 'gloria'? The emphasis upon it is, to be sure, very great, but no greater than its significance requires. Nor does the word escape from the conceptual pattern of its context. Indeed the subsequent terzina represents a developing analysis of what the poet means by 'gloria', so that even if one had never encountered the word before, its lexical definition could scarcely fail to be apparent. And precisely because of that, a directly Christian reading of the phrase, though evidently not inappropriate, may nonetheless be a distraction. For responding to the phrase as one might with a Paschal enthusiasm, one stands to dislocate the proportions which Dante has set upon it. But with that one will lose also the sense that Dante himself has, so to say, appropriated the word, acquiring by his very carefulness, the right to say that at last he understands it. It is that appropriation, I suggest, which the man of good will prizes at its proper worth. This, however, is a point which may most clearly be understood if one turns finally to the presentation of character in the *Paradiso*.

Now my purpose is not to investigate at length Dante's method of characterisation in the *Paradiso*, but to demonstrate, from two of its most important sequences – the Examination Cantos, where Dante himself is the speaker, and Beatrice's speech in Canto Seven – a certain relation between the treatment of character and the reception of the doctrine that Dante himself desires to convey. There is, however, one feature of the characterisation which does have a bearing upon my theme. Thus, with striking regularity and in a manner unprecedented in the previous canticles, the identification of the blessed souls is made a point of ceremonial interest, and the bestowing of names becomes the occasion frequently for a display, at once, of rhetoric and respect.[15]

The most obvious instance of this is in Canto Ten, where, one by one, the souls of the Christian philosophers are presented to the poet, sometimes by name alone, like Isidore, Bede, and Richard of Saint Vincent (line 131), and sometimes, as with Boethius and Siger, in periphrases which indicate a dominant strain in the temperament or history of the man (lines 124–9, 133–8). Already, however, one has seen how decorously Dante beseeches Cacciaguida to reveal his name, and how Cacciaguida answers, at the expense of fifteen terzine (xv 88–135). Nor is Dante less elaborate in requesting Piccarda's name (iii 37–41), while in Cantos Eight and Nine, every speaker is introduced by a periphrasis, as also are Justinian (vi 1–9), and Saints Peter Damian and Benedict (xxi 113–22, xxii 31–51). Two of these alone, the Cunizza passage and the Peter Damian passage, will serve to indicate the importance of this procedure.

Consider, then, Cunizza's opening:

> In quella parte de la terra prava
> italica che siede tra Rïalto
> e le fontane di Brenta e di Piava,
> si leva un colle, e non surge molt' alto,
> là onde scese già una facella
> che fece a la contrada un grande assalto.
> D'una radice nacqui e io ed ella . . .

(In that part of the perverted land/ of Italy that sits between Rialto/ and the springs of Brenta and Piava,/ there raises itself a hill, and it does not rise very high,/ from which descended once a firebrand/ that made a great assault upon the region around./ Of a single root was I born and that [*firebrand*].)

(*Par.* ix 25–31)

In one aspect, these lines have clearly an ornamental function, and are intended to establish a certain dignity around their speaker. But neither the ornament nor the dignity is hollow. For the personal merit of Cunizza resides in her awareness both of what she is and what she has been. And her rhetorical gestures demonstrate precisely the grip she exerts over the forces and facts which have coloured her existence, be these neutral, like the environment of her birth ('si leva un colle, e non surge molt' alto'), or potentially evil, like her kinship to Ezzelino, the 'facella'. In the periphrasis, then, she defines a number of the lineaments of her temporal being; and, able now unflinchingly to accept what, naturally, she was, and able indeed to 'forgive herself' the 'cagion di mia sorte' (*ibid.* 35), she claims, by this act of naming, a respectful attention to her personal presence.

From this, I hope, it will at once be obvious that the character and purpose of Cunizza's speech are largely similar to those which I attributed earlier to the Volgare Illustre. It is, I suggest, possible to discern this resemblance in all of these naming ceremonies in the

Paradiso. To appreciate, however, more particularly the effect of Cunizza's speech, compare it with such passages as Francesca's:

> Siede la terra dove nata fui
> su la marina dove 'l Po discende
> per aver pace co' seguaci sui.

(The place where I was born sits/ on the coast where the Po descends/ to be at peace with the streams that follow it.)

(*Inf.* v 97–9)

or la Pia's:

> ricorditi di me, che son la Pia;
> Siena mi fé, disfecemi Maremma.

(Remember me, who am la Pia;/ Siena made me, Maremma unmade me.)

(*Purg.* v 133–4)

By any definition, both of these passages are dramatic in idiom, and both are the focus of an imaginative sympathy, by which the reader may comprehend, even where the character itself does not, the complex forces that prevail upon it. Thus Francesca's lines reveal a pathetic sentimentality, as though even the waters, in her view, were drawn together by love. Here, too, there emerges the irony which nerves and motivates the whole of this canto. For the rivers, it seems, are allowed a peaceful consummation such as Francesca, now, can never hope for. Likewise, in la Pia's lines, one hears both the fragile voice of la Pia herself, crystallised in the delicate rhythms of the first line and also, in the pattern of the second line, as at every other moment in *Purgatorio* Canto Five, the elegiac note of temporal dissolution captured in the subdued but unflinching awareness of how life begins and ends. But Cunizza, by her very self-awareness, is independent of such dramatic complexity. Nor do her words reveal any particular trait of character. Dante, indeed, appears momentarily to have lent her his own capacities as a rhetorician. Yet the figure is none the less individual for that. For if she does not demand our sympathy, she demands very clearly a courteous attention to her being and accomplishment.

If Cunizza, then, is a typical case, the characters of the *Paradiso* will form, so to say, a gallery of persons to whose authority and merit a reverence, in Dante's eyes, was seriously due.[16] The importance of this, especially to the presentation of doctrine, may be seen if one turns to the Peter Damian episode, where Dante, upbraided for a question which confuses even 'quell' alma nel ciel che più si schiara' (*that soul in heaven that shows itself most brightly*) (*Par.* XXI 91), is obliged humbly to restrain himself and ask only the name of this great soul:

> Sì mi prescrisser le parole sue,
> ch'io lasciai la quistione e mi ritrassi
> a dimandarla umilmente che fue.

(But his words so cut me short/ that I abandoned the question, and confined myself/ to asking humbly who he was.)

(*ibid.* 103–5)

To which Peter Damian replies by describing, with geographical exactitude, the place in which for most of his life he had served God in contemplation:

> Tra ' due liti d'Italia surgon sassi,
> e non molto distanti a la tua patria,
> tanto che ' troni assai suonan più bassi,
> e fanno un gibbo che si chiama Catria,
> di sotto al quale è consecrato un ermo,
> che suole esser disposto a sola latria.

(Between the two shores of Italy, there rise crags, –/ and they are not very distant from your fatherland –/ so high that thunder sounds far below them,/ and they make a hump that is called Catria,/ beneath which is consecrated a hermitage,/ that used to be devoted only to the adoration of God.)

(*ibid.* 106–11)

But this, considering the arguments of Chapter One, is precisely as it should be. For in circumstances where the source of truth is hidden, one is bound to approach the truth, not directly, but rather through one's knowledge of and respect for the speaker himself. In what we know of him, in his proper person, one is to seek the evidence of authority and trustworthiness. When, as here and in the Cunizza passage, a character manifests so great an awareness of the conditions of his human existence, then certainly what he does reveal will be worthy of regard.

The 'naming ceremonies', then, determine the mode of consent under which the reader is to receive the truths that a character offers him. And, turning to the Examination Cantos (Cantos Twenty Four to Twenty Six', one finds that this same consent is exactly what Dante requires there for his own utterances.

Thus, solemn as these cantos undoubtedly are, one should firstly note that there is nothing dramatic about them. Nothing is at stake.

One is not allowed for a moment to suppose that Dante will fail in the test to which he has been brought. On the contrary, before every question the poet announces, through Beatrice or his saintly examiner, a thorough confidence in his own success, as when Beatrice comprehensively declares to Saint Peter:

> S'elli ama bene e bene spera e crede,
> non t'è occulto . . .

(Whether he loves truly and hopes truly and believes/ is not hidden from you.)

(*Par.* XXIV 40–1)

The significance of this for one's response to Dante's argument is obvious. For what is asked of the reader is no involvement, nor concern about the outcome, but, initially, an attention to the figure of the 'buon Cristiano' (*Par.* XXIV 52), Dante himself. We are to recognise, that is, how one man has understood the Christian truth, and to see how, in his person, it might triumphantly be celebrated. If, therefore, Dante does speak out, on matters that have already been concluded, the purpose must clearly be, as Saint Peter says, to 'glorify' the truth (*ibid.* 43–5).

At the same time, there is evidently some sense in which the reader is to learn from what Dante tells him. For, as one saw in Chapter Two, Dante does intend to strengthen the hope of himself and others by speaking of it (*Par.* XXV 43–5). However this need not, I think, imply that we are to be 'stimulated' by Dante's words, nor even exactly persuaded by them. I may best enforce my point by considering Getto's analysis of the 'credo' at *Paradiso*, Canto Twenty Four lines 130–2, which runs:

> E io rispondo: Io credo in uno Dio
> solo ed etterno, che tutto 'l ciel move,
> non moto, con amore e con disio.

(And I replied: I believe in one God/ single and eternal, who moves the whole heaven –/ himself not moved – with love and desire.)

In Getto's view, this terzina displays a syntactical movement which is at once rigorously unified and marked and measured by great pauses (*scandito a grandi pause*). It seems that these echoes multiply, reaching us from infinity (*sembrano molteplicarsi echi che giungono dall' infinito*), so that the name of God, dominating the whole reply, reverberates in our ears, as does the definition of God's uniqueness and eternal existence, and the concept of the cosmic order (*Aspetti della poesia di Dante*, p. 79). In his confrontation, then, with the

Infinite, Dante is possessed of a vigorous conviction (*energica convinzione*) (*ibid*. p. 80), and impelled by this, he offers to the reader a uniquely fashioned phrase in which, directly, he may appreciate the moment of the poet's intuition. So the emphasis upon 'Dio' is is indeed a stimulus to an exceptionally acute understanding of God. Similarly, the movement of the syntax is commended, not for any logical function, but as a special form of the poet's cosmic awareness.

But this interpretation, I venture, is at fault in two respects. Firstly, to render Dante's phrasing 'vibrant', Getto is obliged practically to recreate the poet's actual syntax, so that a simple organisation of concepts may appear as an interlacing of holy 'echoes'. And this merely as a distortion is dangerous enough. But, granted that the poet's understanding is as energetic as Getto desires, one would still not expect of a 'credo' so disruptive and extraordinary an idiom.[17] These words must confess, after all, to the tenets by which the poet has lived since the time of his baptising – an occasion which he recalls in 'Se mai continga'. The confession then will be a grave one, in view, alike, of the poet's responsibilities to his God, and to his own person. Consequently one may expect of it rather a wholehearted carefulness of utterance than any exuberant epiphany.

I suggest, then, that even the pauses and emphases of which Getto speaks may be seen as a burden to the normal logic of syntax, and a witness to the strength of Dante's intellectual engagement. Here, if anywhere, the poet must attain to a clearness of articulation. And precisely because he does so, one must follow him with a carefulness equivalent to his own. Taken in this way, however, the value of the passage will reside in a recognition of the commitment which the poet has brought to bear, even more than in the excitements of realising the truth itself. For these excitements we must ourselves become bearers of our own philosophical destinies. And Dante's successful example should give us heart for that.[18]

Now the Examination Cantos, and the 'credo' in particular, are emblematic of Dante's procedure in the whole of the *Paradiso*. But an emblem of even greater force is the image of Beatrice, especially as she appears in Canto Seven. For in this canto she is possessed of a centrality more evident than at any other point, save only in the Earthly Paradise. And the issues which are discussed in this canto are themselves of the most fundamental importance.

But comparing the presentation of Beatrice here with her appearance in the Earthly Paradise, the difference is very striking. For no sequence in the *Commedia* is more truly dramatic than the latter. Its themes of pride, and of personal guilt and of revelation are the themes of the greatest drama. The setting and the structure of its dialogue, with the choric intervention of the angels are again dramatic, while in the progressive beating of its rhythmic development there is an immediacy of force that may stand comparison, say, with the final scene of Mozart's *Don Giovanni*, or the Porter scenes in *Macbeth*. Thus of the moment at which he hears the angels sing, Dante writes:

> ma poi che 'ntesi ne le dolci tempre
> lor compartire a me, par che se detto
> avesser: 'Donna, perché sì lo stempre?',
> lo gel che m'era intorno al ristretto,
> spirito e acqua fessi, e con angoscia
> de la bocca e de li occhi uscì del petto.

(But when I heard in the sweet harmonies/ their sympathy for me, exactly as if they had said:/ 'Lady, why do you so unnerve him?',/ the ice that was tightened around me,/ turned to breath and water and with anguish/ of the mouth and of the eyes issued from my breast.)

(*Purg*. XXX 94–9)

But of drama such as this, there is none in Canto Seven. For here Beatrice does not actuate any particular scene of guilt and redemption, but defines and clarifies the subject. She, furthermore, is the only speaker,[19] and the rhythm of the canto is designed, like Cunizza's art, to draw attention wholly to the propositions of the speaker herself. The canto, in short, is something of an aria, in which, through Beatrice's voice, the poet arrives at a formula, authoritative for himself at least, of his belief in the Incarnation.[20] And to seek to share in this aria, as though in a drama, would be to obscure its intrinsic virtuosity.[21] The style itself, however, prohibits such a participation.

Consider, firstly, how the rhythm rather divides the canto than unifies it.[22] In at least three places, the progress of the argument is stayed by an emphasis of exceptional weight, as though deliberately to isolate a moment of importance. So even the opening of the sequence is announced with a certain formality, at *Paradiso* VII 16:

> Poco sofferse me cotal Beatrice
> e cominciò, raggiandomi d'un riso
> tal, che nel foco faria l'uom felice.

(Beatrice suffered me thus only a short time/ and began, raying over me a smile/ such that would make a man happy in the fire.)

More emphatic still is the pause which occurs at line 34, as a solemn introduction to the heart of the mystery:

> Or drizza il viso a quel ch'or si ragiona:
> questa natura al suo fattore unita,
> qual fu creata, fu sincera e buona.

(Now direct your sight to that which is to be argued now:/ this nature, united to its maker,/ such as it was created, was pure and good.)

However, the most significant case is at line 94:

> Ficca mo l'occhio per entro l'abisso
> de l'etterno consiglio, quanto puoi
> al mio parlar distrettamente fisso.

(Fix now your eyes within the abyss/ of the eternal counsel, concentrating as much as you can/ strictly upon my words.)

Here the pattern of thought is all but identical with the pattern of of the Peter Damian passage. For the demand is that, while the eyes of the listener are fixed upon the ineffable abyss, his attention to the speaker should be as strict as it may possibly be. The very awareness, it seems, of the transcendent, is to inspire in him a respect for what in fact may be said. The emphatic interruption here of the rhythmic continuity, as to a lesser extent in the other passages, is the formal claiming of this attention.

Now this emphasis is highly characteristic in its function of the *Paradiso* at large. And I shall have more to say of it in Chapter Six. To conclude, however, I would only point out how closely the emphasis co-operates with a stability in the particular terzine.[23] For instance, in the passage I have quoted above, 'Or drizza il viso', the rhythmic disposition of:

> qual fu creata, fu sincera e buona

concentrates our expectancies immediately on the grammar of the repeated 'fu'. In the development of his position, it is important for Dante to establish, equally, that man at his creation was good, and that this goodness became a thing of the past. And this the repetition does establish. Out of context, perhaps, the 'fu' might generate by its evocation of the remote past the pathos of Paradise entirely lost. But this possibility is annulled by the very doctrine which Beatrice expounds. The whole terzina where the reasons for the loss of Paradise are clearly envisaged reflects a liberation from such sentiment in its own finality of form. Likewise consider Beatrice's first speech, beginning at line 19:

> Secondo mio infallibile avviso,
> come giusta vendetta giustamente
> punita fosse, t'ha in pensier miso;
> ma io ti solverò tosto la mente...

(According to my unerring judgement,/ how just vengeance should have been justly/ executed, has set you thinking;/ but I will quickly release your mind.)

Here the unshakeably imperative structure which begins with 'Secondo mio infallible avviso', leads to the

> come giusta vendetta giustamente
> punita fosse...,

where 'giusta ... giustamente' is designed purely to clarify a concept, and in no way to stimulate a tension or a sense of dramatic voice. In this regard, one might add, the phrase is wholly unlike the apparently similar phrase that Pier della Vigna utters at *Inferno* XIII 70–2:

> L'animo mio, per disdegnoso gusto,
> credendo col morir fuggir disdegno,
> ingiusto fece me contra me giusto.

(My mind, through a contemptuous feeling, thinking by death to escape contempt,/ made me unjust against my just self.)

In *Paradiso* Canto Seven instances comparable to those I have considered occur in the 'dannando ... dannò' of line 27, and in the superbly steady syntax of the lines following 'Ficca mo l'occhio...', where, with the 'quanto' of line 100 and the 'tanto ... quanto' of lines 106–7, the mystery of the Incarnation is confidently translated into the conventional grammar of human apprehension. But of such effects I shall have more to say in the two final chapters.

Here, for a last time, I would only point out how distant is the mode I have described from any in which the poet might seek, for the 'anxious energy' of his investigations, a personal sympathy. A stability arises in the *Paradiso* from the interaction of linguistic carefulness and the emphasis of rhythm. And the value of the poetry lies precisely there. For suppose, by way of illustration, that a member of a community had, by his own choice and intention, entirely realised in his own behaviour an orthodox pronouncement.[24] In such a case, the meaning of a pronouncement might remain unimpeachably orthodox.[25] Yet its form would display a particular consummation of that meaning, and no one who failed to recognise that this consummation was the product of individual intention would be likely to achieve a similar realisation in his own behaviour. The example is one to be received at a distance, with an admiring recognition of the formal accomplishment, and a deference, unobscured by sympathy or the coincidence of opinion, for the individuality of the act. This is the courtesy that Dante requires, for himself and others, in the *Paradiso*.

5

WORD AND IMAGE IN THE *PARADISO*

It is time now to turn one's attention wholly to the analysis of Dante's text. In the present chapter I shall consider, in point of style, the diction and imagery of the *Paradiso*. In the next chapter I shall consider its general organisation, as reflected both in the structural characteristics of the single canto, and in the bearing which, stylistically, one canto may have upon another. I shall not attempt a comprehensive survey of the canticle. But from the examples that I shall be concerned with, I would hope to demonstrate the principles that one might employ in an extended examination, and to show how the various features of Dante's style do, according to these principles, consort together. I shall continue as well to examine the differences in style between the *Paradiso* and the first two canticles. Finally, to complete my study of recent criticism, I shall in the main choose passages for consideration which other critics have already analysed in the light of their own particular theories.

On the question, then, of diction, few critics are likely to prove more formidable than Luigi Malagoli, whose interest in the *Paradiso* is attested in a variety of stylistic and historical studies.[1] The notion of poetic diction to which Malagoli contributes is precisely and strenuously consistent with the principles I have set myself to question. However from my present point of view the especial difficulty of his work is that frequently he adduces as the surest confirmation of his interpretation a feature of the style to which I, too, would look as being the surest confirmation of mine. So his cardinal purpose, like my own in the first chapter, is to demonstrate that the word in Dante, unlike the word in Romantic or even Modern poetry, has no tendency to overreach itself or strain beyond its natural limit (*Linguaggio e poesia nella 'Divina Commedia'* (Genoa, 1949), p. 64). Moreover, the alternative which Malagoli offers to Romantic and Modern style, appears at first hardly to differ from that which I have offered in discussing 'stability'. For the characteristic forms of Dante's utterances are, he maintains, 'firm and sculptured' (*ferme e scolpite*) (*ibid*. p. 64).

There is, however, a greater divergence here than the difference in the phrasing might suggest. For where, by speaking of stability – in a sense that Dante himself appears to sanction – I mean to indicate the form and product of a deliberate rationality, Malagoli's phrase is one of several which he uses, metaphorically, to excite in the reader a feeling for the physicality or 'haeccitas' of Dante's diction. Others are 'pittoricità', 'frontalità', 'spazialità, and the familiar 'valore concreto'. The word, in short, is for Malagoli a 'thing' to be contemplated as much as understood.

Clearly this position is consistent with that which earlier I attributed to Eliot. But Malagoli is even more vigorous than Eliot in his pursuit of its consequences. The word, he insists, is an object, to be appreciated in isolation from the syntactic or semantic logicality of its context. From this he argues that the whole of a poetic structure may be seen as alogical, roundly affirming that Dante has no love for logical determinants, since his sensibility is wholly 'figural' (*Linguaggio e poesia*, p. 27). I need not emphasise how unwelcome I find this. Yet precisely here an even sharper embarrassment arises. For in Malagoli's view the origin of Dante's 'pictorial' and hence alogical mode of diction is to be found in the very qualities of rhythmic shape and emphasis which are evidence, I think, of an analytic deliberation.

Thus, Malagoli is concerned to illustrate, as especially typical of the *Paradiso* a style of pauses and clear-cut effects of relief (*delle pause e dei netti rilievi*) ('Il linguaggio del *Paradiso*', 47). Dante, he argues, so handles the terzina as to create a rhythm of momentary emphases, a strongly marked succession of separated notes (*di note per sé stanti*), in which the poetry progresses through successive arcs (*procede per tanti archi successivi*) (*ibid.* 47). Rhythm is the 'vital stimulus to imagination' (*animatore della fantasia*) (*Linguaggio e poesia*, p. 78).[2] It is exactly through the emphasis which rhythm allows, that Dante elicits from the single word or phrase the 'savour of things' (*sapor di cosa*), 'the sense of things standing by themselves' (*senso di cosa a sé stante*) (*Linguaggio e poesia*, p. 10).

Now one may very gladly admire the vigour and indeed the originality of Malagoli's emphasis upon the 'pauses and sharp relief', the 'spezzature', as he puts it, of Dante's style. Certainly the notion of a rhythmic 'spezzatura' in the *Paradiso* (*Linguaggio e poesia*, p. 28) is, I believe, indispensable to the analysis not only of diction and imagery, but also of the canticle in its broadest movements. Yet there is little reason, save a predilection for the imaginative word, to suppose that the 'spezzatura' need act in the way that

Malagoli suggests. It is strange, too, considering that Malagoli derives his analysis from an historical examination of Italian style (see especially *Lo stile del duecento*), to find him expressing so vehement a suspicion of the part that syntax may play in poetry. For historically one cannot disregard the importance to Dante of syntactic construction.[3]

Consider, then, where Malagoli's interpretation of the following passage would lead, and the alternatives one might offer to it. The passage describes the bearing of St Francis at an audience with Pope Innocence:

> Né li gravò viltà di cuor le ciglia
> per esser fi' di Pietro Bernadone,
> né per parer dispetto a maraviglia;
> ma regalmente sua dura intenzione
> ad Innocenzio aperse . . .

(Nor did cowardliness of heart bear down his brows/ for being the son of Pietro Bernadone,/ nor that he appeared amazingly despised;/ but regally his severe intention/ he revealed to Innocence.)

(*Par.* XI 88–92)

The word that particularly concerns Malagoli is 'regalmente', which is one of several he discusses in a section on the adverb in Dante (*Linguaggio e poesia*, pp. 26–8). Believing, however, that the poet 'has no love for the adverb as a logical determinant' (*ibid.* p. 27), and that even so obviously syntactical a feature will for Dante approximate to a noun in function, displaying his 'taste for the substantive' (*ibid.* p. 1), Malagoli asserts that 'regalmente' here is utterly transfigured, acquiring in place of its adverbial force a pictorial power (*una potenza rappresentativa*) and forming the centre of an image (*ibid.* p. 27). Image and emotion, he concludes, are gathered up in this adverb, so that it comes to express not merely a grammatical mode but a whole state of mind.

Let me agree firstly that the rhythm of the passage does bring 'regalmente' into relief. At the same time, consider how much is to be lost if one supposes that the adverb is 'transfigured'. For Dante's concern here is, precisely, with the 'mode' and manner in which the dialogue between a Pope and his inferior was conducted. It is not the glamour of 'regality' itself that matters, but regal behaviour. And even to see completely the picture of this behaviour, one must allow the adverb, emphatic though it is, its normal function in controlling the movement and implication of the verb. 'Regalmente' is the central concept (but no more than that) in a scene where 'manner' is a dominant motif; and, paradoxically, to take it as a noun, or as a dazzlingly present 'thing' is to obscure at once the outline of Dante's own description. Nor is that all. For Dante's intention here is not entirely – or even perhaps primarily – to describe. Rather, in depicting the scene, he seeks to enunciate the particular and possibly militant concept, that a private person such as Saint Francis may at times comport himself with a regal confidence towards his sovereign.[4] And, certainly, one will forfeit the deliberate force of this point if one disturbs the emphatic progress of Dante's syntax.

Similar conclusions are suggested by the gerund[5] 'cangiando' in the following lines which describe the progress in time of the Roman Empire until Justinian's accession:

> e sotto l'ombra de le sacre penne
> governò 'l mondo lì di mano in mano,
> e, sì cangiando, in su la mia pervenne.

(and under the shadow of the sacred wings/ it [*the Roman Eagle*] there governed the world from hand to hand,/ and, changing thus, came into mine.)

(*Par.* VI 7–9)

Here again one may agree that the 'arc' of the rhythm does afford a prominence to 'cangiando', and the word, without doubt, is exactly placed and forcefully realised. Nevertheless Malagoli speaks as though 'cangiando' were the epitome of Dante's meaning. The gerund he asserts is 'sweepingly pictorial', comprehending in its perspective the entire history of the Empire and its Emperors (*Linguaggio e poesia*, p. 30).[6] But there are two objections to this. In the first place the reading encourages an unruliness of response. For once one concentrates upon 'changingness' itself, isolating the word and prohibiting its gerundival function, it will be difficult to repress images of a kind associated with other processes of change, as, for instance, the image of temporal mutability, or of chance. The word will become ambiguous, and may indeed touch, as the concept of change so easily does, an elegiac note. But Dante's concern is with the simple progress of historical fact. He is describing, so to say, the mechanism by which Justinian became an Emperor, and with the accuracy of such description, verbal 'autonomy' (*Linguaggio e poesia*, p. 32) or complexity of effect is clearly inconsistent. Nor, in fact, is this complexity admissible unless one ignores, as Malagoli does, the significance of the 'sì' in 'sì cangiando'. This is my second objection.

For 'sì' is no less emphatic than 'cangiando'. Yet allowing this, one will strictly limit the nature of the 'changingness'. The change is *thus*, and not otherwise. Which is to say that one should understand it in relation to the details which precede 'cangiando' in the sentence. Then, too, it is with 'sì cangiando' that the rhythmic and grammatical shape of the terzina begins to emerge, so that one will suspend the moment of one's final attention until the arrival of the statement to which the 'sì cangiando' is pointing – the 'in su la mia pervenne'. The finality of this phrase, which by any standard is highly satisfying, would be impossible if, overlooking the emphasis of the transitional 'sì', one supposed that the poet had gathered all his meaning into a single suggestive fragment. Here, then, as elsewhere, the final simplicity of Dante's word proves inconsistent with a graphic or dramatic liveliness. Yet the achievement of the poet in this verse is precisely to make comprehensible, for himself no less than for his reader, an historical movement to which he still looked as a tributary of his present existence.[7]

Valuable, then, as the concept of the 'spezzatura' is, I would question Malagoli's application of it. And, while agreeing that the 'spezzatura' is exceptionally noticeable in the *Paradiso*, I insist that its importance here is to enforce the very mode of analytical stability which is largely absent from the earlier canticles.

Compare, then, the following passages, all of which contain either an adverb or a gerundive phrase:

(i) Io vidi più di mille in su le porte
da ciel piovuti, che stizzosamente
dicean: 'Chi è costui . . .'

(I saw more than a thousand above the gates/ of those rained down from Heaven, who viciously/ said: 'Who is he . . .')

(*Inf.* VIII 82–4 (discussed by
Malagoli, *Linguaggio e poesia*, p. 28))

(ii) (*of the 'fessura di Malebolge'*)
e vidila mirabilmente oscura . . .

(I saw it wonderfully dark)

(*Inf.* XXI 6 (discussed by
Malagoli, *ibid.* p. 28))

(iii) Vedea colui che fu nobil creato
più ch'altra creatura, giù dal cielo
folgoreggiando scender, da l'un lato.

(I saw him who was created noble/ more than any other creature, come from heaven/ thunderbolting down, on one side)

(*Purg.* XII 25–7 (discussed by Malagoli, *ibid.* p. 34))

(iv) E come ninfe che si givan sole
per le salvatiche ombre, disïando
qual di veder, qual di fuggir lo sole...

(And like nymphs who would pass alone/ through the shades of the woodland, desiring/ the one to see, the other to escape the sun)

(*Purg.* XXIX 4–6 (discussed by Malagoli, *ibid.* p. 35–6))

(v) così quelle carole, differente-
mente danzando...

(thus these carollers, diverse-/ ly dancing...)

(*Par.* XXIV 16–17 (discussed by Malagoli, *ibid.* p. 27))

(vi) Sì come quando il colombo si pone
presso al compagno, l'uno a l'altro pande,
girando e mormorando, l'affezione...

(Just as when the dove sets itself down/ close to its mate, the one displays to the other,/ circling round and murmuring, its affection)

(*Par.* XXV 19–21 (discussed by Malagoli, *ibid.* p. 32))

(vii) Guardando nel suo Figlio con l'Amore
che l'uno e l'altro etternalmente spira,
lo primo e ineffabile Valore...

(Looking upon his Son with the Love/ that the one and the other eternally breathe,/ the original and ineffable Prowess)

(*Par.* X 1–3)

For 'stizzosamente' (i), and 'folgoreggiando' (iii), it would be hard to better Malagoli's reading. Both words, from their emphatic position, emanate a field of energy leading one, beyond an interest in their syntactical function, to reconstruct the picture which the poet himself entertained. This in part is a consequence of their onomatopoeic vitality. But the effect may arise even where onomatopoeia is absent. Thus 'mirabilmente' (ii) is more remarkable as an expression of frozen irony than for any part it plays in syntactical formulation. The purpose of a critical reading would be to determine what complexity of thought and emotion induced the poet to picture

Malebolge, of all places, as *wonderfully* dark. Somewhat similarly 'disïando' (iv) also transcends the limits of its grammatical context. For throughout the *Purgatorio,* as Malagoli acutely observes, constructions such as 'andar cogliendo' and 'va cercando' have performed a most important function, in creating the intuitive image of a perpetual and purposeful activity (*Linguaggio e poesia*, pp. 35–6), so that one's reception of 'disïando' cannot fail to be enhanced by a memory of its precursors. In the synthesis of the whole canticle, it does indeed 'unveil a scene' and depict 'a state of feeling' (*Linguaggio e poesia*, p. 36).

Turning, however, to the *Paradiso*, one finds firstly with 'differente-mente' (v) that the disposition of the lines draws attention precisely to the adverbial character of the word. As with 'regalmente', Dante's cardinal concern is again with the mode of the dance – the diversity of the 'carol'.[8] And the energy of the emphasis is turned towards, and contained within the larger purposes of the sentence. Likewise, the lovely 'girando e mormorando', though in some degree onomatopoeic, has little in common with 'folgoreggiando', superb though that is, too. For the phrase interrupts not at all the grammatical consequence. Indeed the richness of the verse resides not in imaginative impression, but in the variety of purely descriptive detail which Dante, by the suppleness and proportion of the period, is able to encompass. The penetrating sanity of these lines would have been impossible, had Dante been unable to manipulate the grammar of 'girando e mormorando'.

The most impressive illustration of my point, however, is the 'Guardando' of Canto Ten. Strangely, Malagoli pays no special attention to this.[9] Yet 'Guardando' possesses an indisputably substantive quality, for while the actual subject of the sentence is 'lo primo e ineffabile Valore', 'Guardando' demands at once that one should confront and envisage the 'Looking of God'. So there emerges from the first line a verbal picturing of the Trinity – the Son of God and the Love of God being brought into conjunction with the infinite activity of His creative gaze. Furthermore, 'Guardando', being the first word after the canto-break is, of course, exceptionally emphatic.

Yet precisely with this emphasis, there begins the poet's analysis of the notion of Divine activity. Pausing upon the 'picture' of God's 'Looking', it is the conceptual significance of the phrase, and not any 'concrete' image which answers most satisfactorily to one's awakened interest. The majesty of the emphasis and the majesty of the concept are exactly suited. If 'Guardando' is intended as a representation of God in His first person, one must allow that Dante has understood very exactly the grammatical character of the gerund, playing with theological nicety upon the infinitive construction and the notion of Divine infinity in action,[10] so as to define at least one aspect of what he believes his God to be. So there may be nothing here of the echoing strangeness of 'disïando', nor the sensuous brilliance of 'folgoreggiando'. But there is an unshakeable circumspection in the choice of word, and as always this circumspection has its counterpart in a certain exultant rationality, as within the confines of linguistic convention the poet devises an effectual sign for his Creator. In the end, it is no impossible picture of the Deity that we see but the self-confident finesse of the responsible artist.[11]

Though Malagoli's notion of the 'spezzatura' is of outstanding importance, his view of Dante's diction manifests the extreme consequences to which the theories I spoke of earlier may lead. However, Malagoli's position is by no means the only one to which these theories point. Pre-eminent among his critics, are those who, while still insisting upon the imaginative nature of poetic diction, demand a closer attention than Malagoli pays to the 'tension' of the poetic word. The concept of tension, and its counterpart 'violence', are of central importance in modern stylistic studies. And one cannot ignore those few but impressive passages in the *Paradiso* to which the notion has been applied.

What, though, is 'tension' in poetic diction? A serviceable if brief definition is offered by Bruno Porcelli when he affirms the validity for Dante's work of the law in stylistics that the expressivity of a word in any context is proportionate to its distance from the linguistic area in which normally it would appear (*Studi sulla 'Divina Commedia'*, p. 144). So 'tension' arises where a poet conspicuously departs in his language from some predictable norm of usage.[12] The most obvious cases are, of course, those where the poet has devised a linguistic innovation. Thus Terracini in support of the expressive liberty which he wishes to attribute to the poet, cites the following line from the Venus cantos:

s'io m'intuassi, come tu t'inmii

(If I in–you–ed myself, as you in–me yourself [i.e. *If I were in you as you are in me*].)

(*Par.* IX 81)

The formations of 'm'intuassi' and 't'inmii' are indeed not without parallel in the *Paradiso*.[13] But is one bound to agree with Terracini who, finding them 'violent', demands that one should regard such formations as truly expressive images (*Analisi stilistica*, p. 36)? Surely in the very clearness of their morphological structure these phrases betray an analytic deliberation, which makes them rather 'stable' than 'expressive'. Terracini himself in fact gives weight to this conclusion, noting their connection with 'an aristocratic tradition of scholastic language' (*ibid*. p. 36).

More difficult to construe as stable are the phrases upon which Porcelli concentrates (*Studi sulla Divina Commedia*, pp. 141–66), where Dante offers an apparently deliberate 'violence'.[14] Consider the following example:

> Ma dì ancor se tu senti altre corde
> tirarti verso lui sì che tu suone
> con quanti denti questo amor ti morde.

(But say, too, if you feel other cords/ drawing you towards him, so that you may announce/ with how many teeth this love bites you.)

(*Par*. XXVI 49–51)

For Porcelli the 'tensione espressiva' of such lines resides in their violence of metaphor which is 'that much more emphatic insofar as the subject is a spiritual one' (*Studi sulla Divina Commedia*, p. 143). In the discrepancy between the notion of beatitude and the physicality of 'corde' and 'morde', he discerns the continual effort of the poet to find an adequate expression of his intuition of divinity (*ibid*. p. 146).

Now Porcelli's interpretation might be acceptable if one were convinced that the *Paradiso* represented a truly dramatic movement of ascent, and if, more particularly, in the lines I quote, Dante's rhythmic emphasis rested upon 'corde'. Yet the emphasis falls not there but upon the redoubtably undramatic 'altre': 'Are there any *other* cords which draw you to God.' In this way, the 'violence' of the phrase at once evaporates. For one cannot fail to ask, albeit instantaneously, what are the 'cords' which have so far been enumerated, to make '*other* cords' a sensible phrase. This moment of reflection affects one's reading in two ways.

Firstly, it enforces a connection between the single phrase and its context, regulating any eruptive violence. In this respect, the 'altre' acts precisely like the 'sì' in 'sì cangiando', and I need not again pursue this argument to its conclusion. In the second place, however, when with 'altre' the context of the whole is brought into focus, one must surely remember that the arguments of divine love, which are here called 'corde' are elsewhere designated in entirely different ways.[15] At Canto Twenty Six line 24 for example, Dante's love of God is spoken of as a 'target' at which the poet aims his bow. But this is immediately paraphrased, so that Dante's spiritual archery becomes 'filosofici argomenti' and obedience to the philosophical authorities. Then again at line 29 the same love appears as a burning fire, while finally at lines 55–66, the poet offers a list of all the 'morsi', referring in explicitly detailed language to God's acts in the world.

It will be evident, then, that 'corde' so far from being the only adequate expression available to the poet, is, as 'altre' encourages one to see, merely one of a number of phrases which the poet uses to communicate the same concept. It is by no means a 'necessary' phrase. Indeed, its effect, in context is rather that of a simile or a passingly apt analogy than a metaphor. The significance of this may best be seen by comparing this passage with another, from the *Purgatorio*, which undoubtedly is 'violent'.

I refer to the following lines:

> Come balestro frange, quando scocca
> da troppa tesa, la sua corda e l'arco,
> e con men foga l'asta il segno tocca,
> sì scoppia' io sottesso grave carco . . .

(As a cross-bow breaks, when discharged/ with too great a strain, – both string and bow –,/ and the bolt strikes the mark with diminished force,/ so did I burst under the heavy load.)

(*Purg*. XXXI 16–19)

Here the rhythm so falls upon the violent 'frange', 'scocca', and 'tesa' as to stimulate suggestions which positively interrupt the progress of the syntax. With each of these words one is made once more to realise the inner drama which the poet himself, as he writes, is re-experiencing. Indeed, while formally the lines constitute a simile, they display a far more obviously metaphoric quality than the 'corde' passage. For by virtue of the fragmentation, the reader is stimulated to translate each detail of the 'balestro' figure into a psychological or spiritual equivalent. Precisely in that lies the bond of an imaginative or dramatic sympathy.[16]

Returning to the *Paradiso* passage, one finds that even apart from the 'altre', the rhythm and the enjambment, which in the *Purgatorio* passage so sharpen the impact of the single word, are here arranged rather to facilitate the movement of the sense towards its final explication. The pause after 'corde' prepares one for the defining phrase, 'tirarti verso lui'. Likewise, after 'lui', the rhythmic and syntactic caesura articulates the emphasis upon 'sì che', where the goal of Dante's actions is defined for him. And when with the rhyme 'corde:morde', one arrives at the resolution, the rhyme itself, though scarcely a predictable one, strikes a note of elegant and harmonious virtuosity, which, in conjunction with the simplicity of the preceding movement renders the moment of violence a moment, as it were, of shadow-play.

Now it is precisely in the sense of play that the value of these lines resides. For once again, I suggest, one must envisage, in place of 'ansietà', an enjoyment of Dante's intellectual *ludus*. Certainly, in my reading, the 'violence' vocabulary of the *Paradiso* will be seen as ornamental in its function, and I trust that by now ornament may be regarded, at least in Dante's case, as a thing both of spiritual and artistic value. For the virtuosity which produces it is no mere exhibition of skill but the exercise of a profoundly sane and confident spirit. This contention, however, has been connected throughout with an understanding of Solomon's position in Canto Thirteen. In the violence of the following passage – which R. Ramat discusses more effectively than Porcelli – the significance of Solomon's wisdom is again apparent.

> Luce divina sopra me s'appunta,
> penetrando per questa in ch'io m'inventro,
> la cui virtù, col mio veder congiunta,
> mi leva sopra me tanto, ch'i' veggio
> la somma essenza de la quale è munta.

(Divine light is focused upon me,/ penetrating through that in which I am enwombed,/ the virtue of which, conjoined with my sight,/ raises me so much above myself, that I see/ the supreme essence from which it [*the light*] is milked.)

(*Par.* XXI 83–7)

Here, certainly, we find a most remarkable constellation of neologism and 'violence'. Let me concentrate, however, upon 'm'inventro' and 'munta'. To Ramat, these two verbs are rich in associations of animality and matter, laden with the mysteries of procreation and nutrition, and above all, charged with an expressive tension, typical of Dante (*tensione espressiva dantesca*), that draws up physical reality into the spiritual logic of the universe ('Il Canto XXI del *Paradiso*', contained in *Lettura critica della Divina Commedia*, ed. T. di Salvo (Florence, 1969), vol. III, p. 198).[17] From this observation he argues – in terms which are compatible if not explicitly connected with the principles of organicism – that the apparently heterogeneous elements of the canto are collected into a unity which resides not in the intellectual rigour that governs the narrative structure of the canto, but in an extreme and unresting tension that resolves itself in an exceptional but permanently present emotion (*una emozione eccezionale permanente*). And out of this same rhythm, Ramat concludes, there arises the uniqueness of Dante's words, his syntax and his rhythms (*la singolarità della parola, della sintassi, del ritmo dantesco*) (*ibid*. p. 190).[18]

There are three consequences of particular importance in Ramat's argument. Firstly he demonstrates clearly the connection between a certain understanding of the single word and an understanding of the canto structure, which is a matter I shall return to in the next chapter. Secondly, he shows a predictably deep antagonism to the notion of poetic ornament (*ibid*. p. 192). Lastly, and most interestingly, Ramat here carries to a conclusion a suggestion which has all along been implicit in the notion of imaginative expressivity – the suggestion that an interest in the operation of the aesthetic moment will divert the reader from an interest in the poet's own intention.[19] So the poetry of the Saturn cantos is 'the poetry of the dissolution of the individual' (*la poesia della dissoluzione dell'individuale*) (*ibid* p. 194). Indeed, the *Paradiso* as a whole is to be seen as a painful and laborious reconquering of that absolute logic 'in which metaphysically the individual is annulled' (*in cui l'individuale si annulli metafisicamente*) (*ibid*. p. 194).

The last of these three points, which tends, of course, to subsume the other two, is the most important; and if one is to speak of the 'annulment' of the poet, it may seem most appropriate to do so in respect of the Saturn sequence. For these are the cantos of ascetic mysticism, where the individual might well be expected to embrace his own dissolution. Yet asceticism is represented here as a way not to the annihilation of the individual, but to the sustaining of an integral harmony in his being, so that if Beatrice does not smile, and if the blessed souls are silent in this sphere, it is to save the poet from an overwhelming excess of joy. One may indeed discern, in this purposeful abnegation, an echo of the cautious self-limitation which Vergil and Aquinas, in their own ways, each exemplified.[20] It is this lesson, as a discipline and a source of celebration, that the style of the canto follows.

Compare the passage I have quoted only with the following, the first of which is certainly, in Ramat's phrase, 'cari(*o*) di mistero generativo e nutritivo', the second of which contains a form of 'mungere':

Noi andavam con passi lenti e scarsi,
e io attento a l'ombre, ch'i' sentia
pietosamente piangere e lagnarsi;
e per ventura udi' 'Dolce Maria!'
dinanzi a noi chiamar così nel pianto
come fa donna che in parturir sia.

(We were moving on with slow and restricted steps,/ I concentrating upon the shades that I heard/ piteously weeping and lamenting;/ and it chanced that I heard one calling 'Sweet Maria!'/ in front of us in his pain/ as woman does who is in childbirth.)

(*Purg.* XX 16–21)

La divina giustizia di qua punge
quell' Attila che fu flagello in terra,
e Pirro e Sesto; e in etterno munge
le lagrime, che col bollor dissera
a Rinier da Corneto, a Rinier Pazzo . . .

(The Divine Justice here pricks/ that Attila who on earth was a scourge,/ and Pyrrhus and Sextus; and to eternity milks/ the tears, which with the boiling it unlocks,/ from Rinier da Corneto and Rinier Pazzo.)

(*Inf.* XII 133–7)

In the first passage, even discounting effects of rhythm, one finds, in the richest sense, a synthetic structure. Every element contributes to the tonality of the whole. To define its tone, one must remain open, in imagination, to the combination of gravity, loneliness, delicacy and primitive anguish which arises with perfect coherence from the combination of 'io attento', 'passi lenti e scarsi', 'Dolce Maria' and the image of childbirth. Nor is this tonality, which originates in aural and visual impression as well as in concept, unique to these lines alone. At every point in the canto it is extended and modified through images of wrath, crucifixion, and through the overwhelming consolation of the 'gloria' at line 136. Here certainly we may surrender ourselves, with the poet, to the dynamic 'logica assoluta' of which Ramat speaks.

But is such a surrender possible in the *Paradiso* passage? To be sure, the images of 'milking', and of the benign but rapier-like light are themselves suggestive of a spiritual tilth. But to consider only the imagery is to ignore the careful repetition and the studied alteration of related notions like 'focusing' (sopra me s'appunta'), 'penetrating' ('penetrando'), 'joining' ('congiunta'), and 'extracting' ('munta'). The steady progress of these concepts is organised by the disposition of rhythm and syntax, from which there arises an immediately conceptual clarity. Precisely because the passage is so well regulated, the phrases 'm'inventro' and 'munta' are liberated, as they would not be in the *Purgatorio*, where significance is created by the oblique and complex impression of every element of meaning. Their function is that of a grace-note or flourish, the tribute of the poet to the tune he has to play, and even to the discipline that makes his playing possible.

Even more revealing in another way is the comparison with the *Inferno* passage. For Dante's meaning, in both the *Inferno* passage and the *Paradiso* passage, is much the same. In both he envisages the present power of God, enveloping and entering the soul. In both, the power of God is represented in the fullest sense as a mystery. However, the manner of representation is, in the two cases, profoundly different. In the *Inferno*, God's power appears as an all but inconceivable paradox. Thus on the one hand, the Deity, unbearably, wrings tears of agony from the sinners. Yet this very act is a 'milking', and by that description is assimilated to an act of satisfying husbandry. This is a further statement of the 'hard sense' of Hell-Gate: that the Maker of Hell should be Love itself. And 'munta' carries the paradox to its point. Nor is the irony lessened by the knowledge that the sufferers themselves were barren tyrants, 'flailing' the world for nothing save their gain and pleasure.

But mysterious as God must still remain, in the *Paradiso* he need not be approached in paradox. For, in Dante's understanding, it is wholly natural that God should be said to 'enwomb' his creature, and the divine light to be 'milked' from the supreme essence. There exists, that is, in the conventions of Dante's thought, a possible analogy between the earthly acts that 'inventro' and 'munta' denote, and the divine act. Of course, why such analogy should itself be possible is also a mystery. But the Resurrection, which Solomon proclaims, guarantees the possibility, so that in the physical act – an act such as 'milking' – the poet may be confident of a divine correspondence, and celebrate by the comparison both the presence of divinity in the human world, and the compatibility of the human and divine.

The freedom, then, which the poet exercises here is a freedom not to grasp the heart of mystery, but to build around it conventions of his own devising. In 'munta', as in 'corde', one finds, appropriately, no searching metaphor or paradox, but a form of simile or comparison. For in this way the poet manifests the frame of reference in which he finds it right to cast his thought. This conclusion is of importance also in the discussion of Dante's visual imagery in the canticle, to which I now turn.

Among various studies of Dante's imagery, few are more comprehensive than Olivero's *The Representation of the Image in Dante* (Turin, 1936). Unsophisticated though this essay is, there is no other which so explicitly connects the interpretation of Dante's imagery to the principles of the 'esemplastic' imagination.[21] The phrase is Coleridge's, and it is to Coleridge that Olivero appeals, to show how 'setting to work our fantasy is . . . the effect of all true poetry, and this is mainly obtained by means of metaphor' (*ibid.* p. 136). For the poet himself, images are evoked 'unconsciously . . . from his richly stored memory, and they pass swiftly before his inward eye' (*ibid.* p. 5). And precisely in receiving these images, the reader may enter into areas of experience which no ordinary mechanism of the intellect would reveal to him, since, when the mind is struck by a metaphor, it remains 'for an instant wavering between the images of the real subject and its changed reflection in the object' (*ibid.* p. 3).

Olivero's position, of course, is fundamental. But what concerns me in this chapter and the next are two particular developments of it, in the first of which the visual imagery of the poem will be taken as a reflection of the poet's psychic movement, and in the second as an essential constituent of poetic meaning and structure. So in the first case, Porcelli discerns in Dante's imagery a 'continuous germination' (*una germinazione continua*) (*Studi sulla 'Divina Commedia'*, p. 158) out of the poet's subconscious intention, while similarly C. S. Lewis experiences 'the curious feeling that the great poem is writing itself, or, at most, that the tiny figure of the poet is merely giving the gentlest guiding touch . . . to energies which for the most part spontaneously group themselves . . .' ('Dante's Similes', in *Studies in Medieval and Renaissance Literature* (Cambridge, 1966), pp. 76–7). In the second case, one would maintain as, say, T. S. Eliot does that the images must in no way be seen as 'decorative verbiage' (*Dante*, p. 47), and would determine to regard them as 'a serious and practical way of making the spiritual visible' (*ibid.* p. 48). This second position contains, of course, the notion of imagery as a 'linguaggio figurato' which I mentioned in the first chapter.

As to the position which Porcelli and Lewis adopt, it implies, as Lewis proceeds to acknowledge, 'a kind of abdication on the part of the poet', who, conceiving the image, has henceforth only to 'get himself out of the way' (*ibid*. p. 76), allowing the image to create its effect independently.[22] And it is, of course, precisely this notion that I find inappropriate to the *Paradiso*. However, one cannot easily show why the images of the canticle should not 'group themselves' spontaneously until one has considered the typical structure of a whole canto. Here, therefore, I shall examine only whether one needs, with Eliot, to take the particular images as exclusively 'serious' or 'practical' in function.

Consider, then, the following passages

> E come li stornei ne portan l'ali
> nel freddo tempo, a schiera larga e piena,
> così quel fiato li spiriti mali
> di qua, di là, di giù, di sù li mena.

(And as their wings carry along the starlings/ in cold weather, in a broad and full flock,/ thus did that blowing lead the evil spirits here, there, up and down.)

(*Inf*. v 40–3)

> Lo maggior corno de la fiamma antica
> cominciò a crollarsi mormorando,
> pur come quella cui vento affatica...

(The greater horn of the ancient flame/ began to crack against itself, murmuring,/ exactly as if it were strained by the wind.)

(*Inf*. xxvi 85–7)

> Quale allodetta che 'n aere si spazia
> prima cantando, e poi tace contenta
> de l'ultima dolcezza che la sazia,
> tal mi sembiò l'imago de la 'mprenta
> de l'etterno piacere, al cui disio
> ciascuna cosa qual ell' è diventa.

(Like the lark which soars in the air/ first singing, and then falling silent, content/ with the final sweetness that gives her satisfaction,/ thus seemed to me the image of the impress/ of eternal pleasure [*the Justice Eagle*] in desiring which/ everything becomes that which it is.)

(*Par*. xx 73–7)

Eliot examines these verses, which are all supremely dantescan, in *Dante*, pages 18, 22 and 48–9. With his discussion of the first two there is little reason to quarrel. 'We can see and feel the situation... though we do not yet understand the meaning which Dante gives it' (*ibid*. p. 18). In both, the images are undeniably concrete, being sustained, for instance, by the pathos of the verbal enactment 'di qua, di là, di giù, di sù', and the onomatopoeia of 'crollarsi'. One may indeed 'not yet understand their meaning in full'. For, like the cantos to which they belong, these verses are each symbolic fragments – moments, that is, of intuitive energy where the mind may contemplate without restraint the pure complexity of its own impressions. Thus, meditating the 'fiamma antica', one senses ever more deeply the tragic and unrequitable contradiction which arises where human energy encounters the grandeur of divine judgement.[23] Likewise, in the comparison of the lovers and the 'stornei', one discerns the mystery of the weakness of natural creation, and the mystery, too, which distinguishes men from creatures of simple instinct. Neither in Canto Five nor in Canto Twenty Six is there any need, or any encouragement to analyse the image. For the moment, Dante's 'capability' is 'negative'. And his images stand as a vital manifestation of, in Eliot's phrase, 'the logic of sensibility' (*Dante*, p. 51).

But the 'allodetta' passage is in no way comparable. The lines to be sure are visually clear. But their clarity is the product of a meticulous exactitude in descriptive detail.[24] The poet has at some time seen such a bird and listened to it with an all but scientific interest, and his word directs one rather to the sureness of his observation than to the 'logic of his sensibility'. Nothing in the visual detail of the passage disturbs the concision, the proportion, and the integral finality of the terzina. For its duration we are concerned, clear-headedly and simply, with the way in which an 'allodetta' has been seen to behave. Any complexity which may arise from this is not an imaginative complexity but the reflection of an actual complexity, in the world as Dante knew it. Nor does the comparison between the earthly and the heavenly phenomenon arouse any particular tension. For just as Dante is clear about the behaviour of the bird, so is he clear about the relationship of the image and its object. It is a conventional relationship. So in the lines which Eliot does not quote, beginning 'tal mi sembiò . . .', Dante emphasises with studied technicality that he presents only a resembalance of what was itself 'l'imago de la 'mprenta/de l'etterno piacere'. Where an image is so confessedly tenuous in its connection to the object, one cannot easily attribute to it a formal utility. Rather, with Dante himself one must accept that the relation is gratuitous, and doing so begin to recognise, with Dante, the virtue and solemnity that inheres in purely natural description. One may indeed note how in the final lines of this passage the response to 'eternal pleasure' that the Eagle of Justice expresses is one that leads 'each thing' precisely to the attainment of its proper place in the natural world. Yearning for justice, every creature will 'become what truly it is' in the just scheme of creation. And since, once again, Dante insists so strongly upon the love of created order, it will surely be right for him to display in his poetry not the logic of sensibility but the wisdom of Solomon and the joyous pursuit of science for its own sake. How else, in fact, is one to explain the great procession of bird images which accompanies the 'allodetta' verse. Surely these images cannot all contribute to the 'logic' of the canto. But if, therefore, the images are redundant, their redundancy is by no means inconsistent with the intellectual *ludus*.[25]

Consider a further two examples:

> 'Bastiti, e batti a terra le calcagne;
> li occhi rivolgi al logoro che gira
> lo rege etterno con le rote magne'.
> Quale 'l falcon, che prima a' piè si mira,
> indi si volge al grido e si protende
> per lo disio del pasto che là il tira,
> tal mi fec' io . . .

('Let it be enough for you, and strike on the ground your heels;/ turn your eyes to the lure that is whirled/ by the eternal king with the great spheres'./ Like the falcon, which first stares down at its feet,/ then turns to the call and stretches out/ in the desire for food that draws it there,/ thus I made myself.)

(*Purg.* XIX 61–7)

> Quasi falcone ch'esce dal cappello,
> move la testa e con l'ali si plaude,
> voglia mostrando e faccendosi bello,
> vid' io farsi quel segno . . .

(As the falcon which leaves the hood,/ moves its head, and claps with its wings,/ displaying his zeal and making itself fine,/ thus I saw that sign become.)

(*Par.* XIX 34–7)

Consider, too, the interpretation of them which Irma Brandeis has given. Brandeis's work, which has been praised by Montale, is an attempt to extend and modify T. S. Eliot's principal contention, arguing that the imagery of the *Commedia* changes constantly its character and force in response to the spiritual growth of the pilgrim–protagonist. These developments in the imagery, however, are not, Brandeis maintains, the product of a conscious plan but the expression of an imaginative sensitivity which answers '*wholly* to the quality of each successive moment of experience' ('Metaphor in

The Divine Comedy', *HR*, VIII (1956), 558). The imagery of the poem will thus constitute a set of 'clues' to an ulterior meaning or a further moment of comprehension – clues which are valid as well for the poet in his own search for understanding as for the reader (*ibid.* 559). In the images, the reader will find a wisdom 'so sharp and unified that logical analysis is quite beside the point' (*ibid.* 574). Unlike Eliot, however, Brandeis is concerned not with the quality of Dante's imagery in itself, but with its suitability to the stages of the poet's education, and with the part it plays in revealing, even to the poet himself, the state of his own advancement.

Now this notion has an especial value in, say, the *Purgatorio* passage which I quote. Here, Brandeis makes clear, Vergil 'scolds' the poet into *becoming* a falcon (*ibid.* 567–8). Dante does indeed say that he 'makes' himself a falcon ('tal mi fec' io . . .'), and there occurs a moment of very humane comedy, as the poet, pursuing Vergil's image of the 'logoro', imitates faithfully the gestures of the bird. This is entirely appropriate. For, as Brandeis shows, the poet, in identifying the noble hunter with the hunting spirit of the pilgrim, momentarily comprehends the truth of man's relation to his God – in the fullness of obedience, freedom, pleasure and dignity (*ibid.* 568–9). Furthermore, the impact of this identification involves the reader, too, in an awareness of the secret and potentially sacred empathy which may exist between mankind and the rest of creation.

In comparison with this, the image in the *Paradiso*, Brandeis declares, is 'an unfamiliar, unlifelike concrete'. By which she does not mean to be wholly adverse. For the text of the *Paradiso* 'drives us constantly towards the comprehension of essences', and if Dante does not create a 'concrete Paradise' for the reader to contemplate, then it is precisely because he wishes the reader to rise in imagination beyond the images that his text presents to him (*ibid.* 571). In form, however, the *Paradiso* image is manifestly more stable than the *Purgatorio* image. The all-important 'fec' io' of the *Purgatorio* dissolves here into an ordinary simile, which centres around the simple 'vid'io'. Dante's own relation to the 'falcon' is not dynamically or creatively metaphoric, but the relation plainly of an observer to an object. To Dante himself it clearly is important that he should have 'seen' the Justice Eagle gesture in a particular way, and, equally, that, on earth, he had noted how an actual falcon moves. It is precisely this, however, that Brandeis, demanding that we constantly be 'educated' by the images, cannot allow. Thus in the *Paradiso* 'we are not to stare' at the images. Indeed, such sequences as the 'sky-writing' in the Justice cantos would become 'absurd' if we were to (*ibid.* 570). But would they? One has seen, after all, in 'Imagini, chi bene intender cupe', that Dante positively invites his reader to 'stare', and I suggest that the 'altri pochi', who do not need exactly to be educated by the poet, will be satisfied to stare, admiring, from a distance, the science and art by which the poet establishes his thought. With the falcon, then, as with the lark, one will attend, for the space of the terzina, to the self-contained and self-sufficient description of the bird itself. For the Christian world has been sanctioned to bear a truth to the scientific eye. And the poet himself is free to draw upon its detail in the framing of his personal understanding.

With Brandeis's objection to the 'sky-writing' of the Justice Eagle one arrives at a question which cannot properly be answered until the following chapter. For throughout the canticle there are images, such as the Justice Eagle itself, the Eagle of Justinian, and the images in the final sequences of the work which exert undoubtedly a very extensive influence. Could these at all possess the completeness of the lesser image? I think they can. And my general contention will be apparent if, in conclusion, one considers the following two passages, from the final canto:

> Ne la profonda e chiara sussistenza
> de l'alto lume parvermi tre giri
> di tre colori e d'una contenenza;
> e l'un da l'altro come iri da iri
> parea reflesso . . .

(In the absolute being – profound and shining –/ of the exalted light there appeared to me three rounds/ of three colours and of one encompassment;/ and, as rainbow by rainbow, the one by the other/ appeared to be reflected.)

(*Par.* XXXIII 115–19)

and

> Quella circulazion che sì concetta
> pareva in te come lume reflesso,
> da li occhi miei alquanto circunspetta,
> dentro da sé, del suo colore stesso,
> mi parve pinta de la nostra effige:
> per che 'l mio viso in lei tutto era messo.
> Qual è 'l geomètra che tutto s'affige
> per misurar lo cerchio, e non ritrova,
> pensando, quel principio ond' elli indige,
> tal era io a quella vista nova . . .

(That circling which, thus conceived,/ appears in you as reflected light/ – having been scanned for a while by my eyes –/ within itself, of its own colour,/ seemed to me painted with our [*human*] semblance:/ for which reason my sight was wholly set upon it./ Like the geometer who concentrates wholly/ on the measuring of the circle, and does not discover,/ pondering, that principle which he lacks,/ such was I at this new spectacle.)

(*ibid*. 127–36)

These lines are all, of course, governed by a decisive protestation of inadequacy identical with those which I examined in Chapter One:

Omai sarà più corta mia favella,
pur a quel ch'io ricordo, che d'un fante
che bagni ancor la lingua a la mammella.

(Now will my speech be yet more inadequate,/ even to that which I remember, than that of an infant/ who still bathes its tongue at the breast.)

(*ibid*. 106–8)

In the imagery, what follows is no sequence of paradoxes or of 'clues' but a conspicuously normal presentation of colours, shapes, numbers, and consequences. The fundamental conventions of human understanding are called into play, in the representation of the 'tre giri', 'tre colori', in the 'circulazion' and the 'cerchio'. This representation is sustained by a complete stability in the grammar and the rhythm of the passages, by the definitions offered in such phrases as 'che sì concetta', the articulation of 'dentro da sé, del suo colore stesso', and the leisurely, but precise 'alquanto'. The poet's subject, to be sure, is the supreme paradox. But like the geometer, he is bound to acknowledge his perplexity, and, realising the rules and limitations not only of his art but equally of the human mind, return to a sphere in which the critical intellect is truly at home. Not to do so indeed would be to reject what the paradox itself has to teach him. For in the 'tre giri' one may surely see a new manifestation of the Rainbow of the Covenant, a sign that the earth is for man to inhabit.[26] Certainly when at the heart of his vision Dante describes. 'la nostra effige' it is a confirmation of the place which the human person does hold, through Christ, in Creation. But what else should Dante learn from this, save the surest confidence in himself, as a man, and in the conventions and abilities of the human mind? The normality of his imagery in the final canticle is, I suggest, the triumphant manifestation of such confidence.

6

THE ORGANISATION OF THE CANTO IN THE *PARADISO*

Turning from the details of word and image, my purpose in this final chapter is to examine the way in which Dante has handled the larger movements of the *Paradiso*. I shall consider here the structure that seems to me typical of the single canto, and suggest, too, how as the work develops we are to understand the relationship that exists in the general scheme between one canto and the next. Of course, the issues involved in this discussion are of far-reaching significance and properly perhaps should lead one to a discussion of thematic and narrative motive. However, I shall again limit my own analysis to those particular points of stylistic effect which have, I feel, been obscured in more comprehensive studies. In this regard my contention again is a simple one.

For just as in the single terzina a certain effect of rhythm secures analysis and stability, so does it also, I suggest, in the larger sequences of the work. Thus, in the *Paradiso*, the structural rhythm of a canto so far from encouraging, as in the earlier canticles, a sense of organic connection is inclined rather to isolate particular moments of significance, so that each in itself may carry the impress and authoritative cadence of the poet's deliberations. In fine, the general rhythm of the canticle is one which tends to isolate statements, and is a function of that willingness which the poet displays throughout to interrupt himself.[1] It is entirely at one with his carefulness in the placing of the word. Indeed, stability in the single phrase or image could not perhaps be achieved if the larger movement did not sanction it.[2]

But where earlier I spoke of the 'spezzatura' which the individual terzina manifests – adapting Malagoli's notion – here I would rather speak, in a sense which Fubini has defined, of the rhythm as a rhythm of 'didactic pauses'. And so, even at the height of Dante's vision Fubini observes the didactic pauses in which Dante strives to 'fix' an aspect of the truth he has attained (*fissare un aspetto della verità conquistata*) ('L'ultimo canto del *Paradiso*', *Il peccato di Ulisse*, pp. 131–2). This, especially in relating the didactic pause to the establishment of 'la verità conquistata', indicates very exactly the quality I mean to discuss.[3] Though Fubini himself allows an alternation between these pauses and moments celebrating the rapture (*l'ebbrezza*) of Dante's vision,[4] the aptness of his reading from my point of view is only emphasised when he notes the distance which to the last the poet maintains between himself and the object of his contemplation. The personality of the poet, he asserts, remains to the very end 'sound and entire' in the face of the Divinity (*ibid.* p. 131). The pause is indeed to be seen as evidence of a self-possession in the poet. But precisely this, – an evident firmness in the handling of experience – has throughout been characteristic of the stable phrase.

Consider, then, the structure of the opening canto, and particularly the effect of 'Surge ai mortali . . .' at line 37:

> Poca favilla gran fiamma seconda:
> forse di retro a me con miglior voci
> si pregherà perché Cirra risponda.
> Surge ai mortali per diverse foci
> la lucerna del mondo; ma da quella
> che quattro cerchi giugne con tre croci,
> con miglior corso e con migliore stella
> esce congiunta . . .

(A great flame follows a little spark:/ following me perhaps there will be offered with better words/ a prayer that Cyrrha should answer./ To mortals there rises through diverse channels/ the lamp of the world [*the sun*]; but from that/ which joins four circles with three crosses,/ with better course and with a better star/ conjoined, it issues.)

(*Par.* I 34–41)

Between 'si pregherà perché Cirra risponda' and 'Surge ai mortali . . .', there occurs an unmistakable interruption of the canto rhythm, which may firstly be seen in the phonetic properties of the passage. So in the single word, 'Surge', the weight and resonance of the vowel has no precedent save perhaps for the far less robust notes of 'f*o*rse' and 'migli*o*r'. Following this the whole of the second terzina is more definite and steady in pitch. But rhythm is not a matter of sound alone, and the stronger quality in the second verse must also be attributed to an alteration in, so to say, the dynamics of significance. The diminutive tonality of 'Poca favilla' in line 34, and the 'forse' in line 35 are in direct contrast to the strong and unqualified statement which follows. From 'Surge' one moves with the impetus of new confidence through a sustained and complex period of scientific exposition.[5]

This, then, is the first, and certainly one of the most obvious of Dante's didactic pauses. As to its consequences, one may firstly note its effect upon the imagery of the canticle. In both sections, from line 34 to 36 and from line 37 to 42, the dominant motif is fire and brightness, and taking these passages out of context, it would be simple to construct an imaginative logic for their juxtaposition.[6] Yet the quality of thought informing the two sequences is entirely different, the first being gnomic, the second, carefully scientific. Once one recognises the thoroughness of the pause which intervenes, there is no need to devise an imaginative connection. For with the pause one sees how each utterance within its own sphere is completely self-explanatory and consistent, each in turn attracting to its argument and associated imagery an undivided concentration. The pause, indeed, arrives as something of an enfranchisement, assuring the reader that one particular episode in the argument is now as complete as the poet can make it and freeing him to receive with an equal attention whatever next is laid before him.

Further on in the canto, several effects occur. In the superb continuation of the passage above, one sees how Beatrice, and Dante himself through Beatrice, may gaze upon the sun. The conclusion reads:

> così de l'atto suo, per li occhi infuso
> ne l'imagine mia, il mio si fece,
> e fissi li occhi al sole oltre nostr' uso.
> Molto è licito là, che qui non lece
> a le nostre virtù, mercé del loco
> fatto per proprio de l'umana spece.

(Thus from her movement, instilled through my eyes into my imagination, my own [*movement*] was formed, and I fixed my eyes on the sun beyond our usual practice./ Much is allowed there that here is not allowed/ to our powers, thanks to the place,/ framed as proper to the human species.)

(*ibid.* 52–7)

Like the firm rock of Canto Thirteen, the tableau, involving Dante, Beatrice and the Sun, holds while it lasts one's entire attention. And carrying with it its own gloss in the phrases 'per li occhi infuso/ ne l'imagine mia' and 'oltre nostr' uso', the first of these terzine is so incisively complete that the following 'Molto è licito . . .' might well seem a repetition or intrusion. Allowing, however, a value to this break in continuity, the second terzina, standing apart from its context, acquires a peremptory force demanding as close a scrutiny as any more extensive utterance might.[7] Such, it appears, is the poet's procedure that every accomplished moment, be it lengthy or not, will require of us a similarly complete concentration.

With 'Molto è licito . . .' one may class the four terzine at the centre of the canto, from line 64 to line 75. For each of these attains to an unquestionable finality, and each in turn requires of the reader an unhasty willingness to listen. But the most important example occurs with the last line of the canto, after Beatrice's final address – which ought itself to be regarded as a distinct unit, even though its themes are derived from the earlier sections of the canto. In context the concluding line appears thus:

> 'Maraviglia sarebbe in te se, privo
> d'impedimento, giù ti fossi assiso,
> com' a terra quïete in foco vivo'.
> Quinci rivolse inver' lo cielo il viso.

(It would be amazing in you if, stripped/ of impediment, you had remained below,/ just as on earth stillness [*would be*] in a living flame.)
(*ibid*. 139–42)

One's first inclination may be to consider here only the narrative importance of the ascent, which is clearly present in Beatrice's action. Yet in its rhythmic effect the line does nothing, I contend, to encourage a projection of the reader's interest. On the contrary, the moment is one of authoritative arrest, as vigorous in its own way as Vergil's 'e più non dimandare' (*Inf*. III 96). Words have done all that on this subject they can do, and with Beatrice's gesture, a limit is imposed upon them. Nor does the limit suggest any need for later elaboration. It is rather a seal set upon the fulfilment of an orderly ambition. Having reached it the reader's desire, as at the conclusion of many a single verse, may well be, not to proceed, but to return to where the sequence began, retracing the rhythm of thought and word as they lead towards the security of their resolution.[8]

In these cases, then, the virtue of Dante's 'didactic pause' is certainly to enforce, in its simplicity, the formula of a 'conquered truth'. It would not be difficult to show how different this procedure is from that which Dante follows in the *Inferno* and *Purgatorio*. There are, to be sure, in both of these canticles, episodes which are governed by a spasmodic or an interrupted rhythm. One thinks, for instance, of *Inferno*, Canto Eight and the appearance of the Messo da Ciel. Yet here, as Auerbach magnificently demonstrates, the pauses testify above all to a command of dramatic *tempi* and narrative pace (*Literary Language*, pp. 228–33). Similarly, in *Purgatorio*

Canto Eight, the pauses are the agent of emotion not understanding, serving only to enhance the mystery of the scenes which they control. And comparable effects may be seen, in the three canticles, from the transition between canto and canto.

The following sequences are, I suggest, characteristic. Firstly, *Inferno*, Canto Seventeen line 133 to Canto Eighteen line 3:

> così ne puose al fondo Gerïone
> al piè al piè de la stagliata rocca,
> e, discarcate le nostre persone,
> si dileguò come da corda cocca.
>
> XVIII
>
> Luogo è in inferno detto Malebolge,
> tutto di pietra di color ferrigno,
> come la cerchia che dintorno il volge.

(Thus Geryon placed us at the bottom/ at the foot, at the foot of the jagged cliff,/ and, unburdened of our persons,/ disappeared like a bolt from a string.

XVIII

A place there is in Hell called Malebolge,/ all of iron-coloured stone/ like the circular wall that goes around it.)

Secondly, *Purgatorio*, Canto Nine line 139 to Canto Ten line 4:

> Io mi rivolsi attento al primo tuono,
> e '*Te Deum laudamus*' mi parea
> udire in voce mista al dolce suono.
> Tale imagine a punto mi rendea
> ciò ch'io udiva, qual prender si suole
> quando a cantar con organi si stea;
> ch'or sì or no s'intendon le parole.
>
> X
>
> Poi fummo dentro al soglio de la porta
> che 'l mal amor de l'anime disusa,
> perché fa parer dritta la via torta . . .

(I turned my back, straining to hear the first tone,/ and '*Te Deum laudamus*', it seemed to me/ I heard in a voice mingled with the sweet sound./ Such an impression it gave me – that which I heard – as when someone is singing with an organ;/ so that now one does and now one does not hear the words.

X

When we were inside the threshold of the gate/ which the evil love of souls makes to be little used,/ since it [*the evil love*] gives the appearance of rightness to the false way.)

Lastly, *Paradiso*, Canto Six line 140 – which concludes Justinian's commendation of Romeo – to Canto Seven line 3:

> e se 'l mondo sapesse il cor ch'elli ebbe
> mendicando sua vita a frusto a frusto,
> assai lo loda, e più lo loderebbe.
> VII
> '*Osanna, sanctus Deus sabaòth,*
> *superillustrans claritate tua*
> *felices ignes horum malacòth!*'.

(and if the world knew the heart he had/ begging crust by crust his life,/ praise him highly as it does, it would praise him more.

VIII

Hail holy God of battles/ illuminating highly with your brightness/ the happy fires of these kingdoms.)

The first passage, representing the poet's entry into Malebolge, contains undoubtedly one of the most impressive 'pauses' in the whole *Commedia*. What, though, is its stylistic character? With the disappearance of the hallucinatory Geryon, the canvas, for a moment, becomes entirely clear.[9] But this itself is a menacing thing. The terrible factuality of 'Luogo è in inferno' which obliterates the preceding phantasmagoria is, though in form a simple statement, in effect a most violent stimulus to the imagination. For how is it possible to pretend to so plain a certainty, when the subject, one knows, must be increasingly horrific? Is it not easier to conceive of Hell in the stealth and the speed of Geryon than in the starkness of 'Luogo è in inferno'?[10] The very contrast renders the second phrase a complex one. And it is surely appropriate that the Malebolge, where deceit is a principal theme, at the outset should challenge one to accept as a fact the most appalling unreality. In a single line, the poet announces the key – a very remote one – in which the ensuing division is wholly set.

In the second example, the effect of the transition is even more evidently organic,[11] insofar as the single moment is connected by it to the movement of the canticle at large. For the rhythm which the break induces is the rhythm of the whip and the bridle which sounds in every aspect of the second realm. So at the end of Canto Nine, the pause serves to emphasise the urgent and vivacious image of the *Te Deum* – the hymn interacting in imagination with the massy creaking of the Purgatory gate. Few passages represent more forcefully the penitential mingling of security and joy and vital action. The opening, however, of Canto Ten, to which the pause imparts an equal weight, expresses a wholly different aspect of Purgatory, the 'bridle', in the restraint and ruminative secrecy of its tone. The soul, realising how grievous is the transgression to which 'il mal amor' has led it, realises, too, how conclusively its being is now locked to the Love of God. It is this ambiguity which vivifies the simple description of 'Poi fummo dentro al soglio de la porta'. Once the imagination is so aroused, one may also hear in 'sonando la senti' esser richiusa' ([*by its*] sounding I heard it was shut again) (line 4), a reminiscence of Ugolino's famous verse (*Inf.* XXXIII 46–8), recognising how dissimilar is this new imprisonment.

But no similar continuity or contrast is to be expected of the third example. In theme certainly there is a connection between Cantos Six and Seven. For since at least Canto Three, Dante's prevailing concern has been with, so to say, the contractual conditions of existence, as represented in the making of vows, the pursuit of justice and the rectification of sin.[12] This appears in the first terzina of Canto Seven as a triumphal praise of God the Protector. But that alone need not induce the reader to attempt any imaginative reconstruction of the poet's thought. After all, Dante is himself explicit in the interpretation of his theme throughout, and while an imaginative reading is not impossible, one is likely to obscure, by adopting it, the direct force of this interpretation. In the transition, therefore, one may again find a stimulus rather to deliberation than to dramatic engagement.

Thus, at the end of Canto Six, the pause co-operates with the conditional 'loderebbe' and the subjunctive 'sapesse', to drive us, not onward, but back in a steady consideration of Romeo's position. For though the reader is of 'the world', he may now fulfil the condition of 'se 'l mondo sapesse il cor ch'elli ebbe'. He is indeed acquainted with the truth about Romeo. And Dante's pause invites him, in courtesy to Romeo, to think again of Romeo's history and to praise him for what he truly is.

But after such a meditation the 'Osanna' is bound to appear discontinuous. The poet certainly does not connect it to the narrative until the second terzina, where he discloses who is singing it. Even if the hymn is intended as a thanksgiving for the divine protection of Romeo, one had still better attend to it *as* a hymn and not attempt to relate it otherwise to its setting.[13] For the distress of Romeo, like the distress of Dante himself, who composes the hymn, was unquestionably real. Nor can the poet's celebration of what was for him with equal reality an eternal remedy, properly be reduced to a moment of aesthetic satisfaction. As long as the hymn lasts one gives oneself entirely to the force and meaning of the praise itself. The concentration which this implies is entirely suitable in a canto where the authoritative figure of Beatrice firmly defines, from pause to pause, the essential principles of Christian doctrine.

Now it would be easy to multiply parallels to this transition. For instance, the management both of 'Guardando' at the opening of Canto Ten, and of 'Al Padre . . .' which begins Canto Twenty Seven, is very similar to the management of 'Osanna' here. And when at the last line of Canto Five, Dante prepares for Justinian's history of Rome with

> nel modo che 'l seguente canto canta
> (in the manner which the following canto chants),

the announcement itself is enough to ensure a renewal of concentration. Here, however, what concerns me more is to consider how in general the notion of a 'didactic pause' may modify the appreciation of sequences where other critics have been especially active. In the third section, therefore, I shall examine Contini's reading of Canto Twenty-eight, and, in the following section, Guardini's approach to the final cantos, where also the question of Dante's imagery may finally be resolved.

The one aspect of Guardini's very various work that concerns me here is the interest he shows in the psychology of Dante's vision.[14] It is this which has had the greatest influence upon recent study of the *Commedia*,[15] and Guardini himself accords it especial emphasis in discussing the imagery of the final cantos.[16] Consequently, throughout this sequence, he discerns in the shift from image to image the spontaneous rhythm of a psychic progress, a rhythm which reflects the interaction of the hidden mind with the outward reality of God. In this way Dante's vision is to be understood as an 'opening up' of his spirit, and a 'transformation, by virtue of the object of contemplation, of his personality' (*Studi su Dante*, p. 153). Each image, then, as it occurs, especially in Canto Thirty, is for the poet a new stage in the recovery of his spiritual health. And the Heavenly Rose, Guardini argues, may therefore be seen as the *finis*, 'the essential measure', both of the 'universal macrocosm' and of the 'microcosm of the man Dante' (*ibid*. p. 161). For it is through the image of the Rose – indeed only through this – that the poet conceives the fullness both of creation and of his own being (*ibid*. p. 166). The Rose-image is itself a means to comprehension and to sanity. The choice of the image, Guardini maintains, is not dictated by convention, but is 'born from the inward spirit of the poet' (*ibid.* p. 163). In this way, the moment of its appearance is a moment of supreme synthesis, in which the poet is at last reconciled with himself and with reality.[17] Nor is this act of synthesis inaccessible to the reader, for he, too, will enter into it, when with the vision of the Rose he remembers how the poem began: in the infertility and distress of the Dark Wood.[18]

Now if one were interested only in the subconscious preoccupations of the poet, there would be small reason to object to Guardini's interpretation. Yet this cannot be one's sole, or even primary interest. For here, as earlier, when I considered the mystic and Platonic qualities of Dante's imagination, it is necessary to examine, in the first instance, the account which the poet himself has offered of his psychic lucubrations, and to see clearly the form in which his experiences have been cast. There is no reason why the principles governing the composition of the work should be identical with those which governed its conception in experience. And on this score, Guardini's reading is, I suggest, at fault.[19]

For even in terms of spectacle the Thirtieth Canto is, from the beginning, an evidently sophisticated piece of writing. Its force is undeniable, but so is its moral dignity. If the sequence does represent 'an opening up of the spirit' and a 'transformation of the personality', this opening up is such that the poet can nevertheless control fully as he writes. So at every significant point the canto is punctuated with the didactic pause. Nowhere is this more apparent than in the opening five terzine, where Dante describes the fading of the angelic chorus. The last two of these terzine read:

> Non altrimenti il trïunfo che lude
> sempre dintorno al punto che mi vinse,
> parendo inchiuso da quel ch'elli 'nchiude,
> a poco a poco al mio veder si stinse:
> per che tornar con li occhi a Bëatrice
> nulla vedere e amor mi costrinse.

(Not otherwise the triumph that plays/ always round the point that defeated me,/ seeming enclosed by that which it encloses,/ little by little was extinguished from my sight:/ so that to turn with my eyes to Beatrice/ the seeing nothing and my love constrained me.)

(*Par.* XXX 10–15)

A slow clearing of the scene is accomplished, a 'nulla vedere' introduced in a long declining arc of rhythm, after which a pause inevitably supervenes. With that pause, one prepares to concentrate upon the quiet but intensely actual account which the poet offers of his relation to Beatrice. The poet looks back across the span of his works and days. In Beatrice he recognises the principle upon which his holiness and 'sanity' have depended, 'from the first day when in this life I saw her face . . .' (lines 28–9). Here certainly is a moment of synthesis, but the depth and strength of it is something which, in words, the poet cannot and will not plumb:

> ma or convien che mio seguir desista
> più dietro a sua bellezza, poetando,
> come a l'ultimo suo ciascuno artista.
> Cotal qual io la lascio a maggior bando
> che quel de la mia tuba, che deduce
> l'ardüa sua matera terminando,
> con atto e voce di spedito duce
> ricominciò . . .

(But now it is needful that my pursuit should cease –/ in writing poetry – far short of her beauty,/ as at his final limit must every artist./ Thus as I leave her [*in her beauty*] to a greater proclaiming/ than that of my trumpet, which draws up/ its arduous theme to an ending,/ she, with the voice and gesture of a ready guide,/ began again.)

(lines 31–8)

Thus, in a supreme instance of the inexpressibility topic, the poet accepts that the image of Beatrice exceeds his power. In terms of the spirit, her value is precisely that she does exceed it. For while it is she who makes the Christian truth accessible to Dante, it is her ineffable connection with divinity that gives her word its authority. As to the poet himself, however, how, in transcribing that word can he safeguard her authority if he does not honestly confess to his own limitations?[20] Recognising, then, that there are limits beyond which every poet must prove incapable, he abandons any desire to trace the spiritual value of the image to its source. And by the very abdication of the 'psychological' motive, he ensures that the words he does give to her – whose greater dignity he leaves to the voice of the 'maggior bando' – should be received with a gravely deliberate attention. The pause which ensues before Beatrice's speech is an indication of the care with which her words are to be heard.

Then, too, the very nature of Beatrice's speech is scarcely compatible with Guardini's account. For in this speech the imagery of the scene is explained as clearly as the poet can explain it. To put it simply, the structure of the canto is not a structure of images alone. Even the 'subito lampo' at line 46 is explicated at once in the terzina

'Sempre l'amore' (line 52), while no sooner has one envisaged the 'lume in forma di riviera' (line 61), than one hears how this is merely one of the 'umbriferi prefazii' of the truth (lines 76–8). At the least, one must allow here, as Fubini suggests, an interaction between moments of vision and moments of explanation.[21]

Consider, too, how the presentation of the image is affected by the rhythmic 'spezzatura' in the following passage:

> O isplendor di Dio, per cu' io vidi
> l'alto trïunfo del regno verace,
> dammi virtù a dir com' ïo il vidi!
> Lume è là sù che visibile face
> lo creatore a quella creatura...

(O splendour of God, in which I saw/ the exalted triumph of the realm of truth,/ give me strength to tell how I saw it!/ A light there is above which makes visible/ the creator to the creature.)

(lines 97–101)

Here, impressive as Dante's exclamation is, his purpose is to ask for the power to expound his vision; and with the cry there occurs an evident pause, as though the poet were indeed collecting his energies for the task. We are called, as in the examination cantos, to witness a performance. As soon as this begins, with the firmness and simplicity of 'Lume è là sù...', it is apparent that this will be no emotional performance. Rather, as in Canto Thirty Three, with 'Quella circulazion...', one finds here, along with the stability of the tone, a rigorous adherence to the convention of normal thought. The sequence, to be sure, is a transition from the 'umbriferi prefazii' to the image of the Rose itself. Yet the pause, emphasising the desire for an intellectual clarity, makes it impossible, in the poem, to see any subliminal relation between these images – though in experience one need not deny that it existed. Even when one arrives at the Rose, one finds that the poet, by applying to it a strict vocabulary of shape, movement and gradation, has abstracted the image from the flux of direct experience, offering it, again, as a comprehensible, if inadequate, token of his understanding. Thus:

> Nel giallo de la rosa sempiterna,
> che si digrada e dilata e redole
> odor di lode al sol che sempre verna...

(In the yellow of the sempiternal rose,/ which unfolds by degrees and dilates and breathes back/ the odour of praise to the sun which keeps perpetual spring.)

(lines 124–6)

This passage has all the naturalness of a stable utterance, none of the fleetingness or rare ambiguity of a psychic moment.[22] And this, finally, is emphasised by the fall of the canto break.

For as if, once established, one could retain the Rose as a clear point of reference, Dante in the closing lines of Canto Thirty, enters upon a wholly separate discussion. And when he does return to it he writes:

> In forma dunque di candida rosa
>
> (In the form, then, of a white rose)
>
> (*Par.* XXXI 1)

The significant word is the urbane 'dunque', which assumes that the reader is returning to an image he has already comprehended. The poet is pursuing no line of spontaneous synthesis but a line of clear, almost leisurely recollection. And one may now expect a further meditation upon the picture he has offered.

I should like finally to illustrate, how the arguments I have proposed in this essay might apply in the detailed interpretation of a single canto. The canto, however, which I have chosen to examine, Canto Twenty Eight, is one to which recently Gianfranco Contini has given considerable attention. Indeed, Contini's *lectura* (in *Varianti e altra linguistica*, pp. 477–97) is an outstanding example of how, with the methods of modern criticism, one may revive a sequence which was once regarded merely as a structural device.[23] For that reason alone it is important firstly to note the principal features of Contini's position. Moreover, while to me the tenor of Contini's analysis is unsympathetic, his observations do in several ways anticipate the arguments I have in mind. Contini himself divides the canto into four distinct 'movements' (*ibid.* p. 478), which accurately coincide with the fall of the didactic pause, thus: Dante's vision of the Primum Mobile; the content of this vision (that is, the luminous point and its encirclement); the doubt which Beatrice resolves concerning the contradiction of temporal by eternal nature; and, finally, the list of the angelic orders. Then again, Contini gives considerable weight to the 'palinode' at the end of the canto, where Dante admits to a previous error in naming the angelic ranks (*ibid.* pp. 483–4). This passage certainly is important, if one is to appreciate the modesty which operates in the didactic pause. But the question of the palinode and also of the canto division leads one again to consider what kind of truth the poet means to offer here. On this matter, as will be seen, there arises an elementary disagreement.

Now, unlike Guardini, Contini, is interested, not in the psychic material of the poet's writing, but in the form of words which the text itself displays. Indeed, even analysing the word, Contini denies any Spitzerian interest in 'preoccupations buried in the subconscious' (*ibid.* p. 478). For while, as Spitzer might, he seeks the word in a text which is fundamental and 'revealing' (*ibid*, p. 477), this, in Canto Twenty Eight, is nothing other than 'vero', or its derivatives. And 'vero' must obviously be seen as a word upon which is focused 'the vivid illumination of the conscious mind and even of conscious intention' (*la vivida illuminazione della coscienza, anzi dell'intenzionalità*) (*ibid.* p. 478).

So far, evidently, there is little to choose between Contini's position and my own. Yet if one asks what Contini understands here by the 'truth', the answer leads one back very nearly to the arguments that earlier one saw Joseph Mazzeo adopt. For the type of truth with which Contini is here concerned is one in which intuition and discourse will be balanced precisely, he asserts, in the way that the *De coelesti Hierarchia* of Dionysius suggests they might be (*ibid.* p. 483). Predictably, the forms which embody this truth will not, in any sense, be stable forms. On the contrary, the language of Canto Twenty Eight exhibits a conscious pursuit of the exceptional emphasis (*uno sforzo intenzionale di differenziazione*) (*ibid.* p. 487), which poetically sustains the pressure towards a final revelation. So, for Contini, the most important feature of the canto is the display of a 'neologistic force' (*ibid.* p. 485),[24] which appears in formations such as the 'in—' formation, latinate borrowings like 'alo' (line 23), 'circumcinto' (line 29), 'rape' (line 70) and '*ubi*' (line 95), and etymologies like 'templo' (line 53) (*Varianti e altra linguistica*, pp. 484–6). In all of these Contini discerns, as would Terracini also, the imaginative fusion of 'significante' and 'significato' (*ibid.* p. 484). For in its very strangeness, the word is a precisely expressive formula for the hidden understanding of the poet.

Is Contini's reading, however, the only possible one? Certainly the latinate forms are, in my view, as likely to be stable as expressive in character. What, though, of the more subtle cases such as 'templo' in the lines:

> Onde, se 'l mio disir dee aver fine
> in questo miro e angelico templo
> che solo amore e luce ha per confine . . .

(Hence if it is right for my desire to have its end/ in this wonderful and angelic temple/ which has love alone and light for its boundary.)

(lines 52–4)

Contini here emphasises the undoubted paradox which exists between the sense of limit conveyed by 'templo' (*un sacro recinto*, *ibid*. p. 484), and also by 'fine', and the sense of the unconfinable conveyed by 'amore e luce' (*entità espanse e illimitate*, *ibid*.). The question is, however, whether Dante has allowed this paradoxical notion to make its impact purely as a paradox. Somewhat as in the 'geometer' image of Canto Twenty Eight, it would seem to me doubtful whether he has. And here it is 'templo' itself which prevents the paradox. As Contini points out, 'templo' may well include a play upon the concept of contemplation (*ibid*. p. 484), and if this is so, the word, explaining the function of a 'temple', presents one with an immediately accessible concept. For even without experiencing the tensions of contemplation itself, one knows that the notion of contemplation comprehends the tension and the paradox of which Contini speaks. The poet, to be sure, envisages a time when his own desires will 'end' in a contemplation of the unending. But 'templo' helps rather to resolve than to sharpen the paradox, since a temple is precisely the place where, in human terms, one might resolve it. Strangely, I think, this reading improves even the descriptive clarity of the passage, because it leads one to recognise not only the physical presence of the temple but also the qualities of stillness and intentness which essentially are connected with the notion of a temple.

Consider also the following passage:

> Come rimane splendido e sereno
> l'emisperio de l'aere, quando soffia
> Borea da quella guancia ond' è più leno
> per che si purga e risolve la roffia
> che pria turbava, sì che 'l ciel ne ride
> con le bellezze d'ogne sua paroffia;
> così fec'ïo . . .

(As it is left shining and serenely clear –/ the hemisphere of the air, – when Boreas blows/ from that cheek whence he is more temperate/ because the murk is purged and dissolved that before was troubling [*the sky*], so that the sky laughs for us/ with the beauties of all its districts;/ thus did I.)

(*Par*. XXVIII 79–84)

Here, Contini argues, neologism, phonic effect and rare rhyme all conspire with the dynamic force (*dinamicità*) of the syntax ('thanks to the progress of the subordinate clauses') to make the moment a moment of sublimity, which should be read in context as a passage expressing the elevation of the spirit.[25] At the centre of the whole movement stands the Boreas image itself, translating the scene, by metaphor, into an allegory of truth revealed in all its purity (*allegoria della svelata verità nella sua purezza*) (*ibid.* pp. 495–6). But how appropriate is this reading? The passage, after all, simply does not anticipate the advent of any novel truth. On the contrary, it is retrospective, occupying the very evident pause which follows Beatrice's 'risponder chiaro'. A point of truth has been reached; and the qualities of style in the subsequent lines are fittingly qualities of philosophical celebration, not of expressing urgency. So the grammatical subordination, of which Contini himself allows the force, is as clean and correct as it should be in a scientific description, while the Boreas image, along with the elegantly strange 'roffia: paroffia' rhyme, may easily be seen as ornamental, even as manneristic, in operation.[26] Nor should one flinch from reading the Boreas figure as a simile. For by doing so one allows to the frame of natural observation a proper dignity in the service of superior truths. After the surpassing difficulty of Beatrice's discourse, it is typical of the Dante I have depicted throughout this essay that he should return to the temporal world and evoke its movements in celebration of his triumph.

Consider finally Contini's analysis of the following:

> L'altro ternaro, che così germoglia
> in questa primavera sempiterna
> che notturno Arïete non dispoglia,
> perpetüalmente '*Osanna*' sberna
> con tre melode, che suonano in tree
> ordini di letizia onde s'interna.

(The second ternary that thus buds in that ever-eternal spring/ which the nocturnal Ram does not spoil,/ perpetually unwinters itself [*with cries of*] *Hosannah*/ in three melodies, which sound in the three/ orders of happiness of which it is in-three'd.)

(lines 115–20)

In the face of so hauntingly extraordinary a passage, one hardly cares to bandy interpretations.[27] Nor can I confidently prefer my own to Contini's, especially where he speaks of the phrase 'notturno Arïete'. Even so, it is hard to accept that these verses are as 'violent' as Contini makes them. In his view, the poetry of his passage lies precisely in the way that its component phrases break through the confines of the normal, to rediscover an 'irrational measure' (*una misura irrazionale*), and in these moments of linguistic violence the canto, which at first sight appears to be dominated by a tone of level-headed exposition, is carried explosively towards the comprehension of the inexpressible (*ibid.* p. 497). Yet these verses, I maintain, in their descriptive framework, manifest too firmly conceptual a grasp to support Contini's verbal mysticism. For instance, the 'primavera sempiterna', which one might suppose to act intuitively, is so evident a paradox as to be emblematic in its force,[28] inviting one to countenance, in reason, the discrepancy between time and eternity. Elsewhere in the passage, there is much to encourage analysis and paraphrase. So, 'Sberna', while from one point of view a notably concrete word, is also, as Contini himself remarks, technical in character (*ibid.* p. 496), defining precisely the concept of a movement, in time, out of winter into spring. Even the 'notturno Arïete' – numinous though Contini takes it to be in its 'privatività' (*ibid.* p. 496) – is likewise a reflection of the poet's meteorological scholarship. In the order of nature, at least, the nocturnal rising of the Ram is no mystery but a phenomenon exactly balanced by a daytime rising – the first occurring in autumn, the second in the spring. The phrase, then, is neither more nor less than a learned periphrasis for autumn and like the periphrases of Canto Eight, a part of its value lies precisely in the learning it displays. So even if the eternal world should know no change, Dante cannot speak of it without ackowledging that the realm of nature does change. And the acute awareness which he shows in these lines both of the differences between earth and heaven, and of the nature of the world to which his mind is accustomed, gives a weight of philosophical seriousness to the image. Though this quality may not be the only one which the verse possesses, neither is the exotic and dream-like quality which Contini attributes to it.

Having considered three passages which happily demonstrate how relative not to say foolhardy one's critical pronouncements will often be, I turn with somewhat greater confidence to a survey of the whole canto. For in the main the canto does respond, I think, to the arguments I have offered.

From my point of view, the cardinal passage is the last, where Dante, acknowledging implicitly an error of his own in the *Convivio*, portrays the hilarity of Saint Gregory who discovers, on arriving in Heaven, that the angelic orders are not as he predicted them to be:

> Ma Gregorio da lui poi si divise;
> onde, sì tosto come li occhi aperse
> in questo ciel, di sé medesmo rise.

(But Gregory afterwards departed from him [i.e. *from the authoritative position of Dionysius*]; hence as soon as he opened his eyes/ in this heaven, he laughed at himself.)

(lines 133–5)

Dante, in the preceding canto, has again been attempting to decide the question of the celestial hierarchy, and this concluding sequence is surely an indication of the conditions under which the results of his present speculation are displayed. Once again one is reminded how fallible is human speculation. Yet though such fallibility is, of course, natural to man, it is not irreparable. Indeed it may even be benign. For Gregory's errors have not precluded his entry into Heaven. While Dionysius is shown emphatically to have been exact in his calculation. But if, in this latter case, one asks how this exactitude was achieved, the answer must be: by a conformity to the condition of fallibility, and a consequent attention to the authoritative voice. For as Beatrice insists in the final verse of the canto:

E se tanto secreto ver proferse
mortale in terra, non voglio ch'ammiri:
ché chi 'l vide qua sù gliel discoperse
con altro assai del ver di questi giri.

(And if so very secret a truth was uttered/ by a mortal on earth, I do not want you to be astonished:/ for he who saw it here above, disclosed it to him/ with a great deal else of the truth of these circles.)

(lines 136–9)

St Paul, that is, in the Scriptures has stated authoritatively the truth of the matter, and the success both of Dionysius and of Dante himself is made to depend upon their 'courteous' submission to his word. Against the speculation that betrayed St Gregory, Dionysius and Dante employ merely that 'syllogism' of the Holy Spirit which at Canto Twenty Four line 93 is defined as an attention to 'le vecchie e . . . le nuove cuoia' (the old and new vellums [i.e. *testaments*]).

Dante, then, through confessing his respect for St Paul and Dionysius, makes clear the nature of the response that he expects here for his own deliberations. The repeated 'vero' which Contini has noted is no imaginative curlicue, but a peremptory focus for the minds of the 'altri pochi'. Indeed from the conclusion of Canto Twenty Seven, where he laments the absence of any temporal authority, the poet, in a general way, has emphasised the importance of submission to an authoritative voice. At the beginning of Canto Twenty Eight, the poet himself is obliged wholly to submit, in appreciating those truths that run 'counter to the present life' (line 1), to the word and gaze of Beatrice. Only thus, in a profoundly courteous deference to her authority, can the 'absurdities' of the metaphysical utterance – where the greater is the lesser and the least is greatest of all – be truly acceptable. If, however, one seeks the warrant of Dante's own authority in the canto, it is again to its style and structure that one must look, where from the first one finds evidence of the stable phrase and the didactic pause.

Thus before entering the 'still point' description, Dante rests, as Contini allows, upon the portrayal of his own relation to Beatrice, as if to emphasise the relevance of his attitude here to the reception of the truths that follow:

> riguardando ne' belli occhi
> onde a pigliarmi fece Amor la corda.

(gazing into the beautiful eyes/ from which love had made a cord to capture me.)

(lines 11–12)

From this begins the establishing of the 'rock-like' image itself. In constructing this, the poet continually maintains the human measure, adducing, as the ground for his calculation, the moon and the stars, and tracing through his description a line of physical cause and effect, which, of course, the logic of the syntax entirely supports:

> un punto vidi che raggiava lume
> acuto sì, che 'l viso ch'elli affoca
> chiuder conviensi per lo forte acume...

(A point I saw that rayed forth light/ so sharp that the sight which it burns into/ must close because of its strong piercingness)

(lines 16–18)

and

> Forse cotanto quanto pare appresso
> alo cigner la luce che 'l dipigne
> quando 'l vapor che 'l porta più è spesso...

(Perhaps as close as it seems/ a halo girdles the light that paints it/ when the vapour that supports it is thickest.)

(lines 22–4)

In both of these passages, one notes the typically strict syntax of the 'sì, che' and the 'cotanto quanto'. However, the most impressive feature throughout the canto is the poet's inexorable reliance upon arithmetical enumeration, in a situation where arithmetic has plainly no more than a conventional value. Yet neither God nor arithmetic is mocked. Such terms are sanctioned for man's use, and Beatrice herself invites the poet to apply them to the mystery:

> per che, se tu a la virtù circonde
> la tua misura, non a la parvenza
> de le sustanze che t'appaion tonde,
> tu vederai mirabil consequenza . . .

(so that, if you encircle the inner strength –/ and not the appearance – of the beings that to you appear round,/ you will see a wonderful conformity.)

(lines 73–6)

There follows at the end of the 'still point' sequence, a further pause, and in noting this one should note also the absolute finality which resounds in Beatrice's word:

> La donna mia, che mi vedëa in cura
> forte sospeso, disse: 'Da quel punto
> depende il cielo e tutta la natura.
> Mira quel cerchio che più li è congiunto;
> e sappi che 'l suo muovere è sì tosto
> per l'affocato amore ond' elli è punto'.

(My Lady who saw me, in concern/ severely caught up, said: 'From that point/ hangs the heavens and all of nature./ Gaze at that circle which is most conjoined to it;/ and know that its movement is so swift/ because of the burning love with which it is pierced'.)

(lines 40–5)

There is no flight of enthusiasm here. But the pause, in conjunction with Beatrice's superb imperatives, 'mira' and 'sappi', give to the utterance a thorough clarity and self-possessedness. One may indeed be sceptical about the adequacy of Beatrice's utterance in relation to 'the state of things'. Yet one cannot deny to so gravely deliberate a a verse the respect and consideration that it plainly demands.

From this, one moves into a sequence which, depending as it does upon Dante's questioning, may at first appear to be dialectical in manner. But the poet is not in any direct way 'investigating' what is true. Rather, he is preparing the ground for a further and no less authoritative statement of belief. A confidence in his own ability, as a poet, to produce this statement takes all the tension out of the question that he proffers. Thus:

Onde, se 'l mio disir dee aver fine
in questo miro e angelico templo
che solo amore e luce ha per confine,
udir convienmi ancor come l'essemplo
e l'essemplare non vanno d'un modo,
ché io per me indarno a ciò contemplo.

(Hence if it is right for my desire to have its end/ in this wonderful and angelic temple/ which has love alone and light for its boundary/ I need further to hear how the copy/ and the pattern do not proceed in like manner/ since for myself I contemplate that [*question*] in vain.)

(lines 52–7)

When at length this answer is provided, there occurs a perfect illustration of how in a stable phrase the poet employs the structure of his rational art to define for himself the best of his understanding. Consider only the following verses:

Maggior bontà vuol far maggior salute;
maggior salute maggior corpo cape,
s'elli ha le parti igualmente compiute.

(The greater the excellence the greater the well-being it desires to effect;/ a greater body contains the greater well-being,/ it has parts of equivalent perfection.)

(lines 67–9)

and

tu vederai mirabil consequenza
di maggio a più e di minore a meno,
in ciascun cielo, a süa intelligenza.

(You will see a wonderful conformity/ of more to greater and smaller to less,/ in each heaven as to its intelligence.)

(lines 76–8)

In the first example, the repeated 'maggior', the antiphonic balancing of its opening lines, and the alliteration of 'corpo cape' and 'compiute' are clearly designed to mark out and sustain the development of the notion as the poet conceived it. This is equally true of the pauses and alliteration in the second passage. At the same time, each notion carries with it, so to speak, its own embellishment, as is particularly striking in the second example. For here, while the 'mirabil consequenza' amounts, at first glance to a mere enumeration of the more and the less, there is, nonetheless a gracefulness in the construction, in the dance of the proportions, which, without compromising the rationality of the phrase, shows how delightedly the poet could contemplate the wonderful actualities of creation. A rational simplicity is here its own ornament, and the control that the poet, by his art, exerts over his meaning, is, as he himself understood in the 'Se mai continga' passage, an attestation of his own ability, as a man no less than as an artist.

The triumphal climax of Beatrice's speech effects the pause which, as I have said, precedes the Boreas image. And with that image there begins the final movement of the canto, which is consistently one of celebration. After the strenuously 'leaden-footed' computation of the Heavenly orders, the poet turns back upon the same considerations to honour their importance in the splendid 'L'altro ternaro . . .' verse, and the magniloquent enunciation of the scriptural nouns: Dominazioni, Virtudi, Podestadi, Principati, Arcangeli and Angeli. The very degrees of creation become the 'Angelici ludi' (line 126). Into the *ludus* of creation the poet himself enters, offering, for his part, the best of his verbal and rhetorical skill. Indeed, now that the philosophic task is over it is possible to introduce again, with a note of happy acceptance, the theme of man's intellectual fallibility. It is on this note that the canto pauses with the delightful mention of Gregory's reaction to his own error. By one's own light, of course, the 'verità conquistata' which Dante lays before one may well be unacceptable. After all Dante himself plainly recognises the possibility of error. Yet if it is unacceptable, the poet's example should nonetheless challenge one to formulate with an equal thoroughness the principles of one's own belief. And knowing, as one will, what it means to attempt such a formulation, one may certainly join with the poet in solemnly proclaiming what he himself has decided must be true.

Let me, however, in coming to a conclusion draw attention not so much to the truthfulness that Dante attains in the *Paradiso* through the acceptance of his own fallibility but rather to the joy that in a Canto like the Twenty Eighth accompanies that acceptance. For it is time to offer on my own account if not a palinode then at least a correction to the impression of prevailing severity that in all likelihood my analysis of the *Paradiso* will have produced. Throughout, of course, I have been concerned primarily to illustrate the effects of the discipline to which Dante submitted in writing the canticle. Nor is that emphasis itself one that I at all regret. For the style does, I believe, consistently respond to it. And when this is recognised the *Paradiso* may come to be seen as a model which, though current theory obscures it, retains for the present both interest and value.

Yet no one who has read the *Paradiso* at all sympathetically will be satisfied to suppose that the exemplary discipline or the stability of the *Paradiso* were the only feature of the work that merited discussion. In fact wherever my concern has been with the *Paradiso* itself, I have attempted to account for what, simply, is the happiness of the work by showing the importance in it of the *ludus* or play of Dante's art. This, of course, has implied no contradiction of my general argument. For the mode of celebration that Dante adopts is a product of and not an escape from the orderliness and care of Dante's procedure. Nor indeed is the sense of the *ludus* – though profoundly connected in Dante's case to a particular view of the universe – altogether inapplicable as an example to the modern writer. For certainly the arbitrariness of language is much in the minds of twentieth-century thinkers. And Dante clearly demonstrates wherever he is 'leaden-footed' how in committing ourselves to those words whose significance we can command, we may even so bring stability and substance to our pronouncements. Equally, however, in the *ludus*, he makes clear that the same arbitrariness may, if one accepts the condition, be a liberation and fine occasion for, precisely, the game of art. It is upon this note that I wish to end. While illustrations of the argument may be discovered in any of the cantos I have hitherto considered, the supreme illustration occurs in the Twenty Third canto of the *Paradiso*.

Consider, then, finally the following lines which coming from one of the richest cantos in the whole *Commedia* have themselves been regarded by some critics as the finest that Dante ever wrote:

> Quale ne' plenilunïi sereni
> Trivïa ride tra le ninfe etterne
> che dipingon lo ciel per tutti i seni,
> vid' i' sopra migliaia di lucerne
> un sol che tutte quante l'accendea,
> come fa 'l nostro le viste superne.

(As in serene and clear full-moonlit nights/ Trivia smiles among the eternal nymphs/ who paint the sky in all of its depths,/ I saw, surmounting a thousand lamps, one Sun that fired everyone of them,/ as our [*sun*] does the sights above us.)

(*Par.* XXIII 25–30)

To lines particularly like the first three, no response surely could be more natural than one of admiration for the brilliance of Dante's artistry. In the words of Aldo Scaglione they represent 'a spectacle of pure aesthetic beauty' ('Imagery and Thematic Patterns in *Paradiso* XXIII', contained in T. G. Bergin's *From Time to Eternity*, p. 154). Yet natural as that response might be, even Scaglione, whose analysis demonstrates very sensitively the depth of Dante's art, does not seem willing to allow that 'spectacle' may be the true mode and function of these lines. In common, indeed, with T. S. Eliot and others whose criticism I have discussed he displays in his reading of the Twenty Third canto a thorough mistrust of any element that might purely be ornamental or be taken at all as 'decorative verbiage'.[29] I venture then to suggest that if one is to admit in this passage the value of its evidently spectacular aspect, without reserve and without diminishing its weight and sophistication, one must again return to the notion of the *ludus*. For in this sequence as in every other where the *ludus* is exemplified, the play of Dante's art may itself be regarded as an aspect of the poet's specific freedom and of his commanding sanity in the face of his experience. So acknowledging that the counterpart in Dante's work to linguistic discipline is a triumphant virtuosity of word and image, one may, I think, appreciate even more fully the exhilaration of such a passage than if one insisted, with Scaglione, upon its rigorous adaptation to an imaginative whole.

In two respects, however, Scaglione has himself drawn attention to those features of the passage that suggest pre-eminently the reading I have in mind. Thus one may observe, as Scaglione does, the very striking disproportion that exists between the vehicle and the tenor of Dante's simile (*ibid.* 161–2). Not only is the Trivïa, on any account, more forceful than the description of Christ's presence among the saints, but there even occurs a discrepancy in the central terms of the comparison between the reference to Christ as a 'Sun' and the reference to Trivïa, which is to say, the Moon. Now it is this discrepancy that leads Scaglione to treat the Trivïa image as autonomously a centre of the canto's lyrical imagery, embodying intuitions that the overt logic of the canto cannot realise. Yet there is little need to turn for an explanation to the remoter regions of the mind. For as one saw first of all in the 'Imagini' passage of Canto Thirteen, Dante is quite aware that the images he offers in the *Paradiso* will necessarily be gratuitous and in essence unconnected to the reality of his experience. This is nowhere more likely to be the case than in a passage that tells of the poet's direct experience of Christ. One saw indeed at the opening of the Cacciaguida episode how the poet acknowledges the failure of his powers in the face of Christ's presence. Though in the Twenty Third Canto, the procession of Christ seems to be arranged especially for the benefit of the poet himself, it is a notable feature of the canto that the emphasis of Dante's description should fall not upon the figure of Christ himself but upon the two figures who in different ways are the human vessels of Christ's reality, Beatrice and the Blessed Virgin. Yet if adequacy or exactitude of description is not to be expected, there still remains for the poet the freedom to perform, as it were, within the limits of human comprehension, in honour of the vision he has been granted. The gratuitousness of the image in that case is neither more nor less than the condition under which the virtuosity of the poet happily operates. And if, like Scaglione one finds that the description of Trivïa is marked by the 'static calm of a contemplative mood' (*ibid.* 146), then this, too, is compatible with such a condition. For here as in the 'Imagini' passage, our response must be, not to seek an unattainable connection between the image and the reality, but to contemplate exactly the art that in reality we can see before us. The very lack of connection in fact frees the mind from the urgency that an 'imaginative' structure would have stimulated, allowing one to pause precisely upon the spectacle of the poet's own achievement.

But if the passage illustrates the freedom that the *ludus* may embody, it illustrates also the abiding sanity that throughout the *Paradiso* underlies the poet's rhetorical virtuosity. Once again Scaglione enables one to see this. Thus as he notes (*ibid.* 153–5), the Trivïa image, in substance at least, could hardly fail to have suggested to the medieval mind, through its associations with astrological lore, the occult and irrational forces that superstitiously were thought to operate in the natural world. Yet the sophisticated use to which Dante puts the Trivïa allusion precisely transcends these primitive overtones. One has in fact already seen in the Venus cantos how Dante, with a full understanding of the force that pagan myth may carry, can still stand apart from their immediate attractions, and, confident of the Christian revelation, make use of the myth itself as a decoration to his Christian theme. So it is here. Trivïa, to be sure, was once as for Vergil and Ovid, the goddess Diana in her threefold aspect – goddess of the Moon, of the hunt and of death, – and thus did personify the dangerous and hidden spirit of the natural world.[30] But for Dante there is nothing now to be feared in nature. Even the haunting brilliance of the full moon can be summoned in the phrase 'plenilunïi sereni' to embellish the Christian victory. And the very learning which the poet displays here – as in the rhetorical ornamentation of the Venus Cantos – in referring to the myth at all, is itself the contribution that a man of reason might naturally make to the celebration of the Christian victory.

The clearest evidence, however, of how in my view one is to approach the Trivïa passage occurs in a passage that dominates the Twenty Third Canto even more markedly than the description of Christ's triumph. I mean, of course, that supreme instance of the inexpressibility topos that earlier I cited for its association with the imagery of *De Vulgari Eloquentia* II iv:

> Se mo sonasser tutte quelle lingue
> che Polimnïa con le suore fero
> del latte lor dolcissimo più pingue,
> per aiutarmi, al millesmo del vero
> non si verria, cantando il santo riso
> e quanto il santo aspetto facea mero;
> e così, figurando il paradiso,
> convien saltar lo sacrato poema,
> come chi trova suo cammin riciso.

(If now all those tongues were to sound/ that Polyhymnia and her sisters made/ most rich with their sweetest milk,/ in aid of me, to a thousandth part of the truth/ it would not come, singing of the holy smile and of how great a pureness it gave the holy face;/ and thus, depicting paradise,/ it is right for the consecrated poem to make a leap,/ like one who finds that his path is cut off.)

(*Par.* XXIII 55–63)

In itself, of course, this passage alone might at once dispel the impression that the poet, in recognising the limit of his linguistic powers, was bound to be contented only with austerity of phrase. For certainly Dante here brings to splendid fruition the understanding that he first attained in *Convivio* III iv 3, where, conscious of his inability to rise to the height of his subject, he nonetheless insists that the utterance he can achieve is to be admired as a true product of 'the workshop of the rhetorician' (*la fabrica del rettorico*). So in the present case, though it is fitting not to speak of the ineffable beauty of Beatrice's smile, the poet, as the devotee of Beatrice, indirectly glorifies her influence by demonstrating in the elaborate decoration of the Polimnïa allusion, that he – her servant – is a man whose words may themselves be admired.

However, in regard to the structure of the canto it is this same attitude towards the inexpressible that explains the remarkable independence not only of the Trivïa image in the pattern of the whole, but equally of every other image in the series to which the Trivïa passage belongs. For in a way that I have noted throughout the present chapter, the Twenty Third Canto divides very clearly into a number of distant and self-sufficient movements. At the centre of each movement there stands, usually, an image drawn with exceptional acuteness from the sphere of temporal nature. The Triviä image is one example of this. But others include the superb comparison of Beatrice to a mother bird which so steadily demands one's attention at the opening of the canto:

> Come l'augello, intra l'amate fronde,
> posato al nido de' suoi dolci nati . . .

(As the bird among the beloved branches,/ settled upon the nest of her sweet offspring)

and at line 79:

> Come a raggio di sol, che puro mei
> per fratta nube, già prato di fiori
> vider, coverti d'ombra, li occhi miei . . .

(As in a shaft of sunlight that flows purely/ through a broken cloud, a meadow of flowers once/ my eyes saw (*though I was still*) under shadow.)

Yet the origin and purpose of these passages will by now be readily apparent. Incomprehensible as the triumph of Christ must remain, save to those who witness it themselves, still the artist may testify to its significance by sounding in his images those notes that are most comprehensible to the human ear.

Nor in the end could any procedure be more appropriate to the theme of this particular canto. For while, in the first section, its subject is the universal victory of Christ and in the second the courtly harmony over which, in Paradise, the Virgin Mary reigns, it is equally a canto in which Dante himself fully comprehends the victory that he himself has now achieved.[31] So in the narrative progress of the canticle, Dante, with the last moments of Canto Twenty Two, arrives at a liberating vision of where exactly, within the perspectives of the universe, the earth stands, marking his own detachment with a smile at its 'ignoble showing'. At the same time, as he takes up his position in the Sphere of the Fixed Stars, he is also preparing himself for the ceremonial testing of his faith that follows in Cantos Twenty Four, Twenty Five and Twenty Six. Indeed, confident of his acceptance in Heaven, he will soon enunciate, in Canto Twenty Five, his longing for a comparable acceptance in his native Florence. In one aspect, then, this canto is the very point at which the discipline of the poet – the *strenuitas* that he learned as well from Cacciaguida and Aeneas as from Aquinas – reveals its reward. By virtue precisely of that he has earned for himself a place among the 'soldiery' of the Church Triumphant. But Dante is not a soldier alone. He is equally, within the code of a divine courtliness, the lover of Beatrice. And in the Twenty Third Canto, which, in portraying the place of the Blessed Virgin in Heaven, is the supreme representation of the courtly life, Dante proves his claim to participate, according to his own peculiar virtues and abilities, in the celebration of ultimate civility. The play of art which dominates the style of this canto is, one may conclude, a spectacle of Dante's own devising, equivalent, in its own way, to the dance that the Angel Gabriel performs, when, taking on the appearance of a crown of light, he again descends to encircle the Virgin:

> per entro il cielo scese una facella,
> formata in cerchio a guisa di corona,
> e cinsela e girossi intorno ad ella.

(down through the heaven there descended a torch,/ formed in a circle in the fashion of a crown,/ and it encircled her and turned about her.)
(lines 94–6)

CONCLUSION

The cardinal purpose of my argument has been to suggest how a poet, by assuming a certain modesty in the face of his experience, may acquire authority for his words and exhibit in his writing a particular kind of truthfulness. Dante's own modesty is dictated to him by his Christian understanding of the world. Yet his example is not, I think, applicable only to Christian experience. Many of the themes upon which the poet has traditionally spoken – the themes, say, of love, of pain, and of universal order – are ineffable in a very similar way to Dante's theme of divinity. Indeed, precisely because they are so, one is accustomed to value the imaginative boldness and the delicacy of the poet in defining them. My intention is by no means to deny the value in literature of rarity and force. These after all are qualities which the *Purgatorio* and the *Inferno* consistently manifest. Yet, in the unremitting caution which Dante recommends, not only in the *Paradiso* but also in his theoretical works, there lies the possibility of another type of proceeding. An intelligently worded statement may, one knows, possess a considerable, if not comprehensive power to illuminate or confirm a truth. And Dante's mode of address in the *Paradiso* may finally be compared to the well-considered utterance of a 'yes' or 'no', where a speaker, choosing for himself a final position, with due regard to its meaning and to its consequences, establishes his mastery over an area of thought, and henceforth holds himself responsible for it.

With the truthfulness which Dante exemplifies in the *Paradiso*, I have associated a particular view of poetic form and a particular understanding of the response which a reader might properly offer to it.

So in the style of a work which did, like the *Paradiso*, pretend to authority, one would look to find, on the part of the poet, a deference towards the normal conventions of speech and thought, as represented, primarily, in syntactic convention. The outcome of this would be – as I have termed it – a stable utterance, where the poet organises his thinking as rigorously as he can within these conventions, and also acknowledges, if only implicitly, that his affirmations are indeed of a relative status.

The proper response to a stable utterance will be the carefulness and the self-possessed attention which is best regarded, I insist, as a form of courtesy. This, I think, is a point of especial importance. For, as one has seen, it has become unnaturally difficult in modern criticism to emphasise the influence that a poet may exert upon the life of the individual. Yet the relationship which a courtesy of the kind I have described will promote is one in which, through the literary medium, individual may again meet with individual.

If these, however, are the dominant issues of the present essay, I am bound, finally, to indicate something of what yet remains to be said about them.

As to the *Paradiso* itself, only in the concluding pages have I suggested at all strongly how the more obviously attractive elements of the canticle might be analysed. I repeat that I in no way want to diminish their force or importance, and hope that the analysis I have offered will be found to apply to many other sequences of the *Paradiso* than those I have discussed. On the other hand, there are certain episodes which although harmonious with the position I have presented, might best be appreciated by comparing them with other works which lie beyond the scope of this essay. Especially in Cantos Four and Five, where Dante discusses so thoroughly the tragic bafflement of the will, the authoritative answer which he provides could well be studied as a contrast to, say, the ironic mode of the great Shakespearian tragedies. But this I have attempted elsewhere.

More generally, I have not even attempted here to suggest what the relation may be, in point of theory, between the mode of writing which I have described and the imaginative mode. In some ways the distinction which my argument implies corresponds to the distinction which Croce draws in *La Poesia* between 'literature' and 'poetry'. However, important as Croce's observations are, there are ways, I believe, in which the 'literary' function may more properly be discharged in verse than in prose.

Two further questions remain. The first of these concerns the philosophy of the argument I have followed. And as the argument stands, I may hope only that it does not irritate the philosophical mind too severely. Yet the problems which have concerned me here have in the past been raised by thinkers like John Holloway, in *The Victorian Sage*, and, more recently, by Professor Mackinnon in *The Problem of Metaphysics*. And I should be happy if the points that I have raised here were seen to have a bearing upon discussions such as these.

Finally, it will, I hope, be apparent that while writing about the *Paradiso*, I have been concerned, even if not explicitly, with the conditions of modern English poetry. Certainly one could wish that the example of Dante's unerring sanity might penetrate, as there is reason for it to do, to the styles and purposes of the modern poet. On that question, however, as Dante himself might have said, it undoubtedly is more fitting to be silent.

NOTES

INTRODUCTION

1. For a survey of the canticle's recent fortune, see G. Paparelli, 'Il problema critico del *Paradiso*', in *Questioni dantesche* (Naples, 1967), pp. 247–307. For the sympathetic reappraisal of the *Paradiso* as typical of the reaction against Croce, see G. Bárberi Squarotti and A. Jacomuzzi, *Critica dantesca* (Turin, 1970), pp. 535–6.

2. G. Getto, *Aspetti della poesia di Dante* (2nd edition, Florence, 1966). A. M. Chiavacci-Leonardi, *Lettura del Paradiso dantesco* (Florence, 1963). M. Fubini, 'L'ultimo canto del *Paradiso*', now in *Il peccato di Ulisse* (Florence, 1966). The attitudes of these critics are extensively reflected in G. Giacalone's recent commentary (Rome, 1969).

3. M. Fubini illustrates one tendency of contemporary criticism when he speaks of the harmony between Dante's verse technique and the techniques of scholastic argument (*Metrica e poesia* (Milan, 1962), vol. I, pp. 197–221). K. Foster, on the other hand, states the question which I have in mind, though he resolves it differently, when he distinguishes the 'genuine insight and intellectual enthusiasm' which characterise Dante's procedure from the 'methodical impartiality' of the true philosopher ('The Mind in Love: Dante's Philosophy', in *Dante: a collection of critical essays*, ed. J. Freccero (Englewood Cliffs, N.J., 1965), pp. 44–5).

4. For the principles and methods of modern Dante criticism see H. Hatzfeld, 'Modern Literary Scholarship as reflected in Dante criticism', *CL.*, III (1951), 289–309; F. Maggini, 'La critica dantesca dal '300 ai nostri giorni', *Questioni e correnti di storia letteraria* (Milan, 1949), pp. 123–66; L. Martinelli, *Dante* (Palermo, 1966); E. Paratore, 'Il più profondo significato delle attuali celebrazioni dantesche', *Tradizione e struttura in Dante* (Florence, 1968), 1–24; M. Sansone, 'Aspetti della interpretazione critica della *Commedia* dal 1920 al 1965', *DMC* (1967), 651–67; N. Sapegno, 'La critica dantesca dal 1921 ad oggi', *ACISD*, vol. II, 263–74; A. Vallone, *La critica dantesca contemporanea* (Pisa, 1953).

5. Cf. H. Hatzfeld, 'Recent Italian Stylistic Theory and Stylistic Criticism', *Studia Philologica et Litteraria in honorem L. Spitzer*, ed. A. G. Hatcher and K. L. Selig (Berne, 1958), pp. 227–8. For the benign influence of Croce, see M. Fubini, 'Rileggendo *La Poesia* di Dante', *CSD*, 7–19; M. Puppo, *Il metodo e la critica di Benedetto Croce* (Milan, 1964), p. 110.

6. For Croce's own argument on this score, see esp. 'Il carattere di totalità della espressione artistica', in *Nuovi saggi di estetica* (1920), p. 129.

7. Cf. H. Hatzfeld, 'Modern Literary Scholarship', 291 and 308. The

sympathy of the historians is also reflected in poets such as Eliot and Pound. And Montale may have hit upon the reason when he speaks of the modern age as 'un nuovo medioevo', 'Dante, ieri e oggi', *ACISD*, vol. II, 317.

8. Thus F. Tateo heralds in the work of C. S. Singleton and R. Montano a 'nuova estetica del poeta-vate, del poeta-teologo' (*Questioni di poetica dantesca* (Bari, 1972), p. 16). Bruno Nardi has been named as the founder of this school of thought; see L. Martinelli, *Dante*, pp. 239–40. See also G. R. Sarolli, *Prolegomena alla Divina Commedia* (Florence, 1971).

9. For the relation between the concept of 'figura' and the drama of historical process, see Auerbach, *Scenes from the Drama of European Literature*, pp. 71–2 of reprint (Gloucester, Mass., 1973). For the full complexity of Auerbach's position, see A. Roncaglia, introduction to *Mimesis* (Italian translation, Turin, 1957).

10. See, for instance, *Commedia: Elements of Structure* (Cambridge, Mass., 1954), pp. 10–11.

11. 'Dramatic' in modern critical usage tends to be synonymous with such terms as 'actualised': see A. Tate, 'The Symbolic Imagination: A Meditation on Dante's Three Mirrors', in *Discussions of the Divine Comedy*, edn I. Brandeis (Boston, 1961), p. 109.

12. E. N. Girardi makes similar demands in 'Dante personaggio', *CSD*, 332–42, criticising even R. Montano – whose work offers a most systematic reappraisal of Dante – for his dependence, ultimately, upon Crocean notions.

13. The mistrust of fundamental questions may be a reaction against 'una troppa prepotente invadenza metodologica' in Croce's approach (Vallone, *La critica dantesca*, p. 23). But Croce himself states the case for a constant attention to principle impeccably in 'La critica letteraria come filosofia', *Nuovi saggi di estetica* (Bari, 1920), pp. 203–19. Even in an age where stylistics claims its own discipline and method the need for such attention is undiminished. See C. Cases: 'I limiti della critica stilistica e i problemi della critica letteraria', *SC*, XI (1955), 46–63, 266–91, and M. Fubini, 'Ragioni storiche e ragioni teoriche della critica stilistica', *GSLI*, CXXXIII (1956), 489–509.

14. See also A. Pagliaro, whose principal works are listed in the Bibliography, and N. Abbagnano, *Possibilità e libertà* (Turin, 1956).

15. See esp. E. Guidubaldi, 'T. S. Eliot e B. Croce: Due opposti attegiamenti critici di fronte a Dante', *Ævum*, XXXI (1957), 147–85.

16. For the derivation of Croce's thought from Romantic concepts of imagination, see G. N. G. Orsini, *Benedetto Croce* (Carbondale, 1961), esp. pp. 34–5, and F. Flora, 'Croce e De Sanctis', in the volume he edited, *Benedetto Croce* (Milan, 1953), pp. 197–229. For Eliot and Romantic thought, see esp. F. Kermode, *The Romantic Image* (London, 1957). Cassirer's debt, and through him, Terracini's, to the idealist philosophers is, of course, fundamental. For the challenge which Dante's work presents to such principles, see M. Petrucciani, 'Dante e le poetiche contemporanee', *Studi in onore di A. Schiaffini* (Rome, 1965), 861–80, and V. Vettori, 'Maestro Dante', in the volume he edited, *Maestro Dante* (Milan, 1962), esp. pp. 229–30.

17. Perhaps the most influential development lies in 'structuralism' (as seen, for instance, in 'Per un approccio strutturalista a Dante', edited F. Casetti and D. Bertocchi in *Lectura Dantis Mystica* (Florence, 1969), 519–30).

But even here a poem is assumed to be an 'organic' whole, as in most 'stylistic' approaches to poetry.

18. Works by della Volpe include *Critica del gusto* (Milan, 1960); *Crisi della estetica romantica* (Rome, 1963); *Schizzo di una storia del gusto*, ed. I. Ambrogio (Rome, 1971); also the entry 'Poetica', in *Enciclopedia dello spettacolo* (Rome, 1961), vol. VIII, cols. 258–62. On della Volpe, see L. Blasucci, *Studi su Dante e Ariosto* (Milan–Naples, 1969), pp. 182–7, and L. Martinelli, *Dante*, pp. 235–6. Works by Calogero include *Estetica, semantica, istorica* (vol. III of *Lezioni di filosofia*) (Turin, 1947); *Studi crociani*, with D. Petrini (Rome, 1930); 'In che senso siamo ancora idealisti?', *DH*, 11–12 (1965), 163–8. On Calogero, see M. Reiser, 'The aesthetics of Guido Calogero', *JAAC*, XXX (1971), 19–26 (where at p. 19, Calogero is described as 'the first writer who challenged the most important tenets of Croce's aesthetic'), and M. Fubini, 'Arte, linguaggio e letteratura', *Belfagor*, III (1948), 269–88, 396–413.

19. Though Croce's philosophy passes through several distinct phases, I assume here a certain consistency in his main principles. Cf. M. Puppo, *Il metodo e la critica di Benedetto Croce*, p. 13, and G. N. G. Orsini, *Benedetto Croce, passim*.

20. Here and generally, see *Aesthetica in nuce*, now contained in Croce's own anthology of his writing, *Filosofia, Poesia, Storia* (Milan–Naples, 1951).

21. Cf. Orsini, *Benedetto Croce*, p. 19.

22. Cf. S. Zink, 'Intuition and Externalisation in Croce's *Aesthetic*', *JP*, XLVII (1950), 210–11.

23. See also G. N. G. Orsini, 'Croce and the Poetic Image', *SP*, X (1956), 1–24.

24. Cf. Croce, 'Il carattere di totalita', p. 126.

25. There is no difficulty for Croce in speaking at once of 'fragmentation' and unity. See 'Frammentismo e poesia', *Letture di poeti* (Bari, 1950), pp. 273–83, esp. 274–5.

26. Cf. L. Tonelli (whose text is the *Paradiso*) *Dante e la poesia dell'ineffabile* (Florence, 1934), esp. p. 23.

27. For Croce on Breglia, see *Conversazioni Critiche*, V (1939), pp. 99–104. For Croce's own argument on this point, see 'Ancora della lettura poetica di Dante', in *Letture di poeti*, pp. 3–20. This essay offers a most accurate prognosis of the ills of modern Dante studies, showing especially how a laborious ingenuity in the interpretation of doctrinal passages may lend them an air of artistic importance.

28. On this, see M. Barbi, 'Poesia e struttura nella *Divina Commedia*', in *Problemi fondamentali per un nuovo commento della Divina Commedia* (Florence, 1955), pp. 7–19, and in relation to the present argument, C. Garboli, 'Struttura e poesia nella critica dantesca contemporanea', *SC*, VIII (1952), 20–44.

29. For Croce on the 'aesthetic personality' see 'L'intuizione pura', p. 18, also Orsini, *Benedetto Croce*, p. 48.

30. Fubini asserts this position against Calogero in 'Arte, linguaggio, letteratura'. Recently, G. Bonelli has revived Croce's main contention in 'La critica estetica: saggio di metodologia letteraria', *AMAT*, XXIII (1972), 251–87.

31. *Estetica, semantica*, p. 28. On this see Fubini, 'Arte, linguaggio, letteratura', esp. 274.

32. However, Calogero does insist, like della Volpe, and against Croce, on the 'radicale oratorietà del linguaggio' and the primacy of 'communication' (*Estetica, semantica*, esp. pp. 240–51). This, I think, is important.

33. The modern antipathy to such a view has recently been expressed very pungently by Richard Wollheim who dismisses as the 'schoolmaster's view of art' the view that 'the production of art was largely concerned with making things which evoked admiration' ('Philosophy and the Arts', in *Modern British Philosophy*, compiled and edited B. Magee (London, 1971), p. 182). But see Chapter Two, below, for Dante's position.

34. Cian, in fact, in his review (p. 61) tends to adopt this view, citing Manzoni's letter to Diodata Saluzzo, November, 1827.

35. Cf. Croce, 'La cosidetta "critica stilistica"', *Letture di poeti*, p. 288. The extremes – against which my own argument is directed, too – may be seen in R. Jakobson and P. Valesio, '*Vocabulorum constructio* in Dante's sonnet "Se vedi li occhi miei"', *SD*, XLIII (1966), 1–33, also P. Valesio, '*Vocabulorum constructio*', *SD*, XLV (1968), 167–77.

36. Thus his opposition to Mallarmé's 'on ne fait pas la poésie avec des idées mai avec des mots', e.g. at *La Poesia* (1942), 3rd edn, p. 241. For his dislike generally of the symboliste aesthetic, see E. Bonora, *Gli ipocriti di Malebolge* (Milan–Naples, 1953), pp. 112–31. Likewise, for his antipathy to stylistic criticism, which in England develops in conjunction with Eliot's writing, see his 'La cosidetta "critica stilistca"', and R. Wellek, 'Benedetto Croce: literary critic and historian', *CL*, V (1953), 75–82. Finally, however, Croce's view of poetic language is not inconsistent with the view of the 'practical critic'. Cf. E. Wasiolek, 'Croce and Contextualist Criticism', *MP*, LVII (1959), 44–54.

37. On Eliot see J. Casey, *The Language of Criticism* (London, 1966); I. Chmielewski, *Die Bedeutung der Göttlichen Komödie für die Lyrik T. S. Eliots* (Neumünster, 1969); M. Praz, 'T. S. Eliot e Dante', in *Machiavelli in Inghilterra*, 2nd edn (Rome, 1943). For a compatibility between Eliot and Croce, see A. Russo, 'Il contributo di T. S. Eliot alla critica dantesca', *ALCGG*, part 2 (1965), 201–32.

38. The notion of the objective correlative may derive from Grandgent's work on Dante (see R. D. K. Banerjee, 'Dante through the Looking Glass', *CL*, XXIV (1972), 138), though it is formulated in the Hamlet essay in *The Sacred Wood*, and clearly sorts with the romantic concept of imagination (cf. Abrams, *The Mirror and the Lamp* (New York, 1953), p. 25). For E. Montale's similar position, as the consequence of 'an intense Dantean experience', see A. Pipa, *Montale and Dante* (Minneapolis, 1968), p. 19, where Montale's own discussion of the question, *Intenzioni*, is also given (pp. 158–71).

39. But in support of Praz, see Casey, *The Language of Criticism*, p. 92.

40. To the reader, certainly, who cannot rise to the intricacy of his thought, Dante may allow the mere beauty of his work to suffice. (See 'Voi che 'ntendendo...', line 61, and the comment by K. Foster and P. Boyde in *Dante's Lyric Poetry* (Oxford, 1967), vol. II, p. 169.) Still, even in the *Vita*

Nuova, he thinks it shameful for a poet to be unable to explain his own meaning (*cap.* xxv).

41. For the opposition of referential language and 'organicism', see M. Krieger, 'Benedetto Croce and the Recent Poetics of Organicism', *CL*, VII (1955), 252–8.

42. For the synthetic as exemplified by the expressive and primitive 'grido di stupore', where all the elements of meaning are collected, globally, into a complex moment, and the analytic by 'Ecco una cosa strana', where the elements are articulated, see C. Segre, 'nota introduttiva' to C. Bally, *Linguistica Generale* (Italian translation, 1963), pp. 28–9.

43. Cf. Croce on primitive speech, *Estetica*, p. 175, and an important passage in *La Poesia*, pp. 18–19. Also B. Terracini, *Analisi stilistica* (Milan, 1966), pp. 36–7. Cf. Chapter Three below.

44. But Croce himself suggests one, when he notes how poets, declaiming their work, 'non li tuonano nè li cantano... ma preferiscono dirli in tono basso... badando solamente a spiccarne bene le parole e a batterne il ritmo' (*La Poesia*, p. 95). To Croce, this indicates a desire to equal as far as possible the rhythm of the inner voice, 'a cui nessuna voce umana è pari'. But one might equally suppose that the poet's manner indicated an *analytic concern* for the structure of his developing thought.

45. Cf. Eliot, 'The Music of Poetry', now in *On Poetry and Poets* (London, 1957), esp. p. 38. Also W. J. Rooney in *The Problem of 'Poetry and Belief' in Contemporary Criticism* (Washington, 1949), p. 103, discussing Eliot's attitude to Dante's 'E 'n la sua voluntade è nostra pace', (*Par.* III, 85).

46. For a sympathetic account of these, see H. Gardner, *The Art of T. S. Eliot*, pp. 62–8.

47. Discomfort over it appears as early as 1931 in Edmund Wilson's *Axel's Castle* (Fontana Library, 1961, pp. 100–1).

48. See *The Anatomy of Nonsense* (Norfolk, Connecticut, 1943), pp. 120–67. For della Volpe's reservations about Winters, see *Critica del gusto*, p. 118.

49. Eliot's view is the reverse of della Volpe's. Thus D. E. S. Maxwell, writing of Eliot's attitude, echoes Eliot's own comment on Donne: 'Rather than elaborating a thinking process, Dante resolves into sensuous imagery the impact of thought upon his sensibility' (*The Poetry of T. S. Eliot* (London, 1952), p. 69).

50. See esp. *Critica del gusto*, pp. 14–16.

51. Thus, for English 'practical criticism' in action, see D. Antona-Traversi, 'Observations on "Io son venuto al punto della rota"', *IS*, II (1938), 65–9.

52. See R. Wellek, *Discriminations*, p. 356.

53. See, in relation to the *Commedia*, *Critica del gusto*, p. 46.

54. Cf. C. Grayson, 'Dante e la prosa volgare', in *Cinque saggi su Dante* (Bologna, 1972), esp. pp. 56–7, and C. Segre, *Lingua, stile, e società* (Milan, 1963). Also see Chapter Three below.

55. There are evident similarities to Vico's thinking in this. For the importance, generally, of Vico in Dante studies, see P. Giannantonio, 'Giambattista Vico, precursore del dantismo moderno', *LA*, x (1969), 52–61.

56. Cf. R. Montano's objections to idealism, especially in Croce, that, in emphasising the freedom of human consciousness, it fails to account for the presence of the concrete individual as author in his work. (*Arte, realtà e storia*, esp. p. 104). I would hesitate, however, to seek the individuality only in terms of his psychological and cultural determinants, as Montano tends to do.

57. Cf. W. M. Urban, 'Cassirer's Philosophy of Language', in *The Philosophy of Ernst Cassirer*, esp. pp. 419–20, 425–6 and 439.

58. On Terracini, see esp. G. Nencioni, 'Orientamenti del pensiero linguistico italiano', *Belfagor*, VII (1952), 249–71.

59. Cf. Cassirer, *The Philosophy of Symbolic Forms*, vol. I, pp. 88–9.

60. Terracini here draws a number of his illustrations from De Sanctis' writing on the Ugolino episode. For De Sanctis' concept of 'organic form', see M. Puppo, 'Il concetto del "vivente" nella critica dantesca di Francesco De Sanctis', *RR*, LXII (1971), 183–91. One notes that P. Dronke finds a notion of the 'organic' in mediaeval aesthetics and in Dante, 'Mediaeval Rhetoric', in *The Mediaeval World*, ed. D. Daiches and A. Thorlby (London, 1973), esp. pp. 331–7.

CHAPTER ONE
The 'modest voice' and the Paradiso

1. I am much indebted to Father Kenelm Foster for showing me his manuscript article on Aquinas and Dante, to appear in the *Enciclopedia dantesca*. This clarified a number of points in this chapter. See also Father Foster's 'St. Thomas and Dante', *New Blackfriars* (April 1974), 148–55, and C. Fabro, 'Tommaso d'Aquino', *Enciclopedia cattolica* (Vatican, 1954), vol. XII, esp. col. 280, on Aquinas's 'sobrietà teologica'. Generally, too, see E. Gilson on the limitations of metaphysics, *Dante and Philosophy* (English translation (Gloucester, Mass., 1968), pp. 121–9, 253–81).

2. One sees how lethal to Cavalcante, in the circle of the heretics, is Dante's ill-considered 'ebbe' (*Inf.* x 63 *et seq.*). When, in the same place at line 39, Vergil asks that Dante's words be 'conte', Landino notes that the word implies the clarity and carefulness of speech which is needed in the avoiding of heresy (quoted G. A. Scartazzini, in the 5th edn of his text and commentary, ed. G. Vandelli (Milan, 1907), p. 90).

3. Cf. M. Aurigemma's excellent *lectura* of Canto XIII *NLD*, pp. 129–46.

4. The theme is, of course, related to Vergil's great injunction at *Purg.* III 37, 'State contenti, umana gente, al *quia*'. For the convergence of Aquinas's thought and classical thought on this point, see M. Apollonio, 'Esperienze e concetto del limite' in *Uomini e forme nella cultura italiana delle origini* (Florence, 1943), pp. 237–93. Few concepts are more important to Dante than that men should consciously be 'content' with their position in existence. Cf., though somewhat differently, K. Foster, 'Dante's Vision of God', *IS*, XIV (1959), 31, and F. Salsano, 'Contento', *ED*, II, 172–3. The intellectual importance of a humble 'contentment' is found as early as the *Convivio*, where it is often associated with references to the Solomon literature. A relevant case

is *Con.* IV vii 9, where translating Proverbs 4. 18, Dante speaks of those who will not bend to the ordained path (in a phrase which exactly foreshadows *Par.* XIII 126: 'Elli non sanno dove rovinano').

5. 'Un'interpretazione di Dante', in *Varianti e altra linguistica* (Turin, 1970), pp. 403–4. Cf. throughout *Par.* XXIX 85–117.

6. One need not dispute Gilson's contention that Siger represents the power of independent reason (*Dante and Philosophy*, pp. 257–81. Yet Gilson underestimates the complexity of the scene in which Siger appears. The very concord of the philosophers in Heaven is a reprimand to the irritations of human reason. Cf. R. Morghen, 'Dante profeta', *LC*, III, pp. 27–8.

7. See J. A. Mazzeo, '*Convivio* IV, xxi, and *Paradiso* XIII: Another of Dante's Self-Corrections', *PQ*, XXXVIII (1959), 30–6, and A. Mellone, 'L' esemplarismo divino secondo Dante', *DV*, IX (1965), 237.

8. On the intellectual life of the Religious Orders, see U. Cosmo, *L'ultima ascesa* (Bari, 1936), chapter 11, and C. Fabro, 'Tommaso d'Aquino', cols. 281–8.

9. Bonaventure earlier acknowledges (XII 143–4) that he is moved to speak by 'l'infiammata cortesia/di fra Tommaso e 'l discreto latin'.

10. S. Pasquazi emphasises how thoroughly Dante had absorbed the monastic spirit, learning, in the words which Dante gives to St Benedict and which echo the Aquinas speech, to 'stay the foot and keep the heart sound' (*Par.* XXII 51), in *All' eterno dal tempo* (Florence, 1966), pp. 285–92.

11. That there is a peculiarly Christian understanding implicit in such a procedure, which demands a recognition at once of God's transcendence and the dignity of the human world, may be seen from the lines: 'Siate, Cristiani, a muovervi più gravi . . .' (*Par.* V 73 *et seq.*) where leaden-footedness is shown to be the proper condition of a vow. The same passage emphasises the importance of respect for the Scriptures. Cf. *Par.* XIX 82–4.

12. P. V. Mengaldo allows 'discrezione' as a synonym for 'distinzione' ('Discrezione', *ED*, II, pp. 490–1). And this is important for two reasons, firstly because 'discrezione', as Mengaldo shows, is for Dante significant in artistic creation (see also Di Capua, Chapter Three below), and secondly because Dante in general attaches a remarkably high value to 'discrezione', especially at *Con.* IV viii 1 *et seq.*, where, notably, one of its 'sweetest fruits' is said to be 'la reverenza che dee lo minore a lo maggiore'.

13. Of recent works which propose the kind of question that I touch upon, I would mention especially D. M. Mackinnon's *The Problem of Metaphysics* (Cambridge, 1974), R. Trigg, *Reason and Commitment* (Cambridge, 1973), also L. J. Cohen, *The Diversity of Meaning* (London, 1966), and R. Kuhns, *Literature and Philosophy* (London, 1971).

14. T. Spoerri, *Introduzione alla 'Divina Commedia'* (Italian translation, Milan, 1966), p. 190, where the 'divina relatività' of the *Paradiso* is claimed as an anticipation of Kant.

15. An interesting case is that of Ripheus, the redeemed pagan (*Par.* XX 118 *et seq.*), who, in view of God's profundity, 'che mai creatura non pinse l'occhio infino a la prima onda', chose, like Solomon, human justice, and was saved by that choice. Vergil, too, though wrong in his information about Ripheus, seems nonetheless to be respected by Dante for his deference to the

hidden will of the Gods ('dis aliter visum', *Aeneid* II 426–8). On Ripheus, see E. Paratore, *Tradizione e struttura*, pp. 34, 76–7, 311–12.

16. Cf. M. Fubini, 'Le sentenze della *Commedia*', *Critica e poesia* (Bari, 1956), pp. 41–7.

17. The Temple Classics *Paradiso* has very appropriately for its epigraph a passage from Saint Bonaventure: 'None partaketh God supremely in the absolute sense, but supremely with respect to himself.'

18. See especially *Paradiso* Canto Thirty.

19. Cf. J. Freccero, 'The Final Image: *Paradiso*, XXXIII, 144', *MLN*, LXXVII (1964), 14–27, and K. Foster, 'Dante's Vision of God', esp. 24.

20. See for instance L. Tonelli, *Dante e la poesia dell'ineffabile*, p. 36, and recently S. Battaglia, *Esemplarità e antagonismo*, esp. pp. 44–6.

21. F. Tateo, *Questioni di poetica dantesca* (Bari, 1972), esp. pp. 173–200. Tateo is particularly important for his discussion of 'Amor, che ne la mente mi ragiona...', and the commentary on this at *Convivio* III iv. Here, even more vigorously than in the *Paradiso*, Dante shows how prepared he is to seek only the proper statement of the 'little' that he can say, when the height of his experience is ineffable. See 'Amor...' lines 9–14, and line 62: 'mi conven contentar di dirne poco'. Cf. F. Montanari, *L'esperienza poetica di Dante* (Florence, 1959), pp. 79–80.

22. Cf. Giacalone, commentary, vol. III, pp. 298–9.

23. Cf. *Con.* III iv 5–13, and *Par.* XXIII 64–6.

24. One of the tasks imposed upon Dante is that he should teach men to be content not to question Providence. Thus Saint Peter Damian (yet again employing the 'foot' image) demands:

> E al mondo mortal, quando tu riedi,
> questo rapporto, sì che non presumma
> a tanto segno più mover li piedi.
>
> (*Par.* XXI 97–9)

25. For a general account of the psychology of speech, see P. Rotta, *La filosofia del linguaggio nella patristica e nella scolastica* (Turin, 1909), esp. Chapter VI, 'La filosofia del linguaggio in rapporto alla psicologia ed alla metafisica scolastica'. See also C. Guerrieri-Crocetti, 'Divagazioni sul *De Vulgari Eloquentia*', *MSD*, 119–29, and 'La razionalità del linguaggio secondo S. Tommaso e Dante', *GD*, XXV (1922), 135–7.

26. For the relation of memory, experience and speech, see B. Nardi, 'Perchè "dietro la memoria non può ire"', *LA*, I (1960), 5–13.

27. Cf. Tateo, *Questioni di poetica dantesca*, p. 189. And see the similar case, at *Par.* XVIII 82–5, where Dante asks for inspiration in the most elevated terms, so that he may speak not directly of God, but like a Ripheus or Solomon, of the vision of Justice, the spelling out of *Diligite Iustitiam*.

28. Thus in the Scartazzini/Vandelli commentary, 20th edn the paraphrase for 'ombra' is 'quella tenue, imperfetta immagine'.

29. See J. Pépin, *Dante et a tradition de l'allégorie* (Montreal and Paris), 1970), pp. 33 and 40. Sapegno recognises the technical force but prefers to give the word an emotional colour, commentary, 2nd edn (Florence, 1968), p. 5.

30. Cf. R. Montano, 'I modi della narrazione in Dante', *CV*, XXVI (1958), 546. Erich Auerbach's concept of 'sermo umilis' is important here and throughout (see *Literary Latin and its Public* (English translation, London, 1965), pp. 25–66, and in relation to Dante, 'Lo stile di Dante', in *Maestro Dante*, ed. V. Vettori (Milan, 1962), pp. 140–51). See also E. Gilson, 'Réflexions sur la situation historique de Dante', *DCV*, 7–8.

31. Cf. A. Guzzo, 'Il *Paradiso* e la critica del De Sanctis', *Rivista d'Italia* (November, 1924), 463, where also Dante's consistent self-possession is taken to be an Italian trait.

32. One of several objections is well defined by M. W. Bloomfield when he writes that the religious symbolism of mediaeval literature is usually underlined by the 'normal meaning of the words', 'Symbolism in Mediaeval Literature', *MP*, LVI (1958), 80.

33. Cf. A. Cairola, 'Il pensiero estetico cristiano nel medioevo e il linguaggio romantico di Dante', in *L'umanesimo in Dante*, ed. G. Tarugi (Florence, 1967), pp. 103–17, J. Pépin, 'Allegoria', *ED*, I, 154; Y. Batard, *Dante, Minerve et Apollon* (Paris, 1952), pp. 72–5. One need not doubt that there was a platonic strain in Dante's spirituality. It does not, however, follow that his style would itself reflect this. Even Plato 'never supposed that absolute beauty and good were capable of being embodied in words' (B. Jowett, *The Dialogues* (Oxford, 1871), vol. I, p. 258).

34. *Structure and Thought in the Paradiso* (Ithaca, N.Y., 1958), pp. 129–30.

35. A stronger argument for the influence of Dionysius is offered by A. Pertusi, 'Cultura greco-bizantina nel tardo medioevo nelle Venezie e suoi echi in Dante', *DCV*, esp. 182–95.

36. For the prevailing importance in Mediaeval aesthetics of clarity and communicative force, see A. K. Coomaraswamy, 'Mediaeval Aesthetic: St. Thomas Aquinas on Dionysius', *AB*, XX (1938), esp. 72–3.

37. For Solomon as the type of the Emperor, taking his authority direct from God, see G. Toffanin on this canto, *LDS*, 449–74.

38. W. Wetherbee notes in twelfth-century Platonism a lack of concern 'with the temporal orientation of the soul in relation to the Last Things' (*Platonism and Poetry in the Twelfth Century* (Princeton, 1972), p. 18).

39. Though, significantly, Mazzeo does not seem to allow this. See his *Mediaeval Cultural Tradition in Dante's Comedy* (Ithaca, N.Y., 1960), p. 113.

40. Bruno Nardi, defining Dante's attitude to the pseudo-Dionysius, emphasises that Christianity and Dante's own thought demand that one 'mantenere intatta la personalità individuale e salvarla dal totale assorbimento e dal nirvana buddistico...', (Sì come rota ch' egualmente è mossa', *SD*, XIX (1935), 94. Cf. C. Garboli, 'Come leggere Dante', *PG* (June, 1965), 31.

41. Solomon is connected to the idea of modest speech throughout Albertano da Brescia's *De arte loquendi e tacendi* (in *Volgarizzamenti del Due e Trecento*, ed. C. Segre (Turin, 1964). Cf. E. R. Curtius on Wisdom IX, *European Literature and the Latin Middle Ages*, English translation (Princeton, 1967), p. 84. For 'sermo umilis' in relation to *Par.* XIV, see E. Bonora, 'Struttura e linguaggio nel *Paradiso* XIV', *GSLI*, CXLVI (1969), 1–17.

42. Somewhat similarly, A. Guzzo, *Studi di arte religiosa* (Turin, 1932), pp. 90–4.

43. A. K. Coomaraswamy, on this and a number of other examples from Dante, emphasises that imagination here is 'deliberately exercised. The vaguer implications of inspiration, enthusiasm, intoxication are lacking' (*The Transformation of Nature in Art* (Dover Books, N.Y., 1956), pp. 175–6).

44. Especially relevant here is Dante's own *Quaestio de aqua et terra, cap.* XX–XXII.

45. '*Ludus*' is suggested by Dante's own use of the word at *Par.* XXVIII 126.

46. I tend to agree with Gilson ('La "Mirabile visione" di Dante', *Il Veltro*, IX (1965), 543–56), at least that the *Paradiso* is a fulfilment of Dante's promise at the end of the *Vita Nuova.*

CHAPTER TWO
Dante's conception of poetic discipline

1. On the didactic cast of medieval rhetoric, see P. Dronke, 'Medieval Rhetoric', contained in *The Medieval World*, vol. II in the series edited by D. Daiches and A. K. Thorlby, *Literature and Western Civilisation* (London, 1973); R. McKeon, 'Rhetoric in the Middle Ages', *Speculum*, XVII (1942), 1–32; A. Viscardi, 'Idee estetiche e letteratura militante nel Medioevo', *Momenti e problemi di storia dell'estetica*, vol. coll. (Milan, 1959), 231–53. However, the most interesting study remains A. Marigo's 'Cultura letteraria e preumanistica nelle maggiori enciclopedie del Dugento', in *GSLI*, LXVIII (1916), 1–42; 289–326. Marigo recognises in the connection between rhetoric and philosophy a 'sincerità spirituale', but is finally unwilling to allow an artistic value to this. For scholastic notions as opposed to (and recommended in place of) modern notions of intellectual poetry, see J. V. Cunningham, 'Logic and Lyric', *MP*, LI (1953–4), 33–41.

2. See also A. C. Charity, *Events and their Afterlife* (Cambridge, 1966), p. 212.

3. Cf. the use which Mengaldo makes of the *Purg.* in his edition of *D.V.E.*, pp. LXXXII–XCI.

4. See G. Francescato on this argument, 'Teoria e realità linguistica', *MD*, 132.

5. Resemblances will be apparent between this argument and A. Pézard's in his great *Dante sous la pluie de feu* (Paris, 1950). My objection is that Pézard points to an enthusiastic and prophetic role for the vernacular which accords ill with Dante's emphasis upon linguistic discipline. See also Pézard's 'Le *Convivio*, sa lettre, son esprit', *Annales de l'université de Lyon*, 3rd series, fasc. IX (Paris, 1940).

6. Cf. Foster and Boyde on Dante's own account of liberality in 'Doglia mi reca', *Dante's Lyric Poetry*, vol. II, p. 296. If justice is a way to the security of the individual (Gilson, *Dante and Philosophy*, p. 178), then, certainly, Dante's own security in exile depended upon the liberality of his patron.

7. The importance of 'martyrdom' in Dante's ethic, both religious and civic, is traced by Di Capua to Dante's experience of exile ('La concezione mistica dell' impero romana', in *Scritti minori* (Rome, 1959), vol. II, esp. pp. 356 and 361).

8. Dante argues in the Epistle to Kan Grande (2–4) that the *Paradiso*, too,

is to be taken as a gift, as though this work were Dante's proper return for liberal patronage.

9. V. Santangelo writes: 'L'attegiamento dell'autosufficienza etica del poeta derivava a Dante da Orazio... Non si può ignorare che Orazio sia il poeta che in molti passi ha affermato che gli basta quel canta senza avere la pretesa di inseguire chimere irragiungibili...' (*Il significato dell'umano nella poetica dantesca* (Palermo, 1968), p. 19; see also p. 79). Cf. A. Schiaffini, '"Poesis" e "Poeta" in Dante', *SPHLS*, esp. p. 85.

10. Cf. Mengaldo, edn, p. XLVII.

11. *Aeneid*, VI 126 *et seq*. In the happier circumstances of the Christian era, Beatrice in the Earthly Paradise may surely be regarded as Dante's own 'Sybil'.

12. M. Fubini descries among the 'geese' the hapless Guittone, *Metrica e poesia*, p. 139, just as S. Santangelo sees Guittone among the venal philosophers of *Con*. III ii 10 ('"Sole nuovo" e "sole usato"', in *Saggi danteschi* (Padua, 1959), p. 111). E. Fenzi, in 'Le Rime per la donna Pietra', *MSD*, pp. 241–5, suggests how Dante, through his devotion to Latin, hoped to assert his position as a poetic leader.

13. Thus on this passage N. Mineo, *Profetismo e apocalittico in Dante* (Catania, 1968), esp. pp. 305 *et seq*.

14. Marigo in his commentary (3rd edn, 1968) notes that the 'strenuitas' which Dante requires at *D.V.E.* II iv 10 is 'espressione guerriera e fa balenare l'idea che anche la poesia è animosa milizia' (p. 195).

15. See M. Casella, 'Le guide di Dante', *AMAT*, I (1947), esp. 24.

16. Images connected with childhood and the renovation of nature pervade the *Purgatorio* from Canto XV onwards, as if at the centre of the poem, Dante recalled the central position in history of Vergil's eclogue. For instance, at XV 3 we find the sphere which plays 'a guisa di fanciullo'; at XVI 85–90 Marco's great child-image; at XX 21 and XXI 96, images of childbirth and nursing. The series culminates in Statius' account of Purgatorial geography (XXI 43 *et seq*. and his discussion of human reproduction in XXV).

17. Schiaffini makes Forese the type of the comic poet (*Momenti di storia della lingua italiana* (Rome, 1953), p. 48). Remembering that Vergil, the great prophet is designated at *Purg*. XXII 57 'canto de' bucolici carmi', it may be that Dante is here extending a 'tragic' standing to all honest poets. On the fluidity of the concepts 'tragic' and 'comic' in these sequences, see E. Paratore, *Tradizione e struttura*, pp. 131–2.

18. Thus at the entry to Purgatory-proper, the Eagle and the Lady are identified when Dante dreams of being lifted by an Eagle and is in fact lifted by Lucia (*Purg*. IX, 19–57). See also C. S. Singleton, 'Virgo or Justice', chapter XI of *Journey to Beatrice* (Cambridge, Mass., 1958).

19. Throughout see J. Wettstein, '*Mezura': l'idéal des troubadours, son essence et ses aspects*' (Zurich, 1945), esp. p. 39.

20. See Wettstein, p. 89.

21. See Gilson, *Dante and Philosophy*, p. 176.

22. See Wettstein, p. 32.

23. It is significant that Dante's vividly personal response to Forese comes only when he hears his *voice*. *Purg*. XXIII 43–5.

24. See U. Bosco, 'Il nuovo stile della poesia dugentesca' in *Medioevo e*

Rinascimento: studi in onore di Bruno Nardi (Florence, 1955), pp. 79–101. For the connection with 'Sumite materiam...', see L. Cocito, 'I problemi di una terzina dantesca (*Purg.* XXIV VV 49–51)', *MSD*, esp. 173–4.

25. Thus in the *Vita Nuova*, XIX 3, Dante conceives spontaneously the line 'Donne ch'avete intelletto d'amor', but puts it away for meditation until he begins to write the subsequent poem.

26. Cf. E. Sanguinetti, drawing attention to *Vita Nuova* XIX, *Il realismo di Dante* (Florence, 1966), pp. 87–9. Also, in general, G. Bonfante, 'Fémmina e Donna', *SPHLS*, pp. 77–109.

27. Bonagiunta recognises that the Guittonians were bound by a 'knot' (*Purg.* XXIV 55–6).

28. Bonagiunta in fact complains of a certain scholastic difficulty in the new style in his sonnet to Guinizelli. See G. Contini, *Letteratura Italiana delle origini* (Florence, 1970), p. 89.

29. Cf. G. Tarozzi, who seeks to assimilate the admiration one feels for a philosophical or moral achievement to aesthetic admiration (*Note di estetica sul 'Paradiso' di Dante* (Florence, 1921), pp. XII–XIV).

30. Thus Foster and Boyde, on 'Amor che ne la mente mi ragiona', lines 51–3, conclude that, for Dante, 'philosophy, simply by being itself... can function as a visible miracle' (*Dante's Lyric Poems*, p. 180). Similarly, in *Monarchia* II 4, Dante takes the institution of the Roman Empire to be a miracle, an occasion for religious amazement.

31. See A. Marigo, ed. and comm. of the *D.V.E.* esp. pp. LVI–CIII, and Mengaldo, ed. and intro. pp. LXIV–LXXVII. Also I. Baldelli, 'Sulla teoria linguistica di Dante', *CSD*, 705–13. The main opposition to this view is offered by G. Vinay, 'Ricerche sul *De Vulgari Eloquentia*, *GSLI*, CXXXVI (1959), esp. 258–71, and 'La teoria linguistica del *De Vulgari Eloquentia*', *CS*, II (1962), 30–42.

32. The theory of the Volgare Illustre, as is widely recognised, is all but inseparable from Dante's political ideals. Thus, for example, the poet's very insistence upon the value of the Sicilian example probably derives from his admiration for the political culture of Frederick II; see B. Panvini, 'L'esperienza dei Siciliani e il volgare illustre di Dante', *DMC*, 236–8, quoting *D.V.E.* I xii 4, and I xii 6. Cf. R. Weiss, 'Links between the *Convivio* and the *De Vulgari Eloquentia*, *MLR*, XXXVII (1942), 159.

33. That one purpose at least of the *Convivio* is to serve as a justification of its author's reputation is shown by Dante's argument in the second chapter of the first book, where he associates himself with Boethius who proved his own worth in the *Consolatio* and St Augustine, who did so by his Confessions. In the *Convivio*, too, it appears that the 'gift' of the vernacular is intended primarily to stimulate good will and philosophical friendship between author and reader (*Con.* I viii 12–13). Indeed in its power to arouse benevolence, the vernacular resembles God himself (*ibid.* 3) – a comparison to which Dante returns at *D.V.E.* I xvi 5. And finally this benevolence in the vernacular may be as important as the information which it conveys. For Dante emphasises that what he has to tell represents no more than the crumbs which fall from the 'beata mensa' (*ibid.* I i 10), while even the utility of the vernacular is shown as an aspect of its liberality (*ibid.* I viii 3).

34. Somewhat similarly, G. Paparelli, *Questioni dantesche*, pp. 48–9.

35. Cf. Mengaldo, ed. p. XLV. Even the vernacular of the *Convivio* is chosen for the benefit not of all Italians, but for 'i principi, i nobili . . . che non hanno tempo e modo di attingere la più alta cultura in latino' (G. Bárberi Squarotti, 'Le poetiche del trecento in Italia', *MPSE*, p. 267).

36. For 'magnalia', Marigo cites Exodus 14. 13, and Acts 2. 11. But, for the connection with foregoing chapter, see *Sirach*, 17 (a work which Dante may have thought by 'Solomon'); this begins 'Deus creavit de terra hominem', and at verse 7 *et seq.* ('posuit oculum ipsorum super corda illorem/ ostendere illis magnalia operum suorum'), 'magnalia' is thrice repeated in connection with man's recognition of his creator.

37. G. Faggin notes the importance of this for the poetic word ('La parola poetica nel *Paradiso*', *Il Veltro*, IX (1965), 649–61), though he interprets the significance of it for the *Paradiso* very differently.

38. In general the rise of the vernacular was not unconnected with the dissemination of millenarian ideals, see A. Monteverdi, 'Lingue volgari e impulsi religiosi', *CNL*, VI–VII (1946–7), 7–21. On the notion that the vernacular is especially favoured, in God's eyes, because it is natural (and naturally humble), see Mengaldo, ed., p. LI.

39. *Cinque saggi su Dante* (Bologna, 1972), pp. 27–31.

40. Vinay places the fourth book of the *Con.* after the writing of the *D.V.E.*, and, observing changes in Dante's political position, argues that from that point Latin was the language he would have chosen ideologically ('Ricerche sul *De Vulgari Eloquentia*' 255–8). Grayson disputes any so exclusive emphasis upon Latin (*Cinque saggi*, pp. 1–31), which is clearly necessary if one is to attribute an ideological significance to the Volgare Illustre.

41. For Sordello as the author of the political 'Lament for Blacatz', see C. Hardie, 'Cacciaguida's Prophecy in Paradiso, 17', *Traditio*, XIX (1963), 283. For the significance of the embrace, see A. Roncaglia 'Il Canto VI del *Purgatorio*', *RLI* (1956), 409–26.

42. At *D.V.E.* I XV 2, Sordello is praised for his willingness to depart from his native tongue, presumably towards a more 'central' and generally grammatical language. On the other hand, Vergil is himself sometimes seen, as a vernacular 'tragedian' might be, in the perspective of his native place, notably in his discussion of Mantuan history in *Inf.* XX, and at *Purg.* XVIII, 82–4, where Dante speaks of Vergil's village, Pietola.

43. The ideal co-existence in Dante's thought of Imperial control and the integrity of the city state is forcefully discussed by Giovanni Gentile in 'La profezia di Dante', *NA*, CXCV (May–June, 1918). See also Gentile's *lectura* on Purg. VI now in *LD*, 789–805. Grayson notes that Vinay suppresses an important emphasis on 'patria' in interpreting the political position of *Con.* IV XXVII 4 (*Cinque saggi*, p. 27). Without this, the importance of 'individuality' would again be obscured.

44. Cf. E. Fenzi, 'Le rime per la donna Pietra', *MSD*, esp. p. 247 *et seq.* Of Arnaut's 'S IM FOS AMORS . . .' (quoted *D.V.E.* II xiii 2), E. Melli writes: Sembra che l'amore gli debba alla fine toccare come per un atto di giustizia ('Dante e Arnaut Daniel', *FR*, VI (1959), 435).

45. S. Pasquazi, '*Purgatorio*, Canto VI', *LDS*, 212, suggests that in the

'crisi politico-religiosa del suo tempo', Dante saw 'qualcosa che faceva pensare a un rinnovarsi particolarmente accentuato della passione di Cristo'. For the city of Florence as a 'woman', see D. Weinstein, 'The Myth of Florence', *Florentine Studies*, ed. N. Rubinstein (London, 1968), pp. 15–44.

46. This interpretation may be disputed, but see Mengaldo, ed., note to p. LXX and p. XLVIII.

47. See Lo Cascio, 'Le nozioni e di nobilità dai Siciliani a Dante', *Atti del Convegno di Studi su Dante e la Magna Curia* (Palermo, 1967), p. 113, who quoting the passage I give here, writes: 'Dante ci ha dato una precisa definizione del termine "cortesia" in quella del corrispondente latino "curialitas"'.

48. In general for the great restoration that the new vernacular will bring after the Fall of Babel, see M. Pazzaglia, *Il verso e l'arte della canzonenel 'De Vulgari Eloquentia'* (Florence, 1967), esp. pp. 99 and 133.

49. E. De Bruyne notes in *The Esthetics of the Middle Ages* (English translation, New York, 1969), p. 205, that the whole *Commedia* is concerned with the *magnalia* and may therefore be thought of as written in the highest style. More accurately, I think, one may see the *Paradiso* as displaying in a supreme sense the magnalia. Cf. E. Paratore, *Tradizione e struttura*, pp. 107–8, and 135.

50. John Holloway has developed an argument similar to mine in *The Victorian Sage* (London, 1953) where, for example, at p. 166, he writes of how in Newman's literary procedure 'The picture ... which Newman shows us of himself seems also to depict an example of what follows from his system'.

51. Cf. H. Gmelin, 'I latinismi del *Paradiso*' (Italian translation contained in *Critica dantesca*, ed. Bárberi Squarotti and Jacomuzzi, esp. pp. 425–8).

52. See W. Binni, 'Il canto XV del *Paradiso*', *CSD*, 620–1. Vergil's lines read:

> tuque prior, tu parce, genus qui ducis Olympo,
> proice tela manu, sanguis meus ...,

St Paul's read:

> 14. et ipsorum obsecratione pro vobis
> desiderantium vos propter eminentem gratiam
> Dei in vobis
>
> 15. gratias Deo super inennarabili dono eius.

53. G. Favati emphasises that Sordello, too, 'sa dire senza ambagi' ('Sordello', *CSD*, 556).

54. See R. Mercuri, 'Conosco i segni de l'antica fiamma', *CNL*, XXXI (1971), 238–93. Also S. Medcalf, 'Vergil's *Aeneid*', in *Literature and Western Civilisation*, ed. Daiches and Thorlby, vol. I, p. 323. On the Earthly Paradise, C. S. Singleton's *Journey to Beatrice*, is indispensable. A. Vallone offers a satisfying account of both Vergil and Beatrice in this sequence. But the most important interpretation remains M. Barbi's in 'Razionalismo e misticismo in Dante', *SD*, XVII (1933), 6–44, and XXI (1937), 5–91.

55. Cf. A. Thorlby, 'The Individual in the Mediaeval World: Dante's *Divina Commedia*', in *Literature and Western Civilisation*, ed. Daiches and Thorlby, vol. II, p. 638.

56. Cf. Barbi, 'Razionalismo e misticismo', part 2, pp. 38–9. With Barbi, however, one should emphasise that Dante does not finally dispense here with reason in favour of mysticism. He is as rational and as mystic as any other Christian. And the appearance of Beatrice ushers in a reign of consummate Christianity not of mysticism.

57. See also on the relation between Latin and vernacular in the final cantos of *Purgatorio*, A. Ronconi, 'Dante interprete dei poeti latini', *SD*, XLI (1964), 5–44.

58. See Paratore's 'Il canto I del *Paradiso*', *NLD*, V (1972), 270–1.

59. For the honest confession of religious guilt in the canzone 'Tre donne', see Barbi, *Problemi di critica dantesca*, 2nd series, pp. 267–76.

60. Cf. generally R. Vivier, 'Les conceptions de la poésie dans la Divine Comédie', *BARRL*, XXXIX (1951), 119, also G. R. Sarolli, *Prolegomena alla Divina Commedia* (Florence, 1971), pp. 284–5.

CHAPTER THREE
The stable phrase

1. Vinay, 'Ricerche sul *De Vulgari Eloquentia*' 260–1, notes that Dante is ambiguous as to whether the Volgare Illustre is a 'language' or a 'style'. R. Montano decides that it must be a style (*Lo spirito e le lettere* (Milan, 1970), vol. I, p. 140), while A. Ewert from a study of Dante's terminology, argues the contrary ('Dante's Theory of Language', *MLR*, XXXV (1940), esp. 360–1). However, from arguments offered by Di Capua and Pagliaro, it would be possible to show that the Volgare Illustre, though artistically created and thence a style, is still intended as a guide in the day-to-day management of linguistic conventions (Di Capua, 'Insegnamenti retorici medievali e dottrine estetiche moderne nel *De Vulgari Eloquentia*', *Scritti Minori*, vol. II esp. pp. 260–1, and Pagliaro, 'I "primissima signa" nella dottrina linguistica di Dante', in *Nuovi saggi di critica semantica* (Florence, 1956), esp. pp. 32–6).

2. *D.V.E.* I ix 2–3.

3. For the consistency of Dante's thought here, see U. Palmieri, 'Appunti di linguistica dantesca', *SD*, XLI (1964), 45–53.

4. Cf. C. Guerrieri-Crocetti, 'Divagazioni sul *De Vulgari Eloquentia*', and 'La razionalità del linguaggio secondo S. Tommaso e Dante'.

5. Cf. Marigo, comm, p. 19, on the conclusion of *D.V.E.* I iii.

6. Cf. Pézard, 'Les trois langues de Cacciaguida), 228: Les hommes ont besoin du latin pour prendre conscience de ce qu'est une langue achevée.

7. See Marigo, comm, p. 189, on *D.V.E.* II iv 3. The reading of *D.V.E.* I x 2 ('secundo quia magis videntur initi gramatice que comunis est . . .'), which Grayson defends (*Cinque saggi*, p. 14), and Mengaldo accepts (*ed.* p. LXIII), also emphasises the effort which individuals must make in their relations with Latin. See, too, on Dante's challenging of the Latin model, A. Ronconi, 'Dante interprete', 5–44, and G. Bárberi Squarroti, 'La retorica dell' etternità' in *L'artificio dell' etternità*' (Verona, 1972).

8. 'Insegnamenti retorica', p. 89. H. Frenzel disputes the simplifying influence of Latin in 'Latinità di Dante', CV, XXII (1954), 16–30. When Dante, however, can write: 'In homine sentiri humanius credimus quam sentire' (*D.V.E.* I v 1), one cannot doubt at least generally his desire to be effective in communication.

9. Di Capua notes a certain fluidity between the notion of discretion in a religious and moral sense, and in its rhetorical application – which in view of my argument in Chapter One is, I think, important. ('Insegnamenti retorica', p. 297). But finally Di Capua is too ready to make 'discretion' a matter only of instinctive good taste. Pazzaglia rightly insists upon its rationality (*Il verso e l'arte*, p. 110). Cf. Pagliaro, commenting on *D.V.E.* I iii 2 ('I "primissima signa" ', p. 224).

10. Neither Pazzaglia nor Pagliaro seem fully to have appreciated the originality of Dante's position in respect of critical theory. The first points us towards the formalist notion of order as found in Jakobson and Valesio's '*Vocabulorum constructio*' (see *Il verso e l'arte*, p. 189), the latter maintains a position not unlike Cassirer's (see esp. *Ulisse* (Milan–Florence, 1967), vol. II, pp. 585–697, and *La parola e l'immagine* (Naples, 1957). For a more vital response to the Volgare Illustre, in its present significance, see R. Fitzgerald, 'The Style that does Honor', *KR*, XIV (1952), 278–85.

11. Cf., esp. for an emphasis upon Dante's attention to syntax, F. Tateo, 'Compositio', *ED*, II, p. 128, and A. Schiaffini, 'Divagazioni e testimonianze sulla retorica nella lingua e letteratura italiana', *ACISR*, vol. II 405 *et seq.*

12. For a full analysis of the rhetorical structure in Dante's own terms, see A. Schiaffini, *Lettura del "De Vulgari Eloquentia" di Dante* (Rome, 1959), pp. 329–32, and Di Capua, 'Insegnamenti retorici', p. 337.

13. 'La prosa del Duecento', *Lingua, stile e societa*, p. 13.

14. F. Groppi, *Dante traduttore* (Rome, 1962), p. 182, cf. Segre, 'I volgarizzamenti del Due e Trecento', *Lingua, stile e societa*, p. 65.

15. In *Realismo dantesco* (Milan–Naples, 1961), esp. 114 *et seq.* See also A. Ronconi, 'Per una semantica dei virgilianismi', *Interpretazioni grammaticali* (Padua, 1958), pp. 81–91.

16. See also A. Vallone, *La prosa del Convivio*, esp. pp. 50–70.

17. At *Par.* XI 52–7 and XII 79–81, Dante handles the etymologies of Ascesi, Felice and Giovanna in a comparable way.

18. On this (and throughout), see C. Muscetta's excellent reading of Canto Eight, *LDS*, pp. 255–92, and also E. Esposito's reading of Canto Nine in *Letture del 'Paradiso'*, ed. V. Vettori (Milan, 1970), pp. 141–66.

19. On this, and on the themes of Canto Eight, see V. Cioffari, 'Interpretazione del Canto VIII del *Paradiso*', *LA*, XIII (1972), 3–17.

20. For a strongly imaginative reading, however, see A. Chiavacci-Leonardi, *Lettura del Paradiso dantesco*, pp. 217–18.

21. Cf. S. Accardo, 'Il Canto VIII del *Paradiso*', *NLD*, VI, pp. 35–6.

22. On Dante's understanding of the Venus myth, see A. Pézard 'Charles Martel au Ciel de Vénus', *Letture del Paradiso*, esp. pp. 71–82.

23. Cf. Esposito's *lectura*, p. 150, also P. Boyde, *Dante's Style in his Lyric Poetry* (Cambridge, 1971), p. 112.

24. Other of the periphrases serve a similar biographical purpose. The verse which introduces Dido (IX 97–9) establishes not only her parentage, but the salient features of her tragedy. Likewise, the periphrasis for Daedalus (VIII 125–6) defines his dominant skill and, again, his peculiar tragedy. Lastly 'facella', for Ezzelino (IX 29), is a reference both to his character and the legend of his birth. 'Facella' at first appears expressive in force. But Dante is using it as a conventional, almost emblematic, designation. And from this arises its stability (Cf. A. Vallone, 'Il Canto IX del *Paradiso*', *NLD*, VI, pp. 53–4).

25. Notably similar, in this respect, is the description of Saint Dominic's birthplace, *Par.* XII 46–54.

26. Cf. E. Raimondi, *Metafora e storia* (Turin, 1970), p. 90.

27. Porcelli, comparing Statius' discourse in *Purg.* XXV with the doctrinal passages of the *Paradiso*, speaks in the former case of 'il motivo dell'alto stupore di Dante per la difficoltà della materia e la complessità del ragionamento e il conseguente profondo senso d'orgoglio'. This, he maintains, is very different from the arduously intellectual concentration of the *Paradiso* (*Studi sulla 'Divina Commedia'* (Bologna, 1970), p. 118).

28. Cf. Muscetta's *lectura*, p. 290.

29. Somewhat similarly, Vallone's *lectura*, p. 62.

30. Giacalone, however, noting the recurrence of the subjunctive in Carlo's speech makes it expressive of a mood 'metastorico, trascendente, superumano ...' (commentary, vol. III, p. 138).

CHAPTER FOUR
Independence and the reader of the Paradiso

1. See, for instance, E. Auerbach, *Literary Language*, pp. 297–303; Y. Batard, *Dante, Minerve et Apollon*, esp. pp. 53–4; U. Bosco, 'The Proem to the *Paradiso*', *FMLS*, I (1965), 147–58; G. R. Sarolli, *Prolegomena alla 'Divina Commedia'*, pp. IX–X; L. Spitzer, 'The Addresses to the Reader in the "Commedia"', *IT*, XII (1935), 143–65; B. Terracini, *Analisi stilistica*, p. 47; also G. Toffanin, *Ultimi saggi* (Bologna, 1960), pp. 41–9.

2. 'Il Canto II del *Paradiso*', *LDS*, pp. 40–5.

3. Battaglia, in his stimulating discussion of troubadour poetry (*La coscienza letteraria del Medioevo* (Naples, 1965), pp. 171–214) raises a number of points which at first appear relevant to Curtius' view, especially in the connection he makes between an aristocratic individualism and a 'poesia "velata" e "strana"' (pp. 211–14). Here, however, as elsewhere, Dante's aristocratic tendencies are an aspect of his humble perseverance in philosophy (cf. Bosco, 'The Proem', 149, and L. Olschki, *Dante, Poeta Veltro* (Rome, 1953), pp. 25 *et seq.*). To argue, similarly, that poet and reader together 'sono chiamati a una decifrazione squisita ma vitale al tempo stesso' (A. Mazza, 'La *Commedia* e alcuni aspetti della poetica del Boccaccio', *AISD* (1967), 444; cf. Sarolli, *Prolegomena*, pp. IX–X, and XVIII and A. Ciotti, 'Il concetto della "figura" e la poetica della visione', *CV*, XXX (1962), 404–5), is to speak in terms appropriate less to Dante's intellectual austerity than to modes which, as Wind shows, characterise the Renaissance (*Pagan Mysteries in the Renaissance*

(Penguin edn 1967)). Something, however, of a mystic test is, perhaps, to be found in, say, *Inf.* IX 61, or *Purg.* VIII 19.

4. For a comparison of this passage with *Par.* II emphasising the humility and exemplary nature of Dante's approach, see G. B. Parma, *Ascesi e mistica cattolica nella 'Divina Commedia'* (Subiaco, 1927), vol. II, pp. 13–14, 308–9.

5. Cf. *Convivio* III 22, where an admiration for the intricacies of astronomy and geodesy distinguishes the philosopher from those whose eyes are fixed 'in the mire of their own foolishness'.

6. Spitzer suggests a similar modification of Auerbach's view in 'The Addresses to the Reader'. He points, too, to the 'roguish' tone of the address at *Par.* V 109 *et seq.*, 'Pensa, lettor...' (151–2). This does at first seem like a 'stimulus'. But then its roguishness or, as I prefer, its urbanity, finally invites one to the sharing of an intellectual 'game'.

7. See A. Momigliano's excellent note (commentary (Florence, 1950), p. 529), and P. R. Olson, 'Theme and Structure in the Exordium of the *Paradiso*', *IT*, XXXIX (1962), 89–104, who, acknowledging a debt to formalism, argues that here there is a 'phonological manifestation of the monistic pathos' (*ibid.* 98).

8. See C. F. Goffis, 'Il canto I del *Paradiso*, *LDS*, p. 11.

9. Notably *Purg.* II 1–9; IX 1–6, and XV 1–6.

10. This is forcefully illustrated in Ungaretti's reading of *Inferno* I (*LD*, pp. 5–23).

11. For the relation, in Dante, between metaphor and mythic or primitive apprehension, see G. Marzot, *Il linguaggio biblico nella 'Divina Commedia'* (Pisa, 1956), esp. *cap.* V, and E. Raimondi, *Metafora e storia* (Turin, 1970).

12. For these, see Giacalone, commentary, vol. III, p. 3.

13. Cf. Goffis, 'Il canto I del *Paradiso*', p. 7.

14. Cf. Croce on the Earthly Paradise, *La Poesia di Dante*, pp. 128–33.

15. There are useful distinctions between the characterisation in each canticle in T. H. Greene's 'Dramas of Self-hood in the *Comedy*' (*From Time to Eternity*, ed. T. G. Bergin (New Haven and London, 1967), pp. 103–36).

16. Cf. R. Montano, 'Erich Auerbach e la scoperta del realismo in Dante e in Boccaccio', *CV*, XXVI (1958), 22.

17. Cf. against Getto's 'mysticising' tendencies, F. Piemontese, 'Dante e la poetica della visione', *HMN*, VII (1952), p. 1046.

18. This not to ask for the poetic assent of which Eliot speaks (*Dante*, p. 36; see also W. J. Rooney, *The Problem of 'Poetry and Belief'*) but for a directly personal assent. Such assent is easier where an affirmation concerns morality rather than fact. But supposing that a speaker is mistaken as to fact, it is still more 'courageous' to disagree than to assume an imaginative interest. Note the very respectful way in which Dante deals with the deluded Plato at *Par.* IV 52–7.

19. On the lack, too, of scenic context, see B. Porcelli, *Studi sulla 'Divina Commedia'*, pp. 111 *et seq.*

20. Cf. *Par.* V 16: 'Sì cominciò Beatrice questo canto...'

21. Only in the Earthly Paradise is the presentation of Beatrice imaginative enough to generate such transcendent meanings as Auerbach and Singleton suggest (*Studi su Dante* (Bologna, 1971), pp. 243–9, and *Journey to Beatrice*,

passim). At most she might 'represent' a being in the knowledge of whose existence the poet has been inspired to organise his life, thought and style. Cf. A. Jacomuzzi, *L' imago al cerchio*, p. 151.

22. For an 'organicist' view of the canto, see C. Galimberti, *LDS* (1968), pp. 219–47.

23. Cf. for the 'forza organica del periodo, il rigore della sintassi', A. Vallone 'Proposte di lettura: il Canto VII del *Paradiso*', *LA*, XII (1971), p. 68.

24. Cf. M. Sansone, 'Il Canto VII del *Paradiso*', *NLD*, p. 23, 'L'atto dell' insegnare è in realtà qui oltre passata nella celebrazione del suo contenuto'.

25. Dante's argument, after all, is firmly founded upon Patristic and Scholastic authority, see C. Galimberti's *Lectura*, 223.

CHAPTER FIVE
Word and image in the Paradiso

1. See by Malagoli; 'Il linguaggio del *Paradiso* e la crisi dello spirito cristiano medievale', *LA*, VII (1966), 40–52; *Linguaggio e poesia nella 'Divina Commedia'* (Genoa, 1949); *Lo stile del Duecento* (1956); 'Lo stile della *Commedia* e lo stile dei Siciliani', *DMC*, 185–91; *Saggio sulla Divina Commedia* (Florence, 1962). On Malagoli, see L. Blasucci, *Studi su Dante e Ariosto*, n. pp. 9–10; L. Martinelli, *Dante*, p. 241; A. Vallone, *La critica dantesca*, pp. 67–72; V. Vettori, *Maestro Dante*, pp. 264–5.

2. Cf. Terracini's comment upon rhythm, *Analisi stilistica*, p. 36, and Getto on Dante's 'credo', discussed in Chapter Four.

3. Cf. A. Scaglione, 'Periodic Syntax', 3 *et seq*. Scaglione's own view, however, would have one see the syntax itself as expressive.

4. Cf. Sordello's criticism of the kings in *Purg*. VII, Dante's own 'coronation' in *Purg*. XXVII, and the prevailing connection in Dante between poverty and nobility.

5. The management of the gerund is a particularly important matter since its abuse can lead to the weakening of syntactical subordination and the primacy of the isolated phrase. See C. Segre, 'La sintassi' in *Lingua, stile e societa*, pp. 122–3, and for Dante's skill with it, *ibid.* pp. 240–1. M. Corti tends, with Malagoli, to see an imaginative force in the gerund, see 'Studi sulla sintassi della lingua poetica avanti lo stil novo', *AMAT*, IV (1953) esp. 341–65.

6. Cf. even more emphatically, Marzot, *Il linguaggio biblico nella 'Divina Commedia'*, p. 21.

7. The fate of the Eagle is traced to its appearance in the strife between the Guelfs and the Ghibellines. And in Dante's own analogue, Romeo, one sees how the destinies of the Empire weigh on the individual. Cf. S. Mariotti, 'Il canto VI del *Paradiso*', *NLD*, V, esp. p. 404.

8. The concept of differentiation is of the highest importance in Dante's view of beatitude. Thus in Canto Four lines 34–6, one hears that the blessed souls:

> tutti fanno bello il primo giro,
> e differentemente han dolce vita
> per sentir più e men l' etterno spiro.

Cf. *Par.* VI 124–6, and – in Beatrice's first discussion of the Heavenly Bodies – *Par.* II 139–40.

9. But see his analysis of 'ardendo in sé' (*Par.* VII 65), in *Saggio sulla Divina Commedia*, p. 31.

10. Cf. *Par.* V 19–20: 'Lo maggior don che Dio per sua larghezza/fesse creando...'. Somewhat similarly, *Par.* XXVI 34–5: 'più che in altra convien che si mova/la mente, amando, di ciascun che cerne...'.

11. Compare the restrained artistry in Dante's use of the gerund here with the 'conceited' use that Guittone makes of it in the lines beginning 'Agricola a nostro Signore' from *Meraviglioso beato* (pp. 227–8 in Contini, *Poeti del Duecento* (Milan–Naples, 1960), vol. I).

12. Cf. E. Sanguinetti, *Il realismo di Dante*, p. 7 *et seq.*, and R. Guardini on the importance in poetry of the 'vera e propria improprietà', *HMN*, XV (1960), 786.

13. Cf., among others, 'incielare' (*Par.* III 97), 'insemprarsi' (*Par.* X 148), 'ingradarsi' (*Par.* XXIX 130), and 'immegliarsi' (*Par.* XXX 87).

14. Cf. L. Blasucci's important 'Le "Petrose" e la "Divina Commedia"', now contained in *Studi su Dante e Ariosto*. P. Boyde in *Dante's Style in his Lyric Poetry* makes a category of the 'violence' figures (p. 132). One may note, however, the importance of rhetorical control, even in the 'Petrose', the most 'violent' of Dante's poems. See on this, A. Jacomuzzi, 'Invenzione e artificio nelle "Petrose", in *Il palinsesto della retorica*, esp. pp. 22–3. Also H. Frenzel, 'Latinità di Dante', *CV*, XXII (1954), 16–30. Note, too, that some of Dante's most violent phrases occur in the episode of Venus, the Heaven of Rhetoric.

15. H. D. Austin, in fact, speaks of lines 49–51, as a 'badly mixed metaphor', but corrects this impression by showing Dante's dependence upon Ezekiel's symbolism, ('Multiple Meanings and their Bearing on the Understanding of Dante's Metaphors', *MP*, XXX (1932), 136–9).

16. From a comparably exalted moment of the *Paradiso*, the 'oltraggio' at XXXIII 57, might appear a victory of poetic boldness over ineffability (see G. Steiner, *Language and Silence* (London, 1967), p. 60), until the presence of the Latin 'ultra' in the word is noted, when it at once becomes a more deliberate coinage, for a 'going-beyond'. Cf. the Latinate 'divelse' and 'impulse' at *Par.* XXVII 98–9. Note that the Casini/Barbi commentary (Florence, 1968), 6th edn vol. III, p. 992, deliberately denies the violence of 'divelse'.

17. Cf. Porcelli, *Studi sulla 'Divina Commedia'*, pp. 142–3.

18. Cf., on 'mungere', Blasucci, 'Le "Petrose"' in *Studi su Dante e Ariosto*, p. 20.

19. Cf. Terracini, *Lingua libera*, p. 54.

20. Cf. S. Pasquazi, *All'eterno dal tempo*, p. 281, speaking of how the great cry at *Par.* XXI, 140, restores Dante 'alle sue proporzioni umane'.

21. A more recent and more subtle account is offered by A. Pagliaro in 'Sul linguaggio poetico della *Commedia*', *Il Veltro*, IX (1965), 589–638.

22. In the essay accompanying the essay I quote, 'Imagery in the Last Eleven Cantos of Dante's "Comedy"' (*ibid.*), Lewis compares the method of his own inquiry with methods used in the study of Shakespeare. This, I think, is a mistake. For there is little evidence, in Dante, of those strange and surely unpremeditated conjunctions of image that, say, E. A. Armstrong has

found in Shakespeare's writing (*Shakespeare's Imagination: a study of the psychology of association and inspiration* (Lincoln, Nebraska, 1963)).

23. Terracini, in a similar vein, has some impressive suggestions in his essay on *Inferno* XXVII (*Analisi stilistica*, pp. 173–205).

24. Cf. *Par.* XXI 34–9. Even the great opening of *Par.* XXIII, 'Come l' augello, intra l'amate fronde...', shows a very close attention to detail. See Chapter Six below.

25. Comparable images, from other spheres of temporal life, are the 'perla in bianca fronte' (*Par.* III 13–15), the dance of philosophers (like ladies 'non da ballo sciolte', *Par.* X 79–81), the 'orologio' (*Par.* X 139–44), and the motes of dust (*Par.* XIV 112–17). Along with the arbitrariness of these comparisons there goes a most acute perception, and a profoundly humane regard for the fashions and furniture of ordinary existence. To employ these minutiae in the context of the *Paradiso* is to proclaim the dignity which Dante believes them to have in God's eyes.

26. Cf. the 'rainbow' image of *Par.* XII 10–18 (which also follows an inexpressibility motif).

CHAPTER SIX
The organisation of the canto in the Paradiso

1. At *Par.* XXIX 79–81, Dante compares the angels, who 'non hanno vedere interciso', with human beings who must 'rememorar per concetto diviso'. The sense of 'diviso' is not entirely clear (see esp. Sapegno, commentary, p. 369). Yet plainly it is related to the awareness of psychological limitation which Dante displays in the ineffability topic. Somewhat similarly, at *Par.* V 16–18, Dante emphasises that Beatrice speaks 'sì com' uom che suo parlar non spezza', which is surely to acknowledge that his own account of her speech will differ precisely in being 'broken'.

2. Something of the 'pause' is, of course, seen and frequently deplored by Crocean critics. See, for instance, M. Rossi, *Gusto filologico e gust poetico*, (Bari, 1942), esp. on the last canto, pp. 129 and 141–2.

3. The early commentators also recognise (though in the *Commedia* as a whole) the value of subdividing cantos, for clarity and didactic force. See, for example, the *Ottimo Commento* (unedited text, 1829), III, p. 7, and da Buti (ed. C. Giannini, 1862), p. 3, on *Par.* I.

4. But throughout 'Arte, linguaggio, letteratura', Fubini objects in principle to Calogero's concept of 'saltuarietà', which is a concept of some significance here.

5. Cf., at the end of the 'address to the reader', *Par.* X 27.

6. As, for the whole canto, Giacalone does (commentary, III, p. 20). See also Giacalone's comment on *Par.* XXIX, 127: 'Ma perché siam digressi assai, ritorci...', (*ibid.* p. 500). Dante acknowledges his own digression, and it is worthwhile considering it as a digression, with its own points of interest, rather than gathering it up, as Giacalone does, into a 'contrapuntal' pattern.

7. Cf. B. Cordati Martinelli, *Lettura scolastica della terza cantica* (Pisa, 1967), p. 43.

8. At times Dante himself asks precisely that one should 'return'. Thus, *Par.* XI 135: 'se ciò ch'è detto a la mente revoche'. Somewhat similarly, *Par.* XIII 46: 'e però miri a ciò ch' io dissi suso...', *Par.* IV 88–9: 'se ricolte/ l'hai comme dei...', and *ibid.* 94: 'Io t' ho per certo ne la mente messo'. With the pauses in Canto One, one may compare several in Canto Four, where the effect is clear, for instance at line 93 ('Ma or ti s' attraversa un altro passo'), line 99 (which prepares for the explanation of Costanza's fate), and at line 118, where Dante takes breath for the great 'aria', 'O amanza del primo amante, o diva'.

9. On Geryon, see G. Cambon, *Dante's Craft*, pp. 80–5.

10. On this see esp. E. Sanguinetti, *Interpretazione di Malebolge* (Florence, 1961), pp. 1–5.

11. In general on the notion of the organic in Dante's canto, see F. Fergusson, *Dante's Drama of the Mind*, pp. 42–5, also on Canto Ten, p. 53.

12. On the connection of *Par.* VI and VII, see M. Sansone, 'Il Canto VII del *Paradiso*', pp. 1 *et seq.*

13. Sinclair, applying his notion of 'relevancy', asks why these lines should contain 'two sacred tongues of history', concluding that this is suitable to Justinian's world view (commentary on the *Paradiso*, p. 113). Where the connection with Justinian is so unemphatic, I would prefer to say that it is suitable directly to Dante's own world-outlook.

14. On Guardini see G. Morra, 'Romano Guardini, interprete di Dante', *Letture classensi*, III (1970), 147–68.

15. In this connection, see A. Jacomuzzi, *Il palinsesto*, p. 163. The principal contributions, recently, to the 'psychiatric' view of Dante are to be found in *Lectura Dantis Mystica* (Florence, 1969). For a survey of psychology and criticism in Italy, see M. David, 'Critica psicanalitica della letteratura', *LTI*, XIV (1962), 450–84.

16. I refer here to the Italian translation of *Landschaft der Ewigheit* (Munich, 1958), contained with other essays in *Studi su Dante*, trans. M. L. Maraschini and A. Sacchi Balestrieri (Brescia, 1967).

17. Cf. Pagliaro on the creative spontaneity of the Rose image, 'Sul linguaggio poeticio della *Commedia*', 628–9.

18. Cf. E. Guidubaldi, 'Dalla "selva oscura" alla "candida rosa"', *Lectura Dantis Mystica*, pp. 352–72.

19. Nor is the form of a kind, like Shakespeare's, to generate a large suggestivity and resonance. Thus when G. Wilson Knight, applying methods which are extremely valuable for Shakespeare, speaks of Dante's images as 'life-forms', the interpretation at once becomes blurred and unmanageable. See his *The Christian Renaissance* (London, 1962), p. 100.

20. For Dante's devotion to the Virgin and to Beatrice as the source of both the humility and confidence that Dante holds in his own powers, see G. S. Tarugi, 'Realtà umana del *Paradiso*', in *L'umanesimo in Dante* (Florence, 1967), pp. 271–2.

21. Tommaseo has no difficulty in finding an allegorical interpretation here, even for the smallest detail of the image, e.g. 'le faville sono gli angeli che gioscono della gioia delle anime, e nel comunicare ad esse la propria, partecipano di quella' (commentary, pp. 752–3).

22. Cf. the hardly less well-measured rose of *Par.* XXII 55–7:

> così m' ha dilatata mia fidanza,
> come 'l sol fa la rosa quando aperto
> tanto divien quant' ell' ha di possanza.

23. For an account of Contini's criticism, see S. Pautasso, *Le frontiere della critica* (Milan, 1972), pp. 20–1.

24. Another feature of Contini's reading – and one which is important in his general view of Dante's poetry – is his concept of the poet's linguistic memory, which produces a system of verbal echoes 'anteriori a qualsiasi programma' (*ibid.* pp. 487 *et seq.*).

25. Cf. here and throughout, A. Frattini, *Il Canto XXVIII del Paradiso* (Turin, 1960), who acknowledges a debt, in respect of theory, to Eliot.

26. Cf. *Par.* XXVII 13–15, where Jupiter and Mars are imagined as 'birds' very oddly changing feather.

27. Malagoli (*Linguaggio e poesia nella 'Divina Commedia'*, p. 28) notes an emphasis upon 'perpetüalmente'. But again, allowing the word too great a weight, one will exchange a clearly articulated description for a density of emotion. Dante is surely too confident of eternity to dwell upon the concept of perpetuity with an affective extravagance.

28. Eliot's adaptation of the line 'Midwinter spring is its own season/ Sempiternal...' (*Little Gidding*) does use the paradox as an expressive necessity.

29. As Scaglione's title suggests, he is concerned to show that beneath the narrative movement of the canto there lies a significant pattern of recurring images. Particularly, he draws attention to repeated evocations of womanhood in its various aspects, beginning with the picture of the mother-bird 'intra l'amate fronde', and culminating in the portrayal of the Virgin Mary. See esp. 165–6, 170.

30. See, for instance, *Aeneid* VI 13 and 35, and Ovid's *Metamorphoses* II 416.

31. Sinclair notes in discussing Canto Twenty Two that Dante stands in that part of the sphere of the Fixed Stars 'which is, so to speak, native to him, the constellation of the Twins under which he was born', and this leads him to emphasise that Dante here is reaping the fruits of following 'his own star'. The end of Canto Twenty Two clearly demonstrates, in Sinclair's view, how salvation for Dante signified the consummation not the transcending of an individual's identity (comm. on the *Paradiso*, p. 329).

SELECT BIBLIOGRAPHY

Abbagnano, N. *Possibilità e libertà*, Turin, 1956.

Abrams, M. H. *The Mirror and the Lamp: Romantic Theory and the Critical Tradition*, New York, 1953.

Accardo, S. 'Il Canto VIII del *Paradiso*', *Nuove Letture Dantesche*, VI, Florence, 1973, pp. 27–44.

Apollonio, M. 'La critica dantesca', *Terzo Programma*, V (1965), 211–43.

'Simbolismo ed emblematica nel commento perenne alla *Commedia*', *Annali dell'Istituto di Studi Danteschi*, I, Milan, 1967, pp. 195–224.

Uomini e forme nella cultura italiana delle origini, 2nd edn, Florence, 1943.

Applewhite, J. 'Dante's Use of the Extended Simile in the *Inferno*', *Italica*, XLI (1964), 294–309.

Armstrong, E. A. *Shakespeare's Imagination: a study of the psychology of association and inspiration*, Lincoln, Nebraska, 1963.

Auerbach, E. *Dante: Poet of the Secular World* (trans. R. Manheim), Chicago and London, 1961.

Literary Language and its Public in Late Latin Antiquity and in the Middle Ages (trans. R. Manheim), London, 1965.

'Lo stile di Dante' (trans. E. Lazzari), contained in *Maestro Dante*, ed. V. Vettori, Milan, 1962, pp. 140–51.

Scenes from the Drama of European Literature: Six Essays (trans. by several hands), Gloucester, Mass., 1973.

Studi su Dante (trans. M. L. De Pieri Bonino and Dante della Terza, with introduction by Dante della Terza), 3rd edn, Milan, 1971.

Aurigemma, M. 'Il Canto XIII del *Paradiso*', *Nuove Letture Dantesche*, VI, Florence, 1973, pp. 129–46.

Austin, H. D. 'Multiple Meanings and their Bearing on the Understanding of Dante's Metaphors', *Modern Philology*, XXX (1932), 129–40.

Baldelli, I. 'Sulla teoria linguistica di Dante', *Cultura e Scuola*, IV (1965), Dante issue.

Banerjee, R. D. K. 'Dante through the Looking-Glass: Rosetti, Pound and Eliot', *Comparative Literature*, XXIV (1972), 136–49.

Bárberi Squarotti, G. *L'artificio dell'etternità*, Verona, 1972.

'Le poetiche del trecento in Italia', *Momenti e problemi di storia dell' estetica*, vol. coll. Milan, 1959, pp. 255–324.

ed. with A. Jacomuzzi, *Critica dantesca*, Turin, 1970.

Barbi, M. *Problemi di critica dantesca* (1st series), Florence, 1934.
Problemi di critica dantesca (2nd series), Florence, 1941.
Problemi fondamentali per un nuovo commento della 'Divina Commedia', Florence, 1955.
'Razionalismo e misticismo in Dante', *Studi danteschi*, XVII (1933), 5–44, and XXI (1937), 5–91.
Batard, Y. *Dante, Minerve et Apollon. Les images de la 'Divine Comédie'*, Paris, 1952.
'Sur quelques métaphores de Dante', *Cahiers du Sud*, XXXVIII (1951), 20–4.
Battaglia, S. *Esemplarità e antagonismo nel pensiero di Dante*, Naples, 1966.
La coscienza letteraria del Medioevo, Naples, 1965.
'Linguaggio reale e linguaggio figurato nella Divina Commedia', *Atti del Congresso Nazionale di Studi Danteschi*, Florence, 1962, 21–44.
Bergin, T. G. 'Dante's Provençal Gallery', *Speculum*, XL (1965), 15–30.
ed. *From Time to Eternity*, New Haven and London, 1967.
Bertocchi, D. (with F. Casetti) 'Per un approccio strutturalista a Dante', *Lectura Dantis Mystica*, Florence, 1969, pp. 519–30.
Bigongiari, D. 'The Art of the Canzone', *Romanic Review*, XLI (1950), 3–13; 81–95.
Binni, W. 'Il canto XV del *Paradiso*', *Cultura e Scuola*, IV (1965), Dante issue, 615–33.
Blasucci, L. *Studi su Dante e Ariosto*, Milan–Naples, 1969.
Bloomfield, M. W. 'Symbolism in Mediaeval Literature', *Modern Philology*, LVI (1958), 73–81.
Bo, C. 'Dante e la poesia italiana contemporanea', *Terzo Programma*, V (1965), 192–9.
Bonelli, G. 'La critica estetica: saggio di metodologia letteraria', *Atti e Memorie dell'Accademia Toscana di Scienze e Lettere* ('La Colombaria'), n.s. XXIII (1972), 251–87.
Bonfante, G. 'Fémmina e Donna', *Studia Philologica et Litteraria in honorem L. Spitzer*, ed. A. G. Hatcher and K. L. Selig, Berne, 1958, pp. 77–109.
Bonora, E. *Gli ipocriti di Malebolge*, Milan–Naples, 1953.
'Struttura e linguaggio nel *Paradiso* XIV', *Giornale storico della letteratura italiana*, CXLVI (1969), 1–17.
Borzi, I. 'L'umana ragione e il fine soprannaturale dell'uomo nella *Divina Commedia*', in *L' umanesimo in Dante*, ed. G. S. Tarugi, Florence, 1967, pp. 73–101.
Bosco, U. 'Il nuovo stile della poesia dugentesca secondo Dante', *Medioevo e Rinascimento: studi in onore di Bruno Nardi*, Florence, 1955, vol. I, pp. 77–101.
'The Proem to the *Paradiso*', *Forum for Modern Language Studies*, I (1965), 147–58.

Boyde, P. *Dante's Style in his Lyric Poetry*, Cambridge, 1971.
Brandeis, I. 'Metaphor in the *Divine Comedy*', *Hudson Review*, VIII (1956), 557–75 (now contained in *The Ladder of Vision*, London, 1960).
ed. *Discussions of the Divine Comedy*, Boston, 1961.
Breglia, S. *Poesia e struttura nella Divina Commedia*, Genoa, 1934.
Brown, M. E. *Neo-Idealist Aesthetics: Croce, Gentile, Collingwood*, Detroit, 1966.
Buck, A. 'Gli studi sulla poetica e sulla retorica di Dante e del suo tempo', *Atti del Congresso Internazionale di Studi Danteschi*, Florence, 1965, vol. I, pp. 249–78.
Bundy, M. W. *The Theory of Imagination in Classical and Mediaeval Thought*, Urbana, 1927.
Cairola, A. 'Il pensiero estetico cristiano nel Medio Evo e il linguaggio romanico di Dante', in *L'umanesimo in Dante* ed. G. S. Tarugi, Florence, 1967, 103–17.
Calogero, G. *Estetica, semantica, istorica* (vol. III of *Lezioni di filosofia*), Turin, 1947.
'In che senso siamo ancora idealisti?' *De Homine*, XI–XII (1965), 163–8.
with D. Petrini, *Studi crociani*, Rome, 1930.
Cambon, G. *Dante's Craft*, Minneapolis, 1969.
Capitini, A. 'Osservazioni sulla poesia del *Paradiso* dantesco', *Italica*, XXIV (1947), 206–11.
Carpi, U. 'Contributo per Montale critico', *Rassegna della letteratura italiana*, 1966, 352–76.
Casella, M. 'Le guide di Dante', *Atti e Memorie dell' Accademia Toscana di Scienze e Lettere* ('La Colombaria'), n.s. I (1947), 1–51.
review of F. Figurelli's 'Il dolce stil nuovo', *Studi danteschi*, XVIII (1934), 105–26.
'Il "Volgare Illustre" di Dante', *Il giornale della cultura italiana*, I (May, 1925), 33–40.
Cases, C. 'I limiti della critica stilistica e i problemi della critica letteraria', *Società*, XI (1955), 46–63; 266–91.
Casey, J. *The Language of Criticism*, London, 1966.
Casini, T. ed. *La Divina Commedia*, 6th edn ('rinnovata e accresciuta, a cura di S. A. Barbi'), Florence, 1967–8.
Cassirer, E. *An Essay on Man* (Bantam edn), New York, 1970.
The Philosophy of Symbolic Forms (trans. R. Manheim), New Haven and London, 1955–7, 3 vols.
Cellucci, L. 'La poetica di Dante e la sua poesia', *Cultura neolatina*, X (1950), 77–97.
Charity, A. C. *Events and their Afterlife*, Cambridge, 1966.
Chiavacci-Leonardi, A. M. *Lettura del Paradiso dantesco*, Florence, 1963.
Chmielewski, I. *Die Bedeutung der Göttlichen Komödie für die Lyrik T. S. Eliots* (Neumünster, 1969).

Cian, V. Review of Croce's *La poesia di Dante*, *Giornale storico della letteratura italiana*, LXXIX (1922), 57–85.
Cioffari, V. 'Interpretazione del Canto VIII del *Paradiso*', *L'Alighieri*, XIII (1972), 3–17.
Ciotti, A. 'Il concetto della "figura" e la poetica della visione nei commentatori trecenteschi della Commedia', *Convivium*, XXX (1962), 264–92; 399–415.
'Rocco Montano e la poesia di Dante', *Convivium*, XXX (1962), 55–62.
Cocito, L. 'I problemi di una terzina dantesca (*Purg*. XXIV, vv. 49–51)', *Miscellanea di studi danteschi*, Genoa, 1966, 167–82.
Cohen, L. J. *The Diversity of Meaning*, 2nd edn, London, 1966.
Contini, G. *Letteratura italiana delle origini*, Florence, 1970.
Varianti e altra linguistica: una raccolta di saggi (1938–1968), Turin, 1970.
Rime, Turin, 1970.
ed. *Poeti del Duecento*, Milan–Naples, 1960, 2 vols.
Coomaraswamy, A. K. 'Mediaeval Aesthetic: St. Thomas Aquinas on Dionysius', *Art Bulletin*, XX (1938), 66–77.
The Transformation of Nature in Art (Dover Books edn), New York, 1956.
Corti, M. 'Studi sulla sintassi della lingua poetica avanti lo stilnovo', *Atti e Memorie dell' Accademia Toscana di Scienze e Lettere*, ('La Colombaria'), n.s. IV (1953), 262–365.
Cordati Martinelli, B. *Lettura scolastica della terza cantica*, Pisa, 1967.
Cosmo, U. *L' ultima ascesa*, Bari, 1936.
Costanza, L. *Il linguaggio di Dante nella Divina Commedia*, Naples, 1968.
Croce, B. *Aesthetica in nuce*, contained in Croce's own anthology of his works, *Filosofia, Poesia e Storia*, Milan–Naples, 1951.
'Ancora della lettura poetica di Dante', contained in *Letture di poeti e riflessioni sulla teoria e la critica della poesia*, Bari, 1950.
Conversazioni critiche, V, Bari, 1939.
Estetica come scienza dell' espressione e linguistica generale (terza edizione riveduta), Bari, 1908.
'Frammentismo e poesia', contained in *Letture di poeti* etc., Bari, 1950.
'Il carattere di totalità della espressione artistica', contained in *Nuovi saggi di estetica*, Bari, 1920.
'La cosidetta "critica stilistica"', contained in *Letture di poeti* etc., Bari, 1950.
'La critica letteraria come filosofia', contained in *Nuovi saggi di estetica*, Bari, 1920.
'La gioia dell'insegnare e dell'apprendere', *Critica* (1949), 137–41.
La Poesia, 3rd edn, Bari, 1942.
La Poesia di Dante, 11th edn, Bari, 1966.
'L'intuizione pura e il carattere lirico dell'arte', contained in *Problemi di estetica*, Bari, 1910.

Cunningham, J. V. 'Logic and Lyric', *Modern Philology*, LI (1952), 33–41.

Curtius, E. R. *European Literature and the Latin Middle Ages* (trans. W. R. Trask), corrected reprint of 1953 edn, Princeton, 1967.

David, M. 'Critica psicanalitica della letteratura italiana dalle origini al Seicento', *Lettere italiane*, XIV (1962), 456–84.

Davie, D. *Purity of Diction in English Verse* (reissue with postscript), London, 1969.

De Bruyne, E. *The Esthetics of the Middle Ages* (abridged version, trans. E. B. Hennessy), New York, 1969.

Della Volpe, G. *Crisis dell'estetica romantica*, Rome, 1963.

Critica del gusto, Milan, 1960.

(a cura di Ignazio Ambrogio) *Schizzo di una storia del gusto*, Rome, 1971.

the entry 'Poetica' in *Enciclopedia dello spettacolo*, vol. VIII, Rome, 1961.

De Lollis, C. 'La fede di Dante nell'arte', *Nuova Antologia*, CCXII (1921), 208–17.

Del Monte, A. 'Dolce stil novo', *Filologia romanza*, III (1956), 254–64.

'"I' mi son un....", *Purg.* XXIV, 52–4', *Studi mediolatini e volgari*, VI–VII (1959), 63–6.

Di Capua, F. *Scritti minori*, Rome, 1959, 2 vols., volume two of which contains 'Insegnamenti retorici medievali e dottrine estetiche moderne nel *De Vulgari Eloquentia* di Dante'.

Di Pino, G. *Studi di lingua poetica*, Florence, 1961.

Di Salvo, T. *Lettura critica della Divina Commedia*, Florence, 1969, 3 vols.

Dragonetti, R. *Aux frontières du langage poétique* (Études sur Dante, Mallarmé, Valéry), Ghent, 1961.

Dronke, P. 'Mediaeval Rhetoric', contained in *The Mediaeval World*, vol. II in the series ed. D. Daiches and A. K. Thorlby *Literature and Western Civilization*, London, 1973.

Eco, U. 'Sviluppo dell'estetica medievale', *Momenti e problemi di storia dell' estetica*, vol. coll. Milan, 1959, pp. 115–229.

Eliot, T. S. *Dante*, London, 1929.

'Deux attitudes mystique: Dante et Donne' (translation by Jean de Menasce of an unpublished Clark lecture), *Chroniques*, III (1927), 149–73.

'Matthew Arnold', contained in *The Use of Poetry and the Use of Criticism*, London, 1933.

'Shakespeare and the Stoicism of Seneca', contained in *Selected Essays*, 3rd edn, London, 1951.

'The Music of Poetry', contained in *On Poetry and Poets*, London, 1957.

Esposito, E. *Gli studi danteschi dal 1950 al 1964*, 'con indice orientativo della critica dantesca 1950–64, di A. Vallone', Rome, 1965.

'Il Canto IX del *Paradiso*', in *Letture del 'Paradiso'*, ed. V. Vettori, Milan, 1970, 141–66.
Ewert, A. 'Dante's Theory of Language', *Modern Language Review*, xxxv (1940), 355–66.
Fabro, G. the entry 'Tommaso d'Aquino' in *Enciclopedia cattolica*, Vatican, 1947–54, vol. VIII.
Faggin, G. 'La parola poetica nel *Paradiso*', *Il Veltro*, IX (1965), 649–61.
Falconieri, J. 'Il saggio di T. S. Eliot su Dante', *Italica*, XXXIV (1957), 75–80.
Favati, G. 'Sordello', *Cultura e Scuola*, IV (1965), Dante issue, 551–65.
Fazio-Allmayer, V. 'Estetica e critica in Benedetto Croce', *Belfagor*, VIII (1953), 262–8.
Fenzi, E. 'Le rime per la donna Pietra', *Miscellanea di studi danteschi*, Genoa, 1966, 229–309.
Fergusson, F. *Dante's Drama of the Mind*, Princeton, 1953.
Fitzgerald, R. 'The Style that does Honor', *Kenyon Review*, XIV (1952), 278–85.
Flora, F. 'Croce e De Sanctis' in *Benedetto Croce*, ed. F. Flora, Milan, 1953, pp. 197–229.
Foster, K. 'Dante Studies in England, 1921–64', *Italian Studies*, XX (1965), 1–16.
'Dante's Vision of God', *Italian Studies*, XIV (1959), 21–39.
'St. Thomas and Dante', *New Blackfriars*, LV (1974), 148–55.
'The Celebration of Order', *Dante Studies*, XC (1972), 109–21.
'The Mind in Love: Dante's Philosophy', in *Dante; a collection of critical essays*, ed. J. Freccero, Englewood Cliffs, N.J., 1965, pp. 43–60.
with P. Boyde, *Dante's Lyric Poetry*, Oxford, 1967, 2 vols.
Francescato, G. 'Teoria e realtà linguistica in Dante', *Miscellanea dantesca*, Utrecht and Antwerp, 1965, 128–37.
Frattini, A. *Il Canto XXVIII del Paradiso*, Turin, 1960.
Freccero, J. 'The Final Image: *Par.* XXXIII, 144', *Modern Language Notes*, LXXIX (1964), 14–27.
ed. *Dante: a collection of critical essays*, Englewood Cliffs, N.J., 1965.
Frenzel, H. 'Latinità di Dante: Riassunto delle teorie di E. R. Curtius', *Convivium*, XXII (1954), 16–30.
Fubini, M. 'Arte, linguaggio, letteratura', *Belfagor*, III (1948), 269–88; 396–413.
Critica e poesia, Bari, 1956.
Il peccato di Ulisse e altri saggi danteschi, Florence, 1966.
Metrica e poesia: lezioni sulle forme metriche italiana dal '200 al Petrarca', Milan, 1962.
'Ragioni storiche e ragioni teoriche della critica stilistica', *Giornale storico della letterature italiana*, CXXXIII (1956), 489–509.
'Rileggendo *La Poesia di Dante*', *Cultura e Scuola*, IV (1965), Dante issue, 7–19.

Galimberti, C. 'Il Canto VII del *Paradiso*', *Lectura Dantis Scaligera: Paradiso* (series directed by M. Marcazzan), Florence, 1968.
Garboli, C. 'Struttura e poesia nella critica dantesca contemporanea', *Società*, VIII (1952), 20–44.
'Come leggere Dante', *Paragone*, XV (1965), 8–42.
Gardner, H. *The Art of T. S. Eliot*, London, 1949.
Garin, E. *Medioevo e Rinascimento*, Bari, 1954, which contains 'Poesia e filosofia nel Medioevo Latino'.
Gentile, G. 'Il Canto VI del Purgatorio', contained in *Letture dantesche*, ed. G. Getto, Florence, 1964.
'La profezia di Dante', *Nuova Antologia*, CXCV (May, 1918), 3–28.
Getto, G. *Aspetti della poesia di Dante*, 2nd edn, Florence, 1966.
'La letterature religiosa', *Questioni e correnti di storia letteraria*, vol. coll. Milan, 1949, pp. 857–900.
Giacalone, G. ed. *La Divina Commedia* (with commentary and critical notes), Rome, 1968–9, 3 vols.
Giannantonio, P. 'Giambattista Vico, precursore del dantismo moderno', *L' Alighieri*, X (1969), 52–61.
Gilson, E. *Dante and Philosophy* (trans. D. Moore), Gloucester, Mass., 1968.
'La "Mirabile Visione" di Dante', *Il Veltro*, IX (1965), 543–56.
'Poésie et théologie dans la Divine Comédie', *Atti del Congresso Internazionale di Studi Danteschi*, Florence, 1965, vol. I, 197–223.
'Réflexions sur la situation historique de Dante', *Dante e la cultura veneta*, ed. V. Branca and G. Padoan, Florence, 1967.
Girardi, E. N. 'Dante personaggio', *Cultura e Scuola*, IV (1965), Dante issue, 332–42.
Gmelin, H. 'Die Sprache des Transzendenten in Dantes *Paradiso*', *Stil und Formprobleme in der Literatur*, Heidelberg, 1959, pp. 189–95.
'I latinismi del Paradiso' (trans. E. Bonora), contained in *Critica dantesca*, ed. Bárberi Squarotti and Jacomuzzi, Turin, 1970, 423–32.
trans. and comm. *Die Göttliche Komödie*, Stuttgart, 1954.
Goffis, C. F. 'Il Canto I del *Paradiso*', *Lectura Dantis Scaligera: Paradiso* (series directed by M. Marcazzan), Florence, 1968.
Grayson, C. *Cinque saggi su Dante*, Bologna, 1972.
Greene, T. H. 'Dramas of Self-hood in the *Comedy*', in *From Time to Eternity*, ed. T. G. Bergin, New Haven and London, 1967, pp. 103–36.
Groppi, F. *Dante traduttore*, 2nd edn, Rome, 1962.
Guardini, R. 'Il linguaggio religioso', *Humanitas*, XV (1960), 779–800.
Studi su Dante (trans. M. L. Maraschini and A. Sacchi Balestrieri), Brescia, 1967.
Guerrieri-Crocetti, C. 'Divagazioni sul *De Vulgari Eloquentia*', *Miscellanea di studi danteschi*, Genoa, 1966, 119–29.
'La razionalità del linguaggio secondo S. Tommaso e Dante', *Giornale dantesco*, XXV (1922), 135–7.

Guidubaldi, E. 'Dalla "selva oscura" alla "candida rosa"', *Lectura Dantis Mystica*, Florence, 1969, pp. 317–72.
Dante europeo, Florence, 1965–8, 3 vols.
'T. S. Eliot e B. Croce: Due opposti attegiamenti critici di fronte a Dante', *Ævum*, XXXI (1957), 147–85.
Guzzo, A. 'Il *Paradiso* e la critica del De Sanctis', *Rivista d'Italia* (November, 1924), 456–79.
Studi d' arte religiosa, Turin, 1932.
Hardie, C. 'Cacciaguida's Prophecy in *Paradiso* 17', *Traditio*, XIX (1963), 267–94.
'Dante and Milton', *Deutsches Dante Jahrbuch*, XLIV–XLV (1965), 82–99.
Hatzfeld, H. 'Modern Literary Scholarship as reflected in Dante criticism', *Comparative Literature*, III (1951), 289–309.
'Recent Italian Stylistic Theory and Stylistic Criticism', *Studia Philologica et Litteraria in honorem L. Spitzer*, ed. A. G. Hatcher and K. L. Selig, Berne, 1958, 227–44.
Holloway, J. *The Victorian Sage: studies in argument*, London, 1953.
Jacomuzzi, A. *Il palinsesto della retorica e altri saggi danteschi*, Florence, 1972.
L' imago al cerchio, Milan, 1968.
Jakobson, R. with P. Valesio, '*Vocabulorum constructio* in "Se vedi li occhi miei"', *Studi danteschi*, XLIII (1966), 7–33.
Kermode, F. *The Romantic Image*, London, 1957.
Knight, G. Wilson. *The Christian Renaissance*, London, 1962.
Krieger, M. 'Benedetto Croce and the Recent Poetics of Organicism', *Comparative Literature*, VII (1955), 252–8.
Kuhn, H. 'Cassirer's Philosophy of Culture' contained in *The Philosophy of Ernst Cassirer*, ed. P. A. Schilpp, Evanston, 1949.
Kuhns, R. *Literature and Philosophy*, London, 1971.
Langer, S. K. 'Cassirer's Theory of Language and Myth', contained in *The Philosophy of Ernst Cassirer*, ed. P. A. Schilpp, Evanston, 1949.
Leo, U. 'The Unfinished *Convivio* and Dante's Re-reading of the *Æneid*', *Medieval Studies*, XIII (1951), 41–64.
Lewis, C. S. *Studies in Medieval and Renaissance Literature*, Cambridge, 1966, which contains 'Dante's Similes' and 'Imagery in the Last Eleven Cantos of Dante's *Comedy*'.
Lo Cascio, R. 'Le nozioni di cortesia e di nobiltà dai Siciliani a Dante', *Atti del Convegno di Studi su Dante e la Magna Curia*, Palermo, 1967, 113–84.
Lord, R. *Dostoievsky: Essays and Perspectives*, London, 1970.
MacKinnon, D. M. *The Problem of Metaphysics*, Cambridge, 1974.
'What is a metaphysical statement', *Proceedings of the Aristotelian Society*, XLI (1940–1), 1–26.
Maggini, F. *Dalle 'Rime' alla lirica del 'Paradiso' dantesco*, Florence, 1938.

Maggini, F. 'La critica dantesca dal '300 ai nostri giorni', *Questioni e correnti di storia letteraria*, vol. coll. Milan, 1949, pp. 123–66.

Maier, B. review of M. Fubini's *Critica e poesia*, *La rassegna della letteratura italiana* (1957), 257–61.

Malagoli, L. 'Dante e noi', *Ausonia*, XX (1965), 11–14.

'Il linguaggio del *Paradiso* e la crisi dello spirito cristiano medievale', *L'Alighieri*, VII (1966), 40–52.

Linguaggio e poesia nella 'Divina Commedia', Genoa, 1949.

Lo stile del Duecento, Pisa, 1956.

'Lo stile della *Commedia* e lo stile dei Siciliani', *Atti del Convegno di Studi su Dante e la Magna Curia*, Palermo, 1967, 185–91.

'Medievalismo e modernità di Dante', *Studi mediolatini e volgari*, IV (1957), 131–76.

Saggio sulla Divina Commedia, Florence, 1962.

Marigo, A. 'Cultura letteraria e preumanistica nelle maggiori enciclopedie del Dugento', *Giornale storico della letteratura italiana*, LXVIII (1916), 1–42; 289–326.

ed. and comm. ('con appendice di aggiornamento a cura di P. G. Ricci'), *De Vulgari Eloquentia*, 3rd edn, Florence, 1967.

Mariotti, S. 'Il Canto VI del *Paradiso*', *Nuove Letture Dantesche*, V, Florence, 1972, pp. 375–404.

Marti, M. *Realismo dantesco e altri studi*, Milan–Naples, 1961.

Martinelli, L. *Dante* (in the series 'Storia della critica'), Palermo, 1966.

Marzot, G. *Il linguaggio biblico nella 'Divina Commedia'*, Pisa, 1956.

Mattalia, D. *La critica dantesca*, Florence, 1950.

Matthiessen, F. O. *The Achievement of T. S. Eliot: an essay on the nature of poetry*, London, 1935.

Maxwell, D. E. S. *The Poetry of T. S. Eliot*, London, 1952.

Mazza, A. 'La "Commedia" e alcuni aspetti della poetica del Boccaccio', *Annali dell' Istituto di Studi Danteschi*, I, Milan, 1967, 436–52.

Mazzeo, J. A. '*Convivio* IV xxi and *Paradiso*, XIII: Another of Dante's Self-Corrections', *Philological Quarterly*, XXXVIII (1959), 30–6.

Mediaeval Cultural Tradition in Dante's Comedy Ithaca, N.Y., 1960.

Structure and Thought in the Paradiso, Ithaca, N.Y., 1958.

McKeon, R. 'Poetry and Philosophy in the Twelfth Century Renaissance', *Modern Philology*, XLIII (1946), 217–34.

'Rhetoric in the Middle Ages', *Speculum*, XVII (1942), 1–32.

Medcalf, S. 'Vergil's *Æneid*', contained in *The Classical World*, vol. I in the series ed. D. Daiches and A. K. Thorlby, *Literature and Western Civilization*, London, 1972.

Melli, E. 'Dante e Arnaut Daniel', *Filologia romanza*, VI (1959), 423–48.

Mellone, A. 'L'esemplarismo divino secondo Dante', *Divinitas*, IX (1965), 215–43.

Mengaldo, P. V. the entry 'Constructio' in *Enciclopedia Dantesca*, vol. II, Rome, 1970.

the entry 'De Vulgari Eloquentia' in *Enciclopedia Dantesca*, vol. II, Rome, 1970.
the entry 'Discrezione' in *Enciclopedia Dantesca*, vol. II, Rome, 1970.
ed. with introduction *De Vulgari Eloquentia*, Padua, 1967, vol. I.
Mercuri, R. 'Conosco i segni de l'antica fiamma', *Cultura neolatina*, XXXI (1971), 238–93.
Mineo, N. *Profetismo e appocalittica in Dante*, Catania, 1968.
Momigliano, A. comm. *La Divina Commedia*, Florence, 1950, 3 vols.
Dante, Verga e Manzoni, 2nd edn, Messina–Florence, 1965.
Montale, E. 'Dante ieri e oggi', *Atti del Congresso Internazionale di Studi Danteschi*, Florence, 1965, vol. II, 315–33.
'Eliot e noi', *L'immagine* (1947), 261–4.
Montanari, F. *L'esperienza poetica di Dante*, Florence, 1959.
Montano, R. *Arte, realtà e storia: l'estetica del Croce e il mondo dell'arte*, Naples, 1951.
'Erich Auerbach e la scoperta del realismo in Dante e in Boccaccio', *Convivium*, XXVI (1958), 16–26.
'I modi della narrazione in Dante', *Convivium*, XXVI (1958), 546–67.
Lo spirito e le lettere, Milan, 1970–1, 2 vols.
Storia della poesia di Dante, Naples, 1962–3, 2 vols.
Suggerimenti per una lettura di Dante, Naples, 1956.
Monteverdi, A. 'Lingue volgari e impulsi religiosi', *Cultura neolatina*, VI–VII (1946–7), 7–21.
Morghen, R. 'Dante profeta', *Letture classensi*, III, Ravenna, 1970, 13–36.
Morra, G. 'Romano Guardini, interprete di Dante', *Letture Classensi*, III, Ravenna, 1970, 147–68.
Muscetta, C. 'Il Canto VIII del *Paradiso*', *Lectura Dantis Scaligera: Paradiso* (series directed by M. Marcazzan), Florence, 1968.
Nardi, B. *Dal 'Convivio' alla 'Commedia'*, Rome, 1960.
Dante e la cultura medievale, Bari, 1942.
'Perchè "dietro la memoria non può ire"', *L'Alighieri*, I (1960), 5–13.
'Sì come rota ch' egualmente è mossa', *Studi danteschi*, XIX (1935), 83–96.
Nelson, L. 'The Rhetoric of Ineffability: toward a definition of mystical poetry', *Comparative Literature*, VIII (1956), 323–36.
Nencioni, G. 'Dante e la retorica', *Dante e Bologna nei tempi di Dante*, Bologna, 1967, 91–112.
'Orientamenti del pensiero linguistico italiano', *Belfagor*, VII (1952), 249–71.
Olivero, F. *The Representation of the Image in Dante*, Turin, 1936.
Olschki, L. *Dante Poeta Veltro*, Rome, 1953.
Olson, P. R. 'Theme and Structure in the Exordium of the *Paradiso*', *Italica*, XXXIX (1962), 89–104.
Orsini, G. N. G. *Benedetto Croce*, Carbondale, 1961.
'Croce and the Poetic Image', *Symposium*, X (1956), 1–24.

Pagliaro, A. *Altri saggi di critica semantica*, Messina–Florence, 1961.
La parola e l'immagine, Naples, 1957.
'Linguaggio e conoscenza dopo l' idealismo', *De Homine*, VII–VIII (1964), 3–24.
Nuovi saggi di critica semantica, Messina–Florence, 1956, which contains 'I "primissima signa" nella dottrina linguistica di Dante'.
Ulisse: ricerche semantiche sulla 'Divina Commedia', Milan–Florence, 1967, 2 vols.
'Sul linguaggio poetico della *Commedia*', *Il Veltro*, IX (1965), 589–638.
Palgen, R. 'Le teofanie nella *Commedia*', *Convivium*, XXXIV (1966), 115–39.
Palmieri, U. 'Appunti di linguistica dantesca', *Studi danteschi*, XLI (1964), 45–53.
Panvini, B. 'L'esperienza dei Siciliani e il volgare illustre di Dante', *Atti del Convegno di Studi su Dante e la Magna Curia*, Palermo, 1967, 236–49.
Le poesie del 'De Vulgari Eloquentia', Catania, 1968.
Paparelli, G. *Questioni dantesche*, Naples, 1967.
Paratore, E. *Tradizione e struttura in Dante*, Florence, 1968.
Parma, G. B. *Ascesi e mistica cattolica nella Divina Commedia*, Subiaco, 1925–7, 2 vols.
Pasinetti, P. M. 'Aspects of Contemporary Italian Criticism', *Romanic Review*, XL (1949), 186–97.
Pasquazi, S. *All' eterno dal tempo*', Florence, 1966.
'Il Canto VI del *Purgatorio*' and 'Il Canto VII del *Purgatorio*', *Lectura Dantis Scaligera: Paradiso* (series directed by M. Marcazzan), Florence, 1967.
Pautasso, S. *Le frontiere della critica*, Milan, 1972.
Pazzaglia, M. *Il verso e l'arte della canzone nel 'De Vulgari Eloquentia'*, Florence, 1967.
Pecoraro, P. 'Il Canto II del *Paradiso*', *Lectura Dantis Scaligera: Paradiso* (series directed by M. Marcazzan), Florence, 1968.
Pépin, J. the entry 'Allegoria' in *Enciclopedia Dantesca*, vol. I, Rome, 1970.
Dante et la tradition de l' allégorie, Montreal and Paris, 1970.
Pertusi, A. 'Cultura greco-bizantina nel tardo medioevo nelle Venezie e suoi echi in Dante', *Dante e la cultura veneta*, ed. V. Branca and G. Padoan, Florence, 1967, pp. 157–97.
Petrocchi, G. 'Dante and Thirteenth Century Asceticism', contained in *From Time to Eternity*, ed. T. G. Bergin, New Haven and London, 1967.
ed. *La Commedia* (secondo l' antica vulgata), Milan, 1966–7, 4 vols.
Petrucciani, M. 'Dante e le poetiche contemporanee', *Studi in onore di A. Schiaffini*, Rome, 1965, 861–80.
Pézard, A. 'Charles Martel au Ciel de Vénus', contained in *Letture del Paradiso*, ed. V. Vettori, Milan, 1970.

Dante sous la pluie de feu, Paris, 1950.
'La langue italienne dans la pensée de Dante', *Cahiers du Sud*, XXXVIII (1951), 25–38.
'Le "Convivio" de Dante; sa lettre, son esprit', *Annales de l'Université de Lyon*, 3rd series, fasc. IX, Paris, 1940.
'Les trois langues de Cacciaguida', *Revue des études italiennes*, XIII (1967), 217–38.
'Regards de Dante sur Platon et ses mythes', *Archives d'histoire doctrinale et littéraire du Moyen Age*, XXIX (1954), 165–81.
'Volgare e latino nella *Commedia*', *Letture classensi*, II, Ravenna, 1969, 93–111.

Piemontese, F. 'Dante e la poetica della visione', *Humanitas*, VII (1952), 1036–48.

Pipa, A. *Montale and Dante*, Minneapolis, 1968.

Porcelli, B. *Studi sulla 'Divina Commedia'*, Bologna, 1970.

Pound, E. *Literary Essays*, edited with an introduction by T. S. Eliot, London, 1960.

Praz, M. *Machiavelli in Inghilterra*, 2nd edn, Rome, 1943.

Puppo, M. 'Il concetto del "vivente" nella critica dantesca di Francesco De Sanctis', *Romanic Review*, LXII (1971), 183–91.
Il metodo e la critica di Benedetto Croce, Milan, 1964.

Raimondi, E. *Metafora e storia: studi su Dante e Petrarca*, Turin, 1970.

Ramat, R. 'Il Canto XXI del *Paradiso*', contained in T. Di Salvo, *Lettura critica del Paradiso*, Florence, 1969, vol. III.

Reiser, M. 'The Aesthetics of Guido Calogero', *Journal of Aesthetics and Art Criticism*, XXX (1971), 19–26.

Roncaglia, A. 'Il Canto VI del Purgatorio', *La rassegna della letteratura italiana* (1956), 409–26.
introduction to Auerbach's *Mimesis* (translated by A. Romagnoli and H. Hinterhauser), Turin, 1957.

Ronconi, A. 'Dante interprete dei poeti latini', *Studi danteschi*, XLI (1964), 5–44.
Interpretazioni grammaticali, Padua, 1958.
'L'incontro di Stazio e Virgilio', *Cultura e Scuola*, IV (1965), Dante issue, 566–71.

Rooney, W. J. *The Problem of 'Poetry and Belief' in Contemporary Criticism*, Washington, 1949.

Rossi, M. *Gusto filologico e gusto poetico*, Bari, 1942.

Rotta, P. *La filosofia del linguaggio nella patristica e nella scolastica*, Turin, 1909.

Russo, A. 'Il contributo di T. S. Eliot alla critica dantesca', *Annali del Liceo Classico 'G. Garibaldi' di Palermo*, II, 1965, 201–32.

Russo, L. *La critica letteraria contemporanea*, Bari, 1946–7, 3 vols.

Salsano, F. the entry 'Contento' in *Enciclopedia Dantesca*, vol. II, Rome, 1970.

Sansone, M. 'Aspetti della interpretazione critica della *Commedia* dal 1920 al 1965', *Atti del Convegno di Studi su Dante e la Magna Curia*, Palermo, 1967, 651–67.
'Il Canto VII del *Paradiso*', *Nuove Letture Dantesche*, VI, Florence, 1973, 1–25.
Sanguinetti, E. *Il realismo di Dante*, Florence, 1966.
Interpretazione di Malebolge, Florence, 1961.
Santangelo, S. *Saggi danteschi*, Padua, 1959, which contains '"Sole nuovo" e "sole usato": Dante e Guittone'.
Santangelo, V. *Il significato dell'umano nella poetica dantesca*, Palermo, 1968.
Sapegno, N. 'La critica dantesca dal 1921 ad oggi', *Atti del Congresso Internazionale di Studi Danteschi*, vol. II, Florence, 1965, 263–74.
ed. and comm. *La Divina Commedia*, 2nd edn, Florence, 1968.
Sarolli, G. R. *Prolegomena alla Divina Commedia*, Florence, 1971.
Scaglione, A. 'Imagery and Thematic Patterns in *Paradiso* XXIII', contained in *From Time to Eternity*, ed. T. G. Bergin, New Haven and London, 1967.
'Periodic Syntax and Flexible Metre in the Divine Comedy', *Romance Philology*, XXI (1967), 1–22.
Scartazzini, G. A. ed. and comm. *La Divina Commedia*, 5th edn, a cura di G. Vandelli, Milan, 1907; also the 20th edn, published as *La Divina Commedia*, 'col commento scartazziniano rifatto da G. Vandelli', Milan, 1969.
Schiaffini, A. 'Dante, Retorica, Medioevo', *Atti del Congresso Internazionale di Studi Danteschi*, Florence, 1965, vol. II, 155–86.
'Divagazioni e testimonianze sulla retorica nella lingua e letteratura italiana', *Atti del VIII Congresso Internazionale di Studi Romanzi*, Florence, 1960, vol. II, 403–22.
Lettura del 'De Vulgari Eloquentia' di Dante (typescript), Rome, 1959.
Momenti di storia della lingua italiana, Rome, 1953.
'Poesis e Poeta in Dante', *Studia Philologica et Letteraria in honorem L. Spitzer*, ed. A. G. Hatcher, K. L. Selig, Berne, 1958, pp. 379–89.
Segre, C. *Lingua, stile e società*, Milan, 1963, which contains 'La prosa del Duecento' and 'La sintassi del periodo nei primi prosatori italiani (Guittone, Brunetto, Dante)'.
'nota introduttiva' to C. Bally, *Linguistica Generale* (trans. G. Caravaggi), Milan, 1963.
Volgarizzamenti del Due e Trecento, 2nd edn, Turin, 1964.
Simonelli, M. ed. *Il Convivio*, Bologna, 1966.
Sinclair, J. D. trans. and comm. *The Divine Comedy* (O.U.P. paperback), London, 1971.
Singleton, C. S. 'Dante and Myth', *Journal of the History of Ideas*, X (1949), 482–502.

Dante Studies. I. *Commedia – Elements of Structure*; II. *Journey to Beatrice*, Cambridge, Mass., 1954 and 1958.
'End of a Poem', *Hudson Review*, VI (1954), 524–39.
Spitzer, L. 'The Addresses to the Reader in the *Commedia*', *Italica*, XII (1935), 143–65.
Spoerri, T. *Introduzione alla 'Divina Commedia'* (trans. M. Cerruti), Milan, 1966.
Steiner, G. *Language and Silence*, London, 1967.
Tarozzi, G. *Note di estetica sul 'Paradiso' di Dante*, Florence, 1921.
Tarugi, G. S. 'Realtà umana del *Paradiso*', *L'umanesimo in Dante*, ed. G. S. Tarugi, Florence, 1967.
Tate, A. 'The Symbolic Imagination: A Meditation on Dante's Three Mirrors', contained in *Discussions of the Divine Comedy*, ed. I. Brandeis, Boston, 1961.
Tateo, F. the entry 'Compositio' in *Enciclopedia Dantesca*, vol. II, Rome, 1970.
Questioni di poetica dantesca, Bari, 1972.
Retorica e poetica fra Medioevo e Rinascimento, Bari, 1960.
Terracini, B. 'Analisi del concetto di lingua letteraria', *Cultura neo-latina*, XVI (1956), 9–31.
Analisi stilistica: teoria, storia, problemi, Milan, 1966.
'L'aureo trecento e lo spirito della lingua italiana', *Giornale storico della letteratura italiana*, CXXXIV (1957), 1–36.
Lingua libera e libertà linguistica, new edn with introduction by M. Corti, Turin, 1970.
Pagine e appunti di linguistica storica, Florence, 1957, which contains 'Il lessico del *Convivio*'.
Thorlby, A. K. 'The Individual in the Mediaeval World: Dante's *Divina Commedia*', contained in *The Mediaeval World*, vol. II in the series *Literature and Western Civilization*, ed. D. Daiches and A. K. Thorlby, London, 1973.
Toffanin, G. 'Il Canto XIII del *Paradiso*', *Lectura Dantis Scaligera: Paradiso* (series directed by M. Marcazzan), Florence, 1968.
Ultimi saggi, Bologna, 1960.
Tommaseo, N. ed. ('con ragionamenti e note'), *La Commedia di Dante*, 2nd edn, Milan, 1854.
Tonelli, L. *Dante e la poesia dell' ineffabile*, Florence, 1934.
Trabalza, C. *Storia della grammatica italiana*, Bologna, 1963.
Traversi, D. A. 'Observations on Dante's Canzone "Io son venuto al punto de la rota"', *Italian Studies*, II (1938), 65–72.
Trigg, R. *Reason and Commitment*, Cambridge, 1973.
Uitti, K. D. *Linguistics and Literary Theory*, Englewood Cliffs, N.J., 1969.
Ungaretti, G. 'Il Canto I dell' *Inferno*', contained in *Letture dantesche*, ed. G. Getto, Florence, 1964.

Urban, W. M. 'Cassirer's Philosophy of Language', contained in *The Philosophy of Ernst Cassirer*, ed. P. A. Schilpp, Evanston, 1949.
Valesio, P. '*Vocabulorum constructio*', *Studi danteschi*, XLV (1968), 167–77.
See also Jakobson, R. and Valesio, P.
Vallone, A. *Dante*, Milan, 1971.
'Il Canto IX del *Paradiso*', *Nuove Letture Dantesche*, VI, Florence, 1973, 45–68.
La critica dantesca contemporanea, Pisa, 1953.
La prosa del 'Convivio', Florence, 1967.
'Proposte di lettura: il Canto VII del *Paradiso*', *L'Alighieri*, XII (1971), 51–68.
Vettori, V. ed. *Letture del 'Paradiso'*, Milan, 1970.
'Maestro Dante', contained in *Maestro Dante*, ed. V. Vettori, Milan, 1962.
Vinay, G. 'La teoria linguistica del *De Vulgari Eloquentia*', *Cultura e Scuola*, II (1962), 30–42.
'Ricerche sul *De Vulgari Eloquentia*', *Giornale storico della letteratura italiana*, CXXXVI (1959), 236–74; 367–88.
Vincent, E. R. 'Dante's Choice of Words', *Italian Studies*, X (1955), 1–18.
Viscardi, A. 'Idee estetiche e letteratura militante nel Medioevo', *Momenti e problemi di storia dell'estetica*, vol. coll. Milan, 1959, 231–53.
Vivier, R. 'Les conceptions de la poésie dans la Divine Comédie', *Bulletin de l' Académie Royale de Langue et Littérature Françaises*, XXIX (1951), 113–29.
Wasiolek, E. 'Croce and Contextualist Criticism', *Modern Philology*, LVII (1959), 44–54.
Weiss, R. 'Links between the *Convivio*, and the *De Vulgari Eloquentia*', *The Modern Language Review*, XXXVII (1942), 156–68.
Weinstein, D. 'The Myth of Florence', contained in *Florentine Studies: Politics and Society in Renaissance Florence*, ed. N. Rubinstein, London, 1968.
Wellek, R. 'Benedetto Croce: literary critic and historian', *Comparative Literature*, V (1953), 75–82.
Concepts of Criticism, New Haven and London, 1963.
Discriminations, New Haven and London, 1970.
Wetherbee, W. *Platonism and Poetry in the Twelfth Century*, Princeton, 1972.
Wettstein, J. '*Mezura*': *l'idéal des troubadours, son essence et ses aspects*, Zurich, 1945.
Whitfield, J. H. *The Changing Face of Dante* (the first of the Barlow Lectures, 1959), published in a supplement to vol. XV of *Italian Studies*, 1960, 1–16.
Wilson, E. *Axel's Castle* (Fontana edition), London, 1961.

Wind, E. 'Contemporary German Philosophy', *Journal of Philosophy*, XXII (1925), 476–93.

Pagan Mysteries in the Renaissance (Peregrine edition), London, 1967.

Winters, Y. *The Anatomy of Nonsense*, Norfolk, Connecticut, 1943.

Wlassics, T. *Interpretazioni di prosodia dantesca*, Rome, 1972.

Wollheim, R. 'Philosophy and the Arts', contained in *Modern British Philosophy*, compiled and edited B. Magee, London, 1971.

Zink, S. 'Intuition and Externalisation in Croce's Aesthetic', *Journal of Philosophy*, XLVII (1950), 210–16.

CANTOS OF THE 'COMMEDIA' CITED IN TEXT

INDEX OF NAMES

INDEX OF TOPICS